HOW
TO
GUIDE

preschoolers

Sunday School Division
The Sunday School Board of the Southern Baptist Convention
127 Ninth Avenue, North
Nashville, Tennessee 37234

Contents

Introduction . . . . Cos H. Davis, Jr. 4

Chapter 1: How Preschoolers
Learn. . . . . Dixie Ruth Crase 6

Chapter 2: How to Teach
Through Activities . . . C. Sybil Waldrop. 21

Chapter 3: How to Teach
Through the Use of
Story Conversation
and Stories . . . . Christine C. McCauley 40

Chapter 4: How to Teach
Through the Use of
Pictures . . . . Christine C. McCauley 55

Chapter 5: How to Teach
Through the Use of
Art Materials . . . . Christine C. McCauley 66

Chapter 6: How to Teach
Through the Use of
Blocks . . . . Patsy Driggers 81

Chapter 7: How to Teach
Through the Use of
Books . . . . Florrie Anne Lawton. 92

Chapter 8: How to Teach
Through the Use of
Homeliving Materials . . Helen Young 104

Chapter 9: How to Teach
Through the Use of
Music. . . . . Sue Raley. 117

Chapter 10: How to Teach
Through the Use of
Nature Materials. . . . . A. Wayne Coley 131

Chapter 11: How to Teach
Through the Use of
Puzzles. . . . . Jewell Wells Nelson 144

Chapter 12: How to Use the Bible
with Preschoolers. . . . Dixie Ruth Crase. 160

Chapter 13: How to Lead
Group-Time
Experiences . . . . S. Alfred Foy 178

Chapter 14: How to Teach
Through the Use of
Audiovisuals . . . . Helen Young 192

Chapter 15: How to Make
Additional Teaching
Materials . . . . Jewell Wells Nelson 203

The Church Study Course 222

Note: Unless otherwise indicated, songs referenced in this book are from the following songbooks:
  †*Songs for the Young Child*
  ††*More Songs for 4's and 5's*
  †††*Music for Today's Child*

Introduction
Cos H. Davis, Jr.

Congratulations! You have made a fine choice. You have decided to sharpen your skills in teaching preschoolers, and *How to Guide Preschoolers* is an excellent resource to use in accomplishing this purpose. The book is a successful attempt to help teachers of preschoolers understand the reasons for and the methods of communicating biblical truths to preschoolers through activities. Several organizations (Discipleship Training, Church Music, Woman's Missionary Union, and Sunday School) of the church have programs for preschoolers. Each of these organizations has distinctive characteristics and terminology. Although the organizational terminology may vary, the way adults relate to the child and guide him should follow the same principle.

As I read the pages of this manuscript, I was impressed with the excellent blend of the practical and the philosophical. For example, one is not only told how to use art activities with preschoolers, but also how these activities can be used to teach biblical truths to young children.

I am sure that you will be interested in reading the first chapter entitled "How Preschoolers Learn." Dixie Ruth Crase gives an excellent background for determining the appropriateness of certain activities with preschoolers.

Sybil Waldrop's chapter on "How to Teach Through Activities" (chapter 2) gives an excellent statement of the philosophy of activity teaching with preschoolers. You will want to read chapter 2 thoroughly

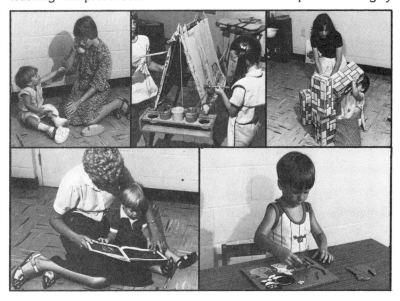

before looking at the chapters which deal with the methods of teaching preschoolers.

Stories and story conversation, pictures, art materials, blocks, books, homeliving materials, music, nature materials, puzzles, how to use the Bible with preschoolers, group time, audiovisuals, and additional teaching materials are the subject areas dealt with in the book *How to Guide Preschoolers.* Each method or activity suggested has one ultimate purpose: to teach biblical truths to preschoolers at their level of understanding.

The methods or activities described in this book should never be thought of as ends in themselves. They are only, and always only, a means to an end. The end or goal of these methods is to help preschoolers become increasingly aware of God. Please read each chapter with this goal in mind.

What are the child's needs? How does the Bible relate to these needs? How can you teach the child what he needs to know? Until Preschool teachers understand the needs of the child and how the Bible relates to him, they are not ready to choose methods. To do otherwise is to make the method an end in itself or an activity without purpose.

Teaching preschoolers is an exciting and rewarding adventure. You have the opportunity to help lay spiritual foundations in the lives of preschoolers. Only eternity will reveal the degree of your influence! This book, *How to Guide Preschoolers,* is a tool to help you complete the stewardship which is yours as a teacher of young children. My prayer is that the material presented in the following pages will be translated into activities to help preschoolers become increasingly aware of God's love and care.

Chapter 1—How Preschoolers Learn
Dixie Ruth Crase

The significance of early experiences in young children's lives is generally recognized. Educators, psychologists, parents, Preschool leaders, and church leaders are convinced of the importance of the first years of life. More emphasis is being placed on the necessity of providing appropriate learning opportunities for preschoolers. This chapter will attempt to answer the following questions:

- Who are preschoolers?
- Why are the Preschool years significant?
- Which learning experiences are uniquely suited to the needs of preschoolers?
- When does learning take place at church?
- Where do young children learn?
- How may preschoolers be encouraged to learn?

Who Are Preschoolers?

The term *preschoolers* generally describes children from birth until entrance in the first grade. Traditionally, most children did not attend school until they were six years old. The years from birth to six encompass tremendous changes in the child's development; thus, the category of preschoolers needs to be divided into separate age groups: babies, creepers, toddlers, twos, threes, fours, and fives. Understanding how preschoolers learn is essential when planning to meet the needs of the children.

How preschoolers learn and the characteristics of each age group provide a general picture or overview of children's development. Keep in mind that children with the same chronological age may vary considerably in specific aspects of their development. In some ways, a nine-month-old is like all other babies of the same age. In some ways, he is like no other baby! Respect for the uniqueness of each child insures that individual attention is given as needed.

Babies

Some individual differences in babies are observable at birth. These differences may influence a baby's health and physical development. When a baby is well, sleeps on schedule, and nurses vigorously, he is off to a good start. His degree of contentment is reflected in parents' and teachers' satisfaction. The child's satisfaction is often a reflection of the satisfaction in his parents' lives. If a baby has difficulty adjusting to his new world, his parents and teachers have more reason to be concerned about his development.

Some observers suggest that babies are a mere bundle of physiological needs and reflexes. When basic physical needs are met, all is well. And yet, from the beginning of life, the need to experience love seems apparent. When denied love, babies fail to thrive and may not survive infancy.

During the first year, babies are in the process of developing a sense of trust. They are learning to trust themselves as well as others. A sense of trust is one of the most important factors in the development of a healthy personality according to educators and psychologists.

Prompt, positive attempts to meet the physical and emotional needs of babies seem to have widespread, favorable results. For example, crying is a primary form of communication during the first weeks of life. When a newborn's crying brings adult assistance, he is likely to cry less at nine months of age than a baby whose crying was often ignored during the early weeks of life. Apparently, babies who learn that they can trust others to meet their needs are happier and more content as they approach the end of infancy.

Newborns venture into their new surroundings through their senses. Visually they have a fixed focus at about seven or eight inches. Isn't it marvelous that the teacher's or parent's face is often about that distance from a baby when he is being fed or changed? Studies indicate that babies are more likely to pay attention to objects that move and have contrasting colors. The human face is sometimes described as an attractive mobile for a baby. Throughout infancy, babies learn through a variety of visual experiences. A "change in scenery" is restful and refreshing at any age.

Authorities on prenatal development suggest that babies have had practice in hearing prior to delivery. After birth, the newborn can be soothed by hearing a familiar voice. Soon a baby coos and babbles to communicate his pleasure and satisfaction. Responsive teachers and parents encourage these vocal practices. Listening to and repeating a baby's sounds promote additional babbling. Talking with and singing to babies positively influences their verbal skills. The infants' attempts to communicate by cooing or babbling have been successful. In addition, babies feel good about themselves. Emotional and social development is enhanced in this warm, supportive atmosphere.

Rooting and sucking reflexes necessary for intake of nourishment are present at birth. Most healthy babies nurse well after a little practice. Feeding the baby does more than meet his nutritional needs. Nursing involves a special opportunity for a physically close, emotionally satisfying experience.

Newborns can differentiate between sweet and salty tastes; they frown if introduced to bitter tastes. Babies continually learn through the sense of taste. "Everything goes to his mouth" is a common description of infant behavior. A variety of clean, safe items to mouth and taste are a part of a well-planned environment for babies.

From birth, the sense of touch helps the newborn to experience his world. Renewed emphasis on natural childbirth suggests that parent-child bonding is an important first experience. Bonding is described as the initial emotional link between child and parent. After the baby's delivery, he may be held and touched by his parents. The immediate physical contact begins to lay the foundation for developing a sense of trust. Holding or patting a baby often comforts him when he is irritated or restless.

Babies need to experience love from thoughtful, sensitive, caring adults who feel God's love. Teachers who lovingly and promptly meet the needs of babies are giving the infants a meaningful introduction to church.

Creepers

Creepers discover new ways to explore their world. They can sit alone, creep, crawl, and even pull themselves up. Because of their increased mobility, creepers can reach objects in the crib or on the floor. Attractive, safe toys are examined visually, handled, mouthed, and banged.

Creepers begin to recognize familiar persons. As babies' emotional attachment to significant persons increases, they are more likely to express fear of an unfamiliar person or an unknown situation. The individuality of creepers is apparent when some children cry and cling to parents as they are separated. Other creepers seem to delight in each new situation. Acceptance of the individuality of children helps teachers and parents to be understanding of each creeper's approach to other persons.

Children are less fearful of unknown children than unknown adults. Most creepers seem to be attracted to other creepers. Initially, creepers react to other children as though they were objects. They may pat, push, or pull each other. They may try to take a plastic rock and stack toy or a covered picture from another preschooler. Creepers are normally easily distracted by a teacher introducing another picture or a book.

The creepers' babbling is increasing and is beginning to sound more like the language the children hear most frequently. Listening and responding to babbling is important. In addition to encouraging the child's development of speech, paying attention to babbling helps the creeper develop positive feelings about himself and his abilities.

Creepers are responsive to appropriate Bible thoughts and conversation. A teacher who smiles and sings, "God loves you, Jeffrey" is helping to lay the foundation for the child's understanding of God.

Toddlers

First birthdays offer several reasons to celebrate. First words and first steps are very often associated with this developmental milestone. Toddlers are ready to begin developing a sense of autonomy or independence.

Unlike the baby who focuses on developing a sense of trust, the toddler strives for new ways to exert his independence. He is no longer a helpless infant, totally dependent upon others for meeting his needs.

Toddlers grow as they have opportunities to choose within appropriate limits. Choosing a doll to hold or a block to stack enhances a child's self-confidence. He may also find necessary limits more acceptable when he can exercise a degree of control over his world. In a well-planned department, toddlers find many opportunities to be successful and few opportunities to meet with frustration or failure.

A toddler's language development is changing from single-word utterances to two-word phrases. Toddlers enjoy turning the pages of appropriate picture books. They can name familiar objects and point to pictures of objects and people with whom they have had experiences.

Although the toddlers' active vocabulary is limited to a few words, they understand much more than they can express verbally. They can follow simple directions. They delight in happy songs and conversation about their activities. As a toddler walks up and down the rocking boat steps, his teacher may say: "Alex is walking up, up, up the steps. Now he is walking down, down, down the steps."

The toddlers' eye-hand coordination has progressed since infancy. The boys and girls easily put a variety of safe household objects in and out of a plastic dishpan or may manipulate an Activity Center for a short while. Working simple puzzles may give some toddlers a sense of satisfaction.

Large motor development involves the toddlers' ability to walk, climb, and slide. Stepping on and off cardboard blocks or rocking in the rocking boat allows toddlers to get the physical exercise they need and want. Pushing or pulling an empty cardboard box is a treat for a child who is practicing his new walking skills. A simple, clear picture of a car, a doll, or a book mounted on each side of the box provides another learning opportunity when the toddler is ready to sit. His teacher may point to the picture and say, "Tell me about your picture." The teacher may say, "Dana, point to the picture of the doll." Toddlers experience love through happy times at church.

Twos

Twos' exuberance for life seems to be reflected in each phase of their development. They can throw, kick, or roll beach balls. Other outside activities such as jumping and running are also accomplished with ease. Cardboard blocks can be built into a tower or placed in a line.

Control over small motor skills is evident as twos complete puzzles with three or four shapes. Exploring various art media is fun as twos experiment with crayons, paint, paste, or play dough.

Two-year-olds are beginning to assume some responsibility for their care. They can assist in removing hats and coats. Most twos are cooperating in the process of toilet training. Children are more likely to be successful if training is delayed until they are mature enough for this new responsibility. Girls usually achieve daytime control sooner than boys.

Twos enjoy water play and washing hands, but they need guidance. As a two-year-old focuses on washing his hands, a teacher may say, "Thank you, God, for hands."

Playing near other children is characteristic of two-year-olds. Often there is little interaction or cooperative play as each child pastes, paints, or stacks blocks. In case of conflicts between children, one child can usually be redirected to another activity.

Two-year-olds are speaking in two- to three-word phrases or sentences. They can point to familiar objects which have been named in a picture book or the Bible. Twos can give their first names and name family members when requested.

Some twos begin to sing simple songs, and all children enjoy a song or conversation about their play (activities). Twos understand appropriate Bible thoughts, stories, and pictures. The boys and girls are growing in their comprehension of God, Jesus, Bible, church, self, family, others, and the natural world.

Threes

Three-year-olds' interest in other persons expands. They usually enjoy playing with other children. Although they are sometimes involved in solitary or parallel play, cooperative play begins to emerge. Leaders and followers can be seen in block play or in homeliving activities.

Parents and teachers often find threes imitating adults' activities. Pretending to cook, clean, care for babies, and go to work are meaningful activities.

Assisting adults in real cleaning tasks or in preparation and serving of foods is also meaningful for threes. Through these experiences, children have many learning opportunities and also develop a close, warm relationship with significant adults in their lives.

Threes' language skills help them talk about their experiences and tell others what they need or want. They can answer simple questions, listen to a short story, describe familiar objects, and talk about pictures of items used in the home.

As threes develop an understanding of similarities and differences, they can group items according to various characteristics. For example, they can sort or match blocks or large beads according to the colors. Threes can work three- to four-piece puzzles. As their eye-hand coordination develops, they can string large beads and build with unit blocks. For three-year-olds, the process of stacking or arranging blocks remains more important than building a specific house, store, or church.

Three-year-olds enjoy exploring various art media. With finger paint, felt-tipped markers, chalk, crayons, or easel brushes, threes produce a variety of scribbles, lines, and circles. In most cases, they are not attempting to draw a specific object or person. Representational drawing comes later. Fine motor skills are developed as threes pour, fill, and empty plastic containers during water play. Play dough can be patted, rolled, squeezed, and punched by threes.

Movement toward independence is enhanced as threes are able to assist in their toileting and washing of hands. They can remove coats and hats and begin to manage large zippers, buttons, or snaps. To do for a child what he can do for himself is to deny him valuable learning

opportunities.

Threes enjoy vigorous outdoor play with opportunities to climb, slide, and run. Outdoor play may set the stage for children and adults to share in their continuing exploration of the natural world. A teacher may say: "God makes the wind blow. Thank you, God, for the wind."

Appropriate Bible thoughts, stories, and pictures are meaningful to threes as they relate to their activities and conversation. Teachers may use pictures, real objects, and the Bible to help threes become more aware of God, Jesus, church, others, self, family, and the natural world.

Fours and Fives

The maturity of fours and fives is apparent in each area of their development. Most fours can speak reasonably well, and few fives have difficulty communicating their ideas and feelings. A lengthened attention span allows the children to enjoy "reading" appropriate picture books. Turning pages, looking from top to bottom, and looking from left to right are prereading experiences. Enjoyment of books and stories is one of the best preparations for learning to read. As children talk about their experiences, a teacher may write the words on paper. Children see their ideas being written and are reminded of the importance of their experiences.

A variety of meaningful songs and simple musical instruments are fun and educational for fours and fives. As they become more aware of church staff members, they may enjoy a visit by the music director who may play an instrument and sing the song "You Are Special," p. 5.†

Four- and five-year-olds' motor skill development allows them to begin to cut with scissors. Their drawings become more representational. They are likely to draw simple persons, houses, trees, or flowers. Children may be invited to talk about their painting, pasting, or cutting.

The ability to work cooperatively with a small group of children is characteristic of fours and fives. They can take turns in activities and during transitions. Appropriate games which involve all children are fun on occasions. Winning or losing should not be emphasized. Successfully following simple directions in games gives older preschoolers a sense of satisfaction.

Fours and fives enjoy choosing among a variety of experiences during activities. Opportunities to name, sort, match, and count objects according to size, shape, color, and texture develop children's classification skills. Perceiving differences and similarities is another prereading skill. Building with unit blocks often includes these skills and the use of transportation toys, family or community figures, or animal figures.

Vigorous physical activities are enthusiastically received by fours and fives. They can be involved in a variety of outside activities such as throwing and catching large balls, galloping, and skipping. With appropriate opportunities, many fives are learning to ride bicycles (with training wheels), skate, and swim.

Although the development of four- and five-year-olds has progressed in dramatic ways since infancy, they continue to depend on adult guidance. They are more comfortable when limits are clearly defined and consistently maintained. Kindness and firmness reassure older pre-schoolers that teachers care enough to guide and redirect them when necessary.

As more fours and fives are enrolled in some type of day-care or kindergarten experience, they are familiar with expectations for group time. Group time at church should be designed to enhance children's understanding of God, Jesus, the Bible, self, family, others, and the natural world. Appropriate games, songs, pictures, and Bible stories for group time are recommended in the periodicals *Preschool Bible Teacher C,*** *Bible Story Time Teacher,*** *The Music Leader,*** and *Start.****

Why Are the Preschool Years Significant?

The importance of first experiences is difficult to overemphasize. Think about some of your "first" experiences. If you are a mother or a father, think of the first time you saw your baby. Do you remember his first step or first word? How did you feel the first time you left your baby with a babysitter?

Although first impressions may not always be accurate, they often influence our initial reactions. First expenences lay the groundwork for subsequent development.

Parents are often given primary credit (or blame) for their children's development. Although other factors influence boys and girls, parents do have the "first chance" to guide their children.

Preschool years in the church are significant, at least in part, because they occur when human development is most pliable. Newborns may vary in temperament at birth. Some babies are basically calm, accept-ing, comfortable individuals. Other newborns are more irritable and more difficult to comfort and soothe. Although these tendencies appear to be inborn, preschoolers are remarkably responsive to the quality of their environment. The following chapters will focus specifically on the preparation of an appropriate environment for preschoolers at each developmental level.

The Preschool years are considered to be crucial because of the rapidity of the child's development during the first five years. During the first year of life, the newborn's weight gain is unparalleled. Babies usu-ally triple their birth weight by the end of the first year. They progress from having little voluntary control over their muscles to having well developed large motor skills and fine motor development at five years of age.

Emotionally and socially, babies begin life with a high degree of egocentrism and little awareness of others' needs. As a maturing five-year-old, the child can fulfill reasonable expectations within a family or a group of children.

The newborn's language is limited to forms of pre-speech com-munication (crying, babbling, body language, or gestures). As an older

preschooler, a child's accomplished performance in understanding and producing language is phenomenal.

The child's use of language is one reflection of his growth in intellectual development. An increasing vocabulary and successful problem-solving skills indicate that the preschooler's mental abilities are expanding. Some authorities suggest that perhaps one half of the child's mental capabilities are begun during these important Preschool years.

A newborn is prepared to experience love from warm, sensitive, caring adults who feel God's love. As a five-year-old, the child's need for love continues, and he is capable of loving himself and others. His appreciation and increased awareness of God, Jesus, the church, the Bible, and the natural world will reflect the quality of learning experiences provided during these formative years.

Which Learning Experiences Are Uniquely Suited to the Needs of Preschoolers?

Learning may be described as a lifetime venture. Some types of experiences seem to match preschoolers' particular learning styles. Activities which are most likely to result in effective learning have some of the following characteristics:

● *Take into account the maturational level of each child.*—Stringing beads may be frustrating, challenging, or boring. If the beads are too small or the end of the string is frayed, a two-year-old may give up in despair. A successful three-year-old may eagerly share his accomplishment with other children or adults. A four-year-old may find the task too simple or repetitious. If following a pattern (for example: one red bead, two blue beads, and three yellow beads) is introduced, the older preschooler may delight in matching colors and numbers of beads.

● *Occur in a warm, supportive atmosphere.*—Unconditional acceptance of children reassures them that they are free to try new learning experiences. A comfortable baby is more likely to reach for a new mobile or try to pull up. The toddler tries to get in the rocking boat if he feels that adults will offer support and encouragement. Sorting and matching games are eagerly explored by confident, secure older preschoolers. When fear of failure is reduced, children are willing to try new challenges.

● *Respect individual interests.*—All children may not be attracted to the same materials or pieces of equipment. A variety of planned activities encourages children to choose activities that lead to experiences which may be personally meaningful.

● *Require active participation of learners.*—In general, preschoolers are more eager learners when their senses of taste, touch, smell, sight, and hearing are involved.

● *Provide opportunities for practice or repetition.*—Watch a baby learning to walk. He delights in practicing his newly acquired skills, although he falls regularly. Favorite songs and stories may be repeated without loss of interest by threes. Successfully pounding a nail into a

stump is likely to be followed by another nail.

● *Acknowledge necessary and appropriate limits in the use of materials or equipment.*—"Play dough must be used on a table or cabinet top." "Unit blocks are for building." "Books and musical instruments are to be handled carefully." "Water stays in the dishpan."

● *Respect rights of children.*—Learning in group experiences requires preschoolers to begin to cooperate in the homeliving area or block area. Taking turns becomes meaningful for fours and fives.

● *Provide firsthand, concrete, sensory activities and motor activities.*— A three-year-old can learn much from a kitten's visit to the department. Seeing the kitten drink milk, listening to it mew, and feeling the soft fur are valid opportunities to help the child know about a kitten. Pictures, books, stories, or poems about kittens take on new meaning as a result of·these firsthand experiences.

When Does Learning Take Place at Church?

Learning occurs during the following times at church:

● *Arrival.*—Advanced planning frees teachers to focus attention on each child from the time he arrives at the door of the department until the end of the session. In the baby department, toys and cribs have been cleaned. Safe, attractive toys or pictures, covered with clear contact plastic, have been placed in each crib. Labels for each child's belongings are ready. A selected recording may be playing. Teachers have arrived in time to spend a few quiet moments in meditation prior to the arrival of the first baby. After the director greets the baby, he will hand him to another teacher who softly sings, "I am happy. . . ." The director will write specific parental suggestions about meeting the needs of the baby during the session on the "Baby's Schedule" card.

In this type of arrival, babies are learning that teachers have carefully prepared for them. The smooth transition from parents to teachers is helpful for children and parents.

● *Activities.*—Much of this book will focus on the learning potential of activities provided for each age group. Children are learning as they paint with a sponge, water a plant, bathe a doll, taste fresh fruit, or look at a book with a friend.

● *Transition.*—After time has been spent in activities, a transition occurs. Materials for some activities may be cleaned, stored, or rearranged. Depending on the age of the children, the boys and girls may need to go to the rest room, wash hands, sleep, or eat. Babies' and creepers' schedules are individualized so that immediate physical needs are balanced with activities. Older preschoolers begin to appreciate the need for nutritious food, cleanliness, rest, and exercise.

● *Group Experiences.*—Whether the group is composed of three children raking leaves or ten four-year-olds listening to the Bible story, their learning is enhanced by being with other children. Younger preschoolers are comfortable playing alone or with one or two other children.

Fours and fives are more capable of accepting the necessary limitations associated with being a member of a group.

• *Extended Session.*—The extended session is designed to extend the learning of children throughout their time at church. The packets *Extended Session for Babies and Ones, Extended Session for 2's and 3's.* and *Extended Session for 4's and 5's*** include recommended schedules of activities to follow. Experiences initiated earlier may be reinforced during the extended session. Children may want to hear the Bible story or sing with the Autoharp used during group time.

• *Departure.*—Preparation for a smooth departure includes having each child's belongings labeled and ready for parents' arrival. One extended session teacher can quietly bring each child to the door as his parents return. This procedure allows other boys and girls to continue their activities until time for their departure. A happy departure is a positive learning experience that helps children want to return to church.

Where Do Preschoolers Learn?
The significance of an appropriate physical setting for preschoolers' development is easily demonstrated. A department which lacks appropriate materials or equipment may be uninviting or unsafe. When adequate lighting, cooling, heating, and ventilating are maintained, children and teachers are likely to be more receptive to positive learning experiences. Pages 105-132 of *Basic Preschool Work** contain informa-

tion regarding size of rooms, location of windows and doors, floor coverings, and recommended equipment for each Preschool age group. Quality substitutes for suggested items can often be produced by creative teachers who care about the children in their department. The importance of cleanliness in the baby department is difficult to exaggerate. As creepers move beyond the crib, the cleanliness, safety, and warmth of the floor become more important. Low open shelves in creepers' and toddlers' departments should be sturdy and offer a variety of colorful, attractive, safe objects to explore. Electrical outlets and cords should be out of children's reach. Good housekeeping promotes a pleasant, uncluttered appearance. This type of arrangement helps children learn proper use and care of materials and equipment.

Subsequent chapters in this book will offer specific suggestions for selection and preparation of materials for each age group. Proper guidance of children in the use of items in each area will also be provided.

Children learn when they are outside the department as well as in the room. Babies and creepers enjoy individual stroller rides through the halls and down the sidewalk. A teacher can stop and let a child touch the damp, green grass or pat the rough brick wall. Fours and fives learn more about their church by visiting the choir room, the church kitchen, or the pastor's office. A visit to the church sanctuary helps preschoolers become more aware of where their parents are during the extended session. The church organist or pianist may be invited to play the song "There's No One Exactly Like Me," p. 12.†††

How May Preschoolers Be Encouraged to Learn?
Most of this chapter has focused on the learner, the preschooler. What about the teacher? What does a teacher need to do and be in order to effectively teach preschoolers? Just as children are developing, so adults need to develop. The following aspects of your development influence your teaching:
● *Physical development.*—How do you feel physically? Are you rested and eager for the children to arrive for teaching-learning experiences? Teachers who are exhausted or feel rushed may lack the patience and tolerance to enjoy vibrant preschoolers. Taking care of your body's physical needs is a must for enthusiastic encouragement of preschoolers' learning.
● *Social-emotional development.*—Studies indicate that teachers need a network of family, friends, co-workers, or neighbors with whom they can share their concerns and aspirations. To express joy is to enhance your happiness; to express grief is to diminish your despair. Feeling good about yourself because of God's unconditional acceptance in turn prepares you to accept children although their behavior may need to be redirected.
● *Intellectual development.*—When did you last read a book or an article about preschoolers or their families? When did you last attend a workshop or conference focused on reaching or teaching preschoolers?

When did you last observe a preschooler and marvel at his development? If you are growing mentally, you are likely to have a deep appreciation for children's daily discoveries.

• *Spiritual development.*—Preschoolers cannot study the Bible for themselves. They can only study your face, sense your feelings, and respond to your actions. The significance of serving as a model for children is an awesome responsibility, a responsibility that can only be assumed with divine guidance.

Summary

The Preschool years are significant because during this period the child's development is rapid and adaptable to the teaching-learning environment. Understanding the characteristics of each age group is essential in attempting to guide the learning experiences. Preschoolers learn everywhere and all the time. Whether the learning is positive or negative is dependent upon the quality of the environment and the attributes of the teacher.

Personal Learning Activities

1. Key words in this chapter are *preschooler* and *learn*. Spell these words down the side of a sheet of paper. Write the first word(s) that come to your mind when you see each letter. When you saw the letter *p*, did you write *peaceful baby* or *playful?* Do this exercise with another teacher, and discuss your responses.
2. Which learning experiences are uniquely suited to the needs of preschoolers?
3. When does learning take place at church?
4. How may preschoolers be encouraged to learn?

Materials for Further Study

Waldrop, C. Sybil. *Understanding Today's Preschoolers.* Nashville: Convention Press, 1982.

Terrell, Jerry D. *Basic Preschool Work.* Nashville: Convention Press, 1981.

Uland, Zadabeth. *Bible Teaching for Preschoolers.* Nashville: Convention Press, 1984.

Kizer, Kathryn and Piland, Harry M. *The Preschool Challenge: Sunday School Outreach.* Nashville: Convention Press, 1985.

Braga, Joseph and Laurie. *Learning and Growing.* Englewood Cliffs: Prentice Hall, 1975.

Baker, Susan, Glennella Key, and Talmadge Butler. *Guiding Fours and Fives in Musical Experiences.* Nashville: Convention Press, 1972.

---

*Available from Baptist Book Stores.

**Available by writing Customer Service Center, 127 Ninth Avenue, North, Nashville, Tennessee 37234; or by calling toll free 1-800-458-2772.

***Available from Woman's Missionary Union, P.O. Box 830010, Birmingham, Alabama 35283-0010.

Chapter 2—How to Teach Through Activities

C. Sybil Waldrop

Using activities to guide young children toward God is a powerful approach. God is the author of using activities in teaching. In Deuteronomy 6:4-7, God commands parents (teachers) to teach young children the love of God as they experience the everyday activities of life. "At church teachers ought to teach the Bible. I didn't bring Kevin here to play. He can play at home," said one parent. Some parents think that play is a waste of time. Some teachers do not see the value of play in teaching biblical truths. To them teaching is a group experience—telling a Bible story; saying a Bible thought; singing a song which has words about God, Jesus, and the church; or telling a child what he can and cannot do. While group experiences are important, a child is learning all the time. He may learn more about the Bible message as he and a teacher respond to each other during informal activities.

What many adults commonly call *play*, teachers at church call *activities*. A distinction can be made between *activity* and *play*.

What Are Activities?
Activity means active involvement. For an activity to occur, a child must select and use the materials. Teaching through activities requires that a child choose and use materials under the guidance of a teacher. An activity has a planned purpose. *Play* takes place as a child chooses and uses materials. He can play without the guidance of a teacher. Play may be done for sheer pleasure.

During weekly workers' meeting, teachers discuss the following questions: What is the purpose of our next session? What should a child think, feel, know, or be able to do as a result of this session? What does the child enjoy doing at church? What is the child's stage of development—what is he ready to learn? What materials and resources will the child choose to use? What guidance is needed by the teacher during the activity to accomplish the purpose for the session? The activity approach to teaching is powerful in the spiritual development of preschoolers.

Activities may be perceived as play. What is play? Play is fun. Play is enjoyable, but play is also a child's work. Play has no extrinsic goal—that is, play is done for the joy of playing and learning, not for other rewards. Play is spontaneous and chosen by the individual. Play is active engagement on the part of the player. Play at church becomes an activity when the teacher uses it to achieve a spiritual purpose.

Activities at church offer a laboratory for relating to others under Christian supervision. A persisting life task is learning how to more ably relate to others. Firsthand experiences in getting along with others provide the best opportunities for learning what the Bible says in this area.

What Is Meant by Teaching the Bible Through Activities?

"We want children to learn the Bible" is a comment made by some parents and teachers. What does it mean to "learn the Bible"? There are those who place more value on facts than on application. Both facts and application are important, but having a child repeat Bible facts is not enough.

Bible content must be understood before it can be applied. To teach a child Bible content which he cannot understand is like feeding meat to an infant. The child is unable to mentally digest these ideas. Such actions deny God's developmental design.

Activities must be planned in keeping with the spiritual purpose. The purpose may be to help the child have experiences in sharing. The story for the session deals with the lad who shared his lunch of two fish and three loaves. Which of these activities would best help the child learn to share?

● Paste two fish and five loaves of bread made of construction paper in the outline of a basket.

● Prepare no-bake cookies to give to a sick child whom the children know.

There are better ways of learning the facts of a Bible story than that of pasting patterned cutouts. Recalling the story with the aid of a picture, or answering questions after a story is told requires less time and more thinking on the child's part. The purpose of the story was not to teach what was in the lunch. The purpose of the story was to relate the way a child shared (or could share). When the child has an opportunity to make cookies and share them, the teacher can retell the story about the boy and the loaves and fish and then use the Bible thought "Be ready to share" (1 Tim. 6:18).

If children are taught Bible facts and verses before they understand the information, they tend to do one of four things:

● Dismiss the Bible facts and verses,

● Distort them,

● Repeat the Bible material for a lifetime without understanding the biblical truths (How many times have you sung the hymn "Come Thou Fount of Every Blessing"[1] and have never asked what is meant by "Here I Raise Mine Ebenezer"?),

● Avoid the Bible.

How important it is to teach preschoolers Bible content which they can understand and use! To be able to teach preschoolers what they can understand, teachers have to know how young children think. (See chapter 5 of the book *Witness to Win*, pp. 75-87 for more information on this subject.) Literal-minded preschoolers (those who interpret words according to their ordinary meanings) have difficulty with "red and yellow, black and white" as it relates to children of the world because these colors are not actual colors of the skin. Calling Jesus by other names—Savior, Lord, Prince of Peace—is confusing to a preschooler who has difficulty understanding how one person can be two or more persons or things at the same time.

The best way to teach the Bible is through examples of love and kindness which require an understanding of each child and his needs and an ability to see things from his point of view. A teacher's lifetime task is maturing in his application of the verse, "Therefore all things whatsoever ye would that men should do to you, do ye even so to them" (Matt. 7:12). A child must receive love and kindness before he can give it. A child learns biblical truths through observing teachers and parents and participating in activities which encourage him to live what the Bible teaches.

Life is primarily a matter of relationships—relationships with God, self, and others. In a Preschool room, activities are suggested which involve art, blocks, books, homeliving, nature, and puzzles (toys). Biblically related resources are used during the activities. These include the Bible, Bible stories, conversation, Bible thoughts, pictures, and songs.

As a child works a puzzle, he learns something about himself and what he can do. He learns about taking turns with others as he waits to work a puzzle. He learns about Jesus as the teacher mentions the picture on the puzzle. The teacher says: "Jesus loves this boy. Jesus loves this girl. And Jesus loves you, Tommy." The suggested materials are selected so that a child can have a sense of accomplishment, and so that he can hear and apply Bible truths about God, Jesus, church, self, others, family, and the natural world. The succeeding chapters of this book will give specific information on how to teach through the use of biblically related materials and activities.

Why Use Activities with Preschoolers?
What does a child learn through activities?
Through activities the child learns new ways of thinking, feeling, and acting. Through activities a child increases his mental capacities as he explores what he can and cannot do with objects and with persons. His curiosity prompts him to try new things. As he attempts activities which are within his realm of challenge, he develops competence, self-control, and self-reliance. As he plays with others, he learns that he has rights and that others have rights. He learns to take turns, which is a readiness for sharing. He learns to cooperate and to take responsibility. Through play activities the child exercises his imagination as he expresses himself through art and in block building. A picture represents real objects or experiences. Blocks become houses, churches, barns—whatever the child imagines them to be. Play activity helps the child in language development as he interacts with adults and other children. Through dramatic play the child experiences a variety of responses in human relationships. The child takes on the roles of others. This imaginative play is the beginning of a way to understand another person's point of

view. The ability to put oneself in the place of another is necessary for one to apply the Golden Rule. Play gives the child the opportunity to solve problems creatively and to express his thoughts and feelings. Through such opportunities he develops a sense of self-control and initiative. Through activities a child learns to walk, jump, run, and climb, as he participates in activities which his body dictates. These developmental tasks are vital to mental, social, emotional, and spiritual development.

Play nurtures the spirit. Through play activities a child senses freedom—the freedom to be himself, to grow, and to develop according to God's plan for him. Play alone is insufficient. The child learns through social interaction—child-to-child, teacher-to-child, and child-to-teacher relationships.

What is God's plan for learning?
God is the designer of the developmental process. The highest of his creation, the human being, requires the longest period of childhood or period of play. Play is the way the child learns best. A child learns through play what he can learn in no other way. Play is not a waste of time; it is serious business.

Teaching through the use of activities was ordained by God. By divine command, parents (teachers) are directed to teach God's love and biblical truths throughout the day as children engage in the ordinary activities of living. The child can then see that the Bible has meaning for each of life's experiences; thus the Bible is used as a guide for daily living. Teaching spiritual concepts to young children at church is best done as God instructed parents to teach.

God commands that teachers love God and keep his commandments. "Do that which is right and good in the sight of the Lord" (Deut. 6:18). Children learn more from the examples of the important adults in their lives than from words. Words take on meaning when children see the words demonstrated in actions.

What did Jesus teach?
Jesus' example with children has a weighty message about young children for teachers of preschoolers today. Jesus warned, "Take heed that ye despise not one of these little ones" (Matt. 18:10). Jesus commanded his listeners to recognize the value of young children. He demonstrated the importance of children by his response to the disciples who asked him to identify the greatest in the kingdom of heaven. Jesus called a little child to him, sat the child among them, and said, "Except ye be converted, and become as little children, ye shall not enter into the Kingdom of Heaven" (Matt. 18:4).

What did Jesus do when he was with children?
"He took them up in his arms, put his hands upon them, and blessed them" (Mark 10:16). Jesus respected the worth of the child and the way each child developed in his unique way. He had reasonable expectations of each child. Jesus taught through actions followed by words. He loved (touched and held them) and blessed them (asked God's

24

blessings upon them).

Why is play important?

The child's natural urge to play is designed by God. The brain of a newborn is incomplete—designed to continue to develop. Surprising to many, the way the brain continues to develop is through motor activity in the form of children's play.

Never again will a child learn so much in so short a time as he does during the Preschool years. During the first five years, the child learns about his world: how things work, what things are, and what the rules are with people and things. The child learns about himself: what his place in the world is, what he can and cannot do, how people feel about him, and in turn how he feels about himself. Much of the preschooler's awareness of his world is learned through the process of play. Thus, during the early years, the period during which a child's occupation is play, his basic outlook on life is formed.

What happens when a child is denied the opportunity to play?

The child in an incubator without human stimulation may show signs of retardation within days. Studies have shown that infants who were diapered and fed but left in their beds to look at drab ceilings and walls, without the stimulation of enticing objects to explore, either wasted away or died. Physical development was severely retarded.

Why encourage individual involvement?

Most parents and teachers give children, birth through eight months, the necessary objects and stimulation; however, within the next few years there are some things which a child must learn on his own. He needs appropriate play materials and adult encouragement. Try teaching a child how to ride a tricycle. Adults can help him get on the tricycle and place his hands on the handlebars, but the child must learn by himself. Play is the way children learn what they can learn in no other way. A child works at play. Observe a child as he practices a newly acquired skill—learning to walk. He persists in practicing even though he falls and bumps himself repeatedly. The presence of a trusted adult who shows joy at the child's attempts and who entices him with a toy or outstretched hands encourages the child to work at the task.

What is the teacher's influence?

During the earliest years of dependence, children are most vulnerable to adult guidance. The young child is more difficult to teach, but more impressionable to teaching. What happens to a child during the earliest years influences him as a youth and adult. The child's basic view of himself, the world, and others is crystallized by age five. His personality is so established that it is difficult, if not impossible, to change; thus, in God's plan early childhood is preoccupied with play. During this time teachers have the greatest influence. So at a time of which the child has little conscious memory, he is started on a path for better or for worse.

Children learn about God's love and the Bible as loving teachers guide them while they play—as they choose activities which are appropriate for their development and interest and which relate to real

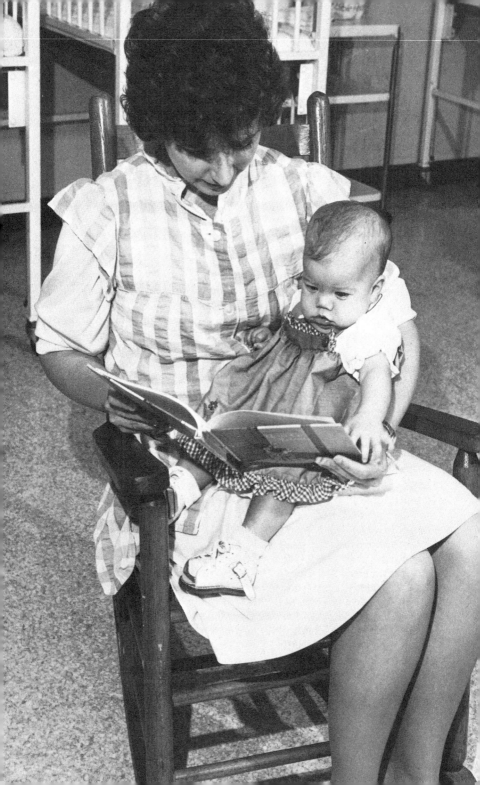

life experiences. The teacher teaches the Bible as he uses a Bible thought, story, picture, or song at a time when a child can understand the relationship of the words to what he is experiencing. In this way, the Bible becomes a book by which to live. Do not underestimate the importance of guiding young children to God. The very best teachers—those who can teach by example—need to be enlisted. What greater impact can a teacher have on the life of a person than to be the individual's teacher during the earliest years when the life is shaped?

What are some optimal learning conditions that encourage wholesome activities at church?

Children deserve to be taught with a planned purpose anytime they are brought to church. Children are always learning. They do not distinguish between Sunday School, Discipleship Training, Mission Friends, Preschool choir, or other times they come to church. They associate church with what happens in their room at church. Since children learn best with familiar and trusted teachers, those persons selected to teach preschoolers must be consistent in their planning and attendance. Anytime preschoolers are in a department at church, there should be *sufficient leadership* to give individualized attention, since children learn best with *adequate pupil-teacher ratios*. Refer to page 66 of *BREAK-THROUGH: Preschool Sunday School Work** for guidelines on pupil-teacher ratios for Sunday School and Discipleship Training. Page 3 of *Building an effective Preschool Choir** contains terminology and pupil-teacher ratios for Preschool choir leaders. Also, the *Missions Friends Leader's Manual** details the distinctives of the WMU program for preschoolers.

Consider other conditions which contribute to the spiritual development of preschoolers.

● *Room Arrangement.*—Preschoolers are active, and a major consideration in the learning environment is space. Space in itself is a form of control for children. Space permits freedom to move with fewer incidents of conflicts with others. If space is insufficient, the director might consider beginning a new department. Refer to pages 111-132 of *Basic Preschool Work* for specific guidelines on room arrangements.

Some principles to consider in room arrangement are:

1. When the child enters the room, he needs to see something inviting. Most children are attracted by homeliving materials.

2. Quiet activities, such as books, puzzles, or nature materials should be grouped together. Activities which produce an appreciable volume of sound such as homeliving, blocks, and music can be grouped together, away from quiet areas. If the homeliving and block areas are too close, traffic problems may arise.

3. Art activities should be close to a source of water.

4. There should be an open space large enough for activities which require free movement as a group. A chair is not necessary for each child. When there is limited space, consider which furnishings can be

removed. Nature materials, books, and puzzles can be used on the floor or placed on windowsills.

• *Appropriate Materials.*—Children are absorbed in activities which they choose. An important condition for optimal learning is met when materials which preschoolers will enjoy are carefully selected to meet the session's purpose.

• *Teaching.*—The teacher is the key to providing effective learning conditions. The teacher is always teaching either positively or negatively. The teacher teaches what he lives. A teacher needs to be aware of each child's needs and interests, knowing that a child's readiness for learning is vital to good teaching. A child can learn only that which can be associated with what he already knows. Therefore, to plan appropriate activities a teacher must know each child's level of understanding and be aware of appropriate materials to challenge each preschooler.

• *Guidance.*—During the Preschool years when children need to develop trust, self-control, and initiative, a teacher plans to use appropriate materials. When he does, a few basic rules are needed:

1. The child is not allowed to hurt himself.
2. The child is not allowed to hurt or annoy others.

When the teacher applies these rules, the child feels safe and secure knowing that he cannot hurt and he will not be hurt.

Punishment has no place at church. Young children learn by imitation—what the teacher does to children, they will do to others. Restrain a child from participating in harmful and destructive activities, while assuring the child of your love.

A child is motivated from within to play; therefore, he does not need external reward to encourage him to play. The teacher reinforces a child's positive actions by noticing him and verbally acknowledging what he has done. In this way a child knows that the teacher is concerned and interested in his activity.

Teachers who aid in effective learning do more observing than talking. Through observation a teacher understands where a child is in his spiritual development. He listens for what each preschooler knows so that he can challenge the child with the next step in his learning. He listens for distortions which the child may have about spiritual thoughts in order to help clarify the preschooler's thoughts.

The wise teacher spends most of his time observing and listening. By observing and listening, the teacher is able to put himself in the place of others and understand from their point of view. Only then can the teacher respond effectively in light of children's needs and apply the Golden Rule (Matt. 7:12).

Refer to chapter 6 of *BREAKTHROUGH: Preschool Sunday School Work*** for additional information regarding the learning environment. *Building an Effective Preschool Choir* (Preschool choir) and *Mission Friends Leader's Manual* (Mission Friends) contain suggestions regarding the learning environment when Preschool choir and Mission Friends groups meet.

What Kinds of Activities Are Desirable to Help Preschoolers Learn?

Guidelines for selecting activities

The following questions serve as guidelines in the selection of appropriate activities for preschoolers:

● Does the activity help a child feel valuable and worthwhile? What does a child think about himself when he is handed a pattern to use? Does the pattern help him think, "I am able and capable; my teacher trusts what I can do," or does this teaching method say to the child: "You are not able to create. I will give you a pattern to use."?

● Can the child experience success with the activity? A child should be able to feel success in what he does at church. Remember that the process is more important than the product. Allow the child to do for himself that which he can do. Allow the child to express what he is thinking and feeling as he works with play materials. To touch up a child's work says to him, "What you did is not good enough." A child who feels successful is willing to take constructive risks to gain more competence.

● Is the activity challenging? For an activity to be challenging, it must be within the range of challenge—not too easy nor too difficult. A child who has the opportunity to use crayons on a large piece of paper can express his thoughts and feelings. The activity is challenging if the child chooses it and continues to use the activity. The use of unstructured materials such as crayons and paper permits the child to practice and increase his abilities to draw and to express his thoughts. He discovers what he can and cannot do with crayons and paper.

● Does the child do the work? Can the child have the feeling of accomplishment expressed in the comments: "Look what I did! I did it all myself." The child learns through doing. When the teacher does the work, the child does not gain the skills for which the activity was planned. To the contrary, he learns dependency and develops a poor self-image.

● Does the activity allow the child to be creative, that is, express himself? Children are made in the image of God with tremendous potential for creativity. Teachers can give children the freedom to develop their God-given capacities, or they can hinder preschoolers' development.

● Does the activity relate to what is important to the child? Effective learning occurs when an activity relates to a child's ongoing needs. The child must be ready to practice the skill, and the information must fit in with what he already knows.

● Will the child be given a choice of an activity? A teacher who allows the child the freedom to choose respects the child's individuality and his need to be self-directed. Choices within reasonable limits encourage self-control and help the preschooler feel that he is trusted.

● Does the activity relate to the purpose for the session? Children are always learning. They are not always learning what we think they are, but an activity should have a purpose.

• Does the child enjoy the activity? For a child to associate happy feelings with experiences at church, activities must be enjoyable. For a child to willingly continue or pursue an activity, he must experience joy or fulfillment. A child's enjoyment of an activity must be considered along with another question: What is he learning from the activity? He may just "love" an activity which is not appropriate for him. For example, he may "love eating chocolate candy or watching television." Real enjoyment helps the child have good feelings about himself, others, and God.

• Does the the teacher accept the child's product or efforts? Avoid evaluating a child's product. The item is his unique contribution and what he has created at this particular time. If the child has joyful experiences, he does not need praise to continue creating. Teachers need to say something which reflects the child's feelings or what is actually on the paper. For example: "It looks like you are enjoying painting today, Johnny. You have painted on the entire piece of paper." The child will let you know if what you said is not accurate.

• Does the activity provide an opportunity for a firsthand experience? Do pictures represent objects or behaviors which the child has experienced? Children and adults learn best from actual experiences. A child may be able to name a picture, "space rocket," for example, if you tell him the right words to say. Unless he has seen a space rocket, he has little understanding of a rocket. What does "manger" or "straw" mean to a child who has never seen or touched these items? To the child a straw may be what he drinks colas through. Firsthand experiences help the child put meaning into the words he hears and the pictures he sees.

• Does the activity provide opportunities for relating to others? Participation in activities with others affords a laboratory of human experience for sharing Bible thoughts, stories, songs, pictures, and conversation when the message relates to the everyday life opportunities of respecting others and sharing.

Kinds of activities

There are four basic kinds of activities (play opportunities planned with a spiritual purpose) which foster creativity, discovery, problem solving, character development, mental competence, language development, self-control, and the ability to get along with others.

• There is play with actions or motions.—During the first two years of life the child gains control of his body movements. Babies are rocked, gently tickled, placed over the foot and swung up and down. Adults control these motions of the baby's body in playful moments of togetherness. The child gains gradual control over his own body movements. He learns to direct his hands to the object he sees and wants. He brings the object to his mouth for further discovery. Early games with motions are peekaboo and pat-a-cake. How important are these early years to gaining automatic control of body movements so that the mind can become involved in more important tasks!

A new stage of development occurs when the child is able to talk. At this time he begins to play with children of his own age. Playfulness takes on the rough-and-tumble motions of jumping, running, hopping, chasing, shoving, and wrestling. This active play usually occurs with groups of the same sex, with boys engaging in more vigorous play than girls.

More complex play occurs as motions combine with ropes, hoops, chants, figures as in hop-scotch, and instructions as in hide-and-seek. Such play offers frequent opportunities to share Bible truths related to getting along with others.

• There is play with objects.—During the crucial first two years known as the sensorimotor period, the child works (plays) at coordinating his body movements and using his senses to acquire and explore objects.

Through his playful exploration of objects (toys), the child gains a basic understanding of such properties as size, shape, texture, and color. He gains a growing understanding of what he can and cannot do with the object. This important knowledge, which continues to be used for a lifetime, is learned during the stage about which we have no conscious memory. When the child learns that an object continues to exist when it is out of his sight, he has reached a mental milestone; thus, object play in infancy forms the structure of the mind and provides a reservoir of mental imagery. You cannot think about something without some mental pictures with which to think.

Object play encourages imagination. The toddler uses a plastic cup for drinking. Later he pretends to drink from an empty cup. At the age of two, the child will pretend to pour milk into a cup before "drinking" from the cup. The child increasingly develops the mental skill of using objects in more complex ways to represent realistic objects and behavior. A block of wood may become a truck. A truck is used for hauling.

By age three, the "family" cooperates in using objects in cooking, and the cooking activity becomes more complex. Cookies are cut. Later they are decorated. They may be shared with another child or with a "sick friend."

At four and five years of age, play becomes even more realistic. A meal is prepared. Guests are coming. Responsibility is taken seriously. Kristin is not ready for group time when the director is. Kristin says: "I've got to finish cooking. Guests are coming."

Play with objects in the block area or homeliving area becomes social play. A child learns to take responsibility; to cooperate; to take turns; to share; to express his thoughts, desires, and feelings; and to respect the rights of others. All this he learns under the guidance of a teacher who, through the use of Bible truths, gives each task a spiritual dimension.

The child's beginning knowledge of cause and effect and means to an end occurs during the first year of life. He drops a spoon from his highchair (cause). The spoon drops to the floor (effect). Mother picks it up (effect); thus he learns to play the "I-drop-it; you-pick-it-up game." He learns to use a stick (means) to reach a block (end—what he wanted to accomplish). Knowing cause and effect and means to an end is vital for a lifetime of making decisions and solving problems.

Objects provide something tangible to share. Shortly after the child is one year old, he will relinquish a toy momentarily. This is a first step to sharing. The teacher says, "Thank you, Stacey," and returns the toy to Stacey's outreached hands. The game has begun. Stacey gives her toy to another for a moment. She hears her teacher say, "Thank you." Stacey mutters her version of "Thank you."

Possession is learned through having objects to hold. For a two-year-old, possession means ownership. "Mine," Jeffrey says as he clutches the book. Conflicts with twos are usually over objects. Conflicts provide opportunities for teaching Christian responses to real problems. A toddler who hurts another in an attempt to get a toy may be surprised when the possessor of the object screams or pulls away from him.

One must possess something in order to take a turn with it (give it up for awhile). One must own an object to share it (give it away). Play with objects in a group setting provides numerous opportunities for young children to gain foundational experiences in sharing.

• There is play with language.—Most play makes use of language. Through playful interaction the child learns to use language for communication. A child learns by imitations. He learns to hold the receiver of the toy telephone to his ear. He has seen it. He mumbles some sounds into it. He has heard such.

Shortly after the first year, he learns to use the word *no*. He has heard the word many times. Motion play such as peekaboo and pat-a-cake involves language. The child needs to experience the real thing (dog), then see pictures of a dog (a representation of the real thing). During playful activities with a book, the teacher shows Jim the picture of a dog. The teacher touches the picture and says, "dog." The child imitates. "The dog goes 'ruff ruff.' " The child makes a barking sound. The child develops a concept of dog; then without a dog or a picture of a dog in sight, the teacher says, "dog." The child imitates the sound of a dog. The use of language is a developmental task at which we can become more and more skillful. Language is used to convey and increase awareness of Bible truths. Don't underestimate the importance of helping a child gain skill in the use of language.

• There is play in the form of games.—Spontaneous games may be played as children initiate them. The resource kits which accompany the Bible Story Time and Preschool Bible Teacher Materials** frequently contain games which involve matching, sorting or grouping, and sequencing (putting pictures in order of what happens first, second . . .). Games are sometimes used during group time for relaxation and while awaiting the arrival of parents. Singing games (example: "This is the way we help at church" to the tune of "Mulberry Bush," p .35)††† may be used for teaching or reinforcing a Bible truth. See chapter 4 (pp. 55-65) and chapter 13 (pp. 184-197) for expanded suggestions on how to use games with preschoolers.

Through the use of desirable activities which relate to the child's everyday needs, and under the guidance of a loving teacher, the child increases "in wisdom and stature, and in favor with God and man" (Luke 2:52).

What Are Some Bible-Related Activities?

What activities are needed to help teachers relate the Christian message to preschoolers? The Bible-related activities are much the same as those used with other age groups, except that those activities used with preschoolers must be understandable for this age child.

The most important way preschoolers learn the biblical message is by being with adults who radiate God's love and care. Additionally, adults must use words, songs, and pictures to help a preschooler become more aware of what the biblical message can mean to him. These Bible-related words, songs, and pictures are interwoven with the activities during each session.

● *Conversation usually precedes any other form of Bible-related activity.*—The use of one word to describe people or things progresses to two words, naming the person or object and describing what they are doing. Short sentences evolve during this process, and by the time a child is six, not only can he listen to extended conversation, but he can converse freely. Conversation is basic to learning. The preschooler is given opportunities to converse as he engages in normal activities as he grows. A child learns to think, then verbally express his thoughts. The child needs to think through his feelings and understandings as he seeks to become a Christian at a later point in his life.

Conversation is used in all activities as you will note in succeeding chapters in this book. An emphasis on story conversation is included in chapter 3.

● *Bible stories told at a child's level of understanding are important avenues of helping the individual become aware of the biblical message.*—Stories and Bible-related activities are vital for preschoolers from two to five years of age. Chapter 3 gives details on using stories with preschoolers.

● *Bible thoughts are the messages from Bible verses in words which preschoolers can understand.*—The biblical message is the thought a child receives from a Scripture passage.

Bible thoughts are woven into each activity as they relate to a child's experience. As you read the succeeding chapters in this book, note how Bible thoughts are used to enhance each activity.

● *Songs are another way to relate the biblical message to preschoolers.*—The use of songs needs to be spontaneous and relate to the activity in which a child is participating. Singing happily to babies and toddlers can help them feel the love and happiness of teachers. Singing to twos and threes usually encourages the children to repeat a song. One three-year-old exclaimed one day as he had repeatedly heard the song "I Like to Go to Church," p. 70,†† "That's my 'savorite' song." Threes, fours, and fives can sing freely with teachers and make up songs. The Bible is full of admonition to sing and thank God. Thank-you songs and other songs with a biblical message need to be used freely with young children. Chapter 9 contains some fascinating information on using music with preschoolers in many different situations.

● *Pictures seem vital to a child's increasing awareness of God, others, and himself.*—From one person or thing per picture to increasing details in a picture, the preschooler grows in his understanding of the Bible and its meaning for him. A child can sing and talk about pictures. He can also tell a story about biblical pictures as he grows. Detailed elaboration on the use of pictures with preschoolers is found in chapter 4.

● *Prayer is another avenue of relating the biblical message to pre-*

schoolers.—Prayers develop as a child hears his parents use simple thank-you prayers for people and things with which he is familiar. A two- or three-year-old can repeat simple prayers. A three-, four-, or five-year-old can listen as simple prayers are spoken and in turn be encouraged to use his own words in talking to God. Spontaneous prayers are encouraged throughout activities as opportunities arise. Especially with the four- and five-year-old, thank-you prayers can be enlarged to asking God for help for himself, others, and things.

Prayer is talking *to* God. Children need to feel that they are talking to God. Use of the same prayer does not help a child grow in learning about prayer. The "God is great, God is good" idea is not a prayer, it is talking about God and not to God.

The use of prayer needs to be a part of a child's understanding of the biblical message. As you read other chapters in this book, note how prayers are a vital part of the child's activities as words, songs, and pictures are used.

• *Giving money at church may be encouraged when the reason for bringing money is explained to older preschoolers and they sense some value in bringing money.*—Jesus certainly stressed meaningful giving. Babies, toddlers, and twos know little about money and may swallow coins. A three-year-old may like to bring money to his department because other members of his family bring money to church. He likes to hear the sound as the money drops in a container. Fours and fives are usually mature enough to remember to have money with them on Sunday. They also like to hear the sound of money as it drops into a container. They can be told that money helps buy the Bible, home books, leisure-reading leaflets, and other things in the room. The money is also given to people who need food, clothes, medicine, and a place to live. If a child finds it difficult to part with his money, respect his right and decision.

The offering container should be seen as a child enters the door, but does not necessarily need to be placed at the door. A child may get the idea that he must pay to gain admission to the room, which is not the biblical message he needs.

Giving is an important avenue to relate the biblical message. A child learns to give of himself in various ways: taking turns with others, and eventually giving of himself and his possessions as he feels secure and senses growing needs around him. Many forms of giving are encouraged as revealed through the suggested activities in this book.

What Are Some Activities for the Extended Session?

The extended session is the continuation of Sunday School or Discipleship Training sessions where the child is being taught while parents attend a worship service. Activities during the extended session afford further opportunities to teach Bible concepts during real life experiences. Specific extended session suggestions are found in the quarterly packets entitled *Extended Session for Babies and Ones, Extended*

Session for 2's and 3's, and *Extended Session for 4's and 5's.*** Listed below are the basic segments of an extended session:

- *Rest Room Time.*—Children learn to take turns washing their hands before eating, and placing their towels in wastebaskets.
- *Snack Time.*—Snack time follows rest room time. Eating provides an opportunity to say thank you to God for food. Babies and creepers eat according to their own schedules. By age two a child can assist in serving the snack. The teacher may say, "Thank you, God, for the apple juice and crackers." Twos, threes, fours, and fives can help serve the juice and crackers.
- *Rest/Listening Time.*—Rest time follows snack time. This portion of the session is for all of the children. Preschoolers need to stop and reflect. They exert much energy trying to relate to other children and need help in resting since they have little skill in this area. Children imitate teachers. Rest/listening time is an opportunity for a teacher to say, "God gives us ears to hear the music." Four- and five-year-olds can say their own thank-you prayer. Teachers lie down with the children during rest time.
- *Activities.*—Activities for extended session are generally the same as or similar to those suggested for Sunday School and Church Training. In keeping with the purpose of the session, children may make visits to different parts of the church, go outside to see a pet, or collect nature items. Such activities are designed to provide firsthand knowledge for children.
- *Outdoor Play.*—Weather permitting, children need fresh air. Outdoor activities give firsthand experiences with the natural world. Children are given opportunities to choose activities which suit their individual needs and interests. Taking turns is a frequent opportunity. Outdoor play is generally planned for the extended session. Pages 133-138 of *Basic Preschool Work** contain guidelines on how to equip and arrange a playground for learning opportunities.

How Do Sunday School, Discipleship Training, Preschool choir, and Mission Friends Activities Differ from Those Used in Vacation Bible School and the Extended Session?

Basically, activities in Sunday School, Discipleship Training, and Vacation Bible School are the same. The activities provide opportunities for children to grow, learn, and think at their full potential. The activities are planned to give children opportunities to

- foster physical development,
- provide mental stimulation,
- promote social awareness,
- encourage a positive self-concept,
- enhance and strengthen curiosity and creativity, and
- develop positive spiritual values.

Vacation Bible School sessions consist of three- to four-hour sessions for five to ten days. Thus preschoolers are given opportunities to have a wider variety of activities because of the extended period of time. There are opportunities to make visits and excursions around the church and in neighboring areas which involve more firsthand experiences. First-hand experiences are vital to a child's learning because these experiences increase a child's understanding of people, the natural world, and his own worth.

A Preschool choir is the basic musical organization for four- and five-year-olds at church. During Preschool choir three or four preschoolers are being led in musical experiences by a teacher. Eighteen preschoolers and several teachers may sing in small groups or in large groups. Preschool choir leaders provide opportunities for preschoolers to grow musically, physically, socially, emotionally, and spiritually.

Mission Friends is the missions education organization for preschoolers provided by the Woman's Missionary Union. The purpose of Mission Friends is to help the child develop an awareness of others and their needs and how he can help.

How Can Preschoolers Who Are Mentally Retarded and Culturally Different Be Incorporated in the Activities at Church?

Mentally retarded preschoolers and culturally-different children have the same basic needs as other children. They need to have their physical needs met, to feel safe, to feel loved, and to learn through challenging activities. They may require more attention than other children in order to feel safe, secure, and loved. With these needs met, they can with guidance turn their thoughts to activities with a spiritual purpose.

Every child learns according to his readiness. The teacher observes the child's readiness and provides materials for challenging activities—neither too easy nor too difficult. Unstructured materials can be used with all learners. How the child uses the materials is based on the child's previous experience, his present abilities, and interests. The mentally retarded may not show as much creative or imaginative power. They may choose activities which require little time. If necessary, the teacher may select activities suggested for children of a younger age in order to meet a particular learner's developmental level.

The teacher needs to give more encouragement and support to the mentally retarded who may be slower to respond. Since children learn by interaction and imitation, a child placed with other children who do not speak his language will quickly learn how to communicate. Learning another language is best done during the Preschool years in an environment in which the child must use the other language in order to be understood. Social interaction is a powerful teacher.

The blind child needs activities which involve the senses of hearing, tasting, smelling, and touching. The deaf child needs activities which involve the senses of touching, tasting, smelling, and seeing.

Any child in an unfamiliar setting needs a source of security. Teachers need to visit the children, be present regularly for each session, and give warm attention to preschoolers so the children can develop a sense of trust in their teachers.

How Do Activities Help Children During Crises?

Such crises as death, moving, illness, divorce, or separation require sensitive teachers and special activities. Activities which permit a child to express his feelings through actions provide a healthy outlet for the child to work through his problems. Not only does the child sense relief, the teachers are able to understand the child's feelings by observing him play out emotions. Unstructured materials have the capacity to encourage the child to use his imagination to express his feelings. Blocks, homeliving materials, crayons or tempera paint with blank paper, and clay are unstructured materials upon which the child acts freely. The materials become whatever the child commands. Music can help children play out their feelings. Books can give the child information to which he can respond creatively. A book about a child experiencing the same problem which he is experiencing gives the preschooler someone with whom to identify. Puzzles which offer the challenge of "work me" absorb the child's mind as he tries to solve a problem, but allows for little creative expression. When a child is experiencing a crisis, the teacher can put into words what the child is feeling: "You feel sad because Daddy is away." "You feel afraid with so many strangers around." (This feeling may occur during a time of death.) "You feel sad because Cha Cha (the child's pet) died." "Daddy and Mother are getting a divorce, and that makes you feel unhappy." Just a few well expressed words let the child know that his teacher is aware of his feelings and cares about those feelings. "You are moving, and you feel sad about leaving your friends."

Summary

Do not minimize the value of play and activities in a child's spiritual development. Play is the window to a child's soul. Through play a teacher is able to see the honest expressions of a child's needs, hopes, fears, and desires.

Personal Learning Activities

1. Why is play important in a child's physical development? social development? emotional development? mental development? spiritual development?
2. Why should preschoolers be allowed to choose from many kinds of activities?
3. What is the value of sensorimotor play (birth-two)? symbolic play (two-five)?
4. List two activities in which children you teach become involved. How can these activities help children develop both physically and spiritually?
5. Name two unstructured play materials. Why are these called unstructured? Why are these materials so important?
6. Prepare a table with appropriate play materials. List the different ways children use these materials.
7. What is the importance of communicating without using words?
8. In a recent conference for Preschool teachers, the following questions were asked: Why aren't Bible story coloring books suggested for art activities? Why didn't the teacher's book suggest that children make sheep cut-outs and paste cotton balls on them last Sunday? (The story was about David and the sheep.) How would you answer these questions?

Materials for Further Study

Caldwell, Max L., compiler. *Witness to Win* (Chapter 5). Nashville: Convention Press, 1978.

Cully, Iris V. *Christian Child Development.* New York: Harper & Row, Publishers, 1979.

Haystead, Wesley. *You Can't Begin Too Soon: Guiding Little Ones to God.* Glendale, California: Regal, 1974.

Ligon, E. M., L. W. Barber, and H. J. Williams. *Looking at Me* (Introduction by Sybil Waldrop). Nashville: Broadman Press, 1979.

Reynolds, Jean K, compiler. *How to Choose and Use Child Care* (Chapter 2). Nashville: Broadman Press, 1980.

---

[1]*Baptist Hymnal* (Nashville: Convention Press. 1975), p. 13.

---

*Available from Baptist Book Stores.

**Available by writing Customer Service Center, 127 Ninth Avenue, North, Nashville, Tennessee 37234; or by calling toll free 1-800-458-2772.

Chapter 3—How to Teach Through the Use of Story Conversation and Stories

Christine Carver McCauley

Young children enjoy a good story today just as they have from the beginning of human history. Storytelling continues to be an important teaching tool, to entertain, and to help the child begin to develop an appreciation of literature.

Activities took first place in curriculum development when educators made teachers aware of the limitations of "transmissive education." Teachers began to see the significance of the concepts that "children learn through doing" and that "children must have firsthand experiences." Some teachers then concentrated on learning new methods and teaching skills. At that point, storytelling took a minor place in teacher-training, and teachers placed less importance on the practice of studying this art. This change of procedure was a loss, because storytelling is an important educational tool, especially in teaching Bible truths and Christian principles. Story conversation or storytelling can never replace a child's firsthand experience, but a teacher can help a child interpret, and have a deeper understanding of what he is experiencing through the use of this valuable teaching tool.

Why Do Teachers Use Story Conversation and Stories with Preschoolers?

Preschoolers know more about people than about words or pictures; consequently, storytelling is the first way in which they can fully understand and enjoy narrative art. Quality narrative art is vitally important to a child's social, emotional, and intellectual development. Through the use of story conversation (conversation about truths related to the preschooler's ability to understand) and stories, a child can learn about his environment, social techniques, and how to communicate with adults and peers.

Conversation and stories help a child's language development. Language is such an important tool in our society that it needs to be cultivated. Teachers should introduce ways of encouraging children in this important aspect of their development. Some of the ways to help children are to encourage them to talk about the story they have heard and to tell Bible and present-day stories themselves. Children should receive positive reinforcement for their efforts. How parents and teachers respond to preschoolers' efforts can make them more verbal or frustrate the children and make them less verbal.

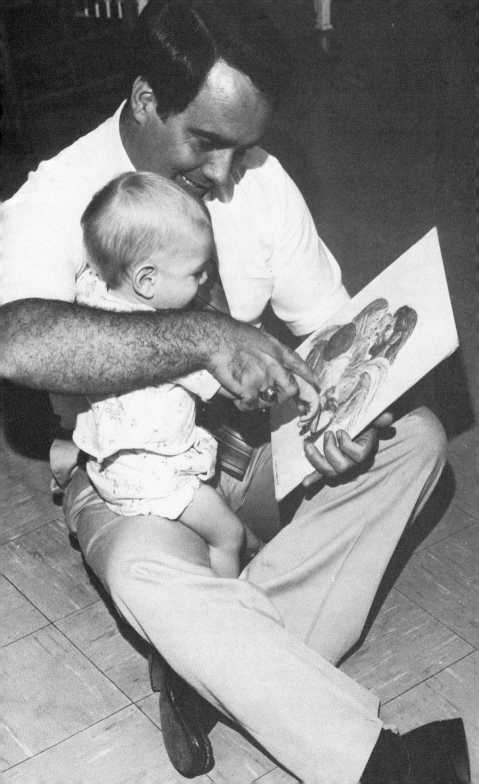

The teacher's speech should be a good example in enunciation and pronunciation. Use a tape recorder to listen to your speech. You may discover that your voice sounds are different from what you imagined.

A child can develop good listening skills as he listens to a story or conversation directed toward him. He can learn to keep in mind a sequence of ideas, increase his vocabulary, and enlarge his background of experiences.

Stories offer opportunity for dramatization. Following the suggestion "Let's pretend that we are the people in the story" may lead to a better understanding of the meaning of the story. Also, teachers may have opportunities to direct the child's undesirable attitudes to others and certain phases of life into wholesome channels.

Story conversation or stories used at the appropriate time can move the emotions and create a mood of awe and wonder for one child or with several children. Teachers need to be sensitive to moments when well-chosen story conversation or a meaningful story can enrich a child's experiences. If children are having satisfying experiences interacting with one another, it is better not to interrupt them, unless you feel the story would be especially beneficial to the learning situation.

As a young child listens to a good story, he can have these vital growth experiences:

- He can see life about him in word pictures that bring him satisfying interpretations.
- He can acquire a better understanding of himself and others.
- His aesthetic sense is sharpened.
- His intellectual growth is stimulated.
- His knowledge increases beyond his environment.

The Preschool years are crucial in the area of the child's spiritual development. Teachers play a major role in this area of development by providing the type of environment where a foundation is laid to help the child grow in increased awareness of God and Jesus. The basic reason for telling Bible stories to young children is to help them form positive foundational understandings of God, Jesus, self, others, family, church, Bible, and the natural world. Bible stories can be used to highlight principles by which one can live a creative, constructive life.

Who Can Benefit Through the Use of Story Conversation and Stories?

Most children can benefit through the use of story conversation and stories. Characteristics and interests of children at different stages should be considered in storytelling. Preschoolers are in the "here and now" stage. They have a short attention span and a limited vocabulary. Story conversation and stories should be selected with these factors in mind.

Bible conversation is a valuable way to help babies, creepers, and toddlers grow in their awareness of God and Jesus. Conversation should be brief with short simply-worded sentences. For example, as a toddler and teacher look at a Bible picture of Baby Jesus at church

in the Read-to-Me Bible (Holman), say: "This is a picture of Baby Jesus at church. Jan, you come to church, too."

Two-year-olds can listen to simple stories, but their interest span is too short for a group time. A teacher may tell the Bible story many times during a session with twos.

Three-year-olds can listen to stories, but the stories should be short and simple. Threes can participate in a short group time, but stories should not be limited to one part of a session.

Four- and five-year-olds are better listeners than younger preschoolers, but two- and three-year-olds still enjoy hearing several sentences from a Bible story. They need stories with simple images, familiar settings, short sentences, and actions in close sequence. Although the vocabulary should remain simple, words are very important, since words are beginning to fascinate the children. Five-year-olds enjoy rhythmic repetition, and they will repeat words that sound alike.

Which Stories Are Appropriate for Preschoolers?

Selecting appropriate stories for preschoolers is very important. Not all stories are suitable for young children. Careful thought should be given to the level of understanding of the age group. Preschoolers are literal-minded (considering only the original meaning of a word) and they think on a concrete level. They are not ready for symbolic terms (terms that refer to something else). Preschoolers cannot make analogies such as Jesus being the light of the world or Jesus as a good shepherd. Frances Dunlop Heron, author of the book *Kathy Ann Kindergartner*, gives adults a graphic picture of how young children think as she relates the incident that happened after a teacher taught the song "The B-I-B-L-E." The words of the song are: "The B-I-B-L-E, that's the book for me. I stand alone on the Word of God. The B-I-B-L-E." Kathy Ann was playing Sunday School with some of her friends at home, and she put the Bible on the floor so they could stand on it. Her father heard the conversation and explained to her that she should not stand on the Bible with her feet. Kathy Ann asked the question, "What other way can you stand?" This is a typical question which we can expect from preschoolers when adults use words and terms they cannot comprehend.[2]

Stories should be read carefully before telling them to children. Check the story for its teaching value. Ask yourself questions such as: "Will the story confuse or frighten the children? What concepts about God and Jesus will it teach?" Confusion can interfere with learning, and many times teachers have more problems clarifying wrong ideas and concepts than teaching correct ones.

Present-day stories, things that happen in real life, are good stories to use with preschoolers. The children enjoy hearing stories about boys and girls who are their age.

Preschoolers have much difficulty in distinguishing between what is real and what is fantasy; therefore, stories should be realistic.

In religious education, the Bible should be the adult's main source for teaching. Our selection of materials, goals, and objectives are somewhat different from those in secular education. Children are at church only a short time; therefore, teachers should make every session a quality learning experience for the boys and girls. This could be the only time they hear about God and Jesus. Our major goal with preschoolers is to help them grow in their awareness and understanding of God, Jesus, church, Bible, self, others, family, and the natural world. Christian principles and Bible truths interpreted by a Christian teacher to the preschooler on his level of understanding are necessary if the above goals and objectives are to be obtained.

Before teachers can become good storytellers, they must know what makes a good story and how to distinguish a good story from an inferior one.

A good story should include a beginning, suspense, climax, and conclusion. Use these steps as guidelines when evaluating stories to be used with preschoolers:

- *Introduction/Setting (Beginning).*—This is a brief introduction of the events to follow. A good beginning captures the interest of the listener in the first few sentences. It must tell about the leading character, put him in the proper setting, and awaken curiosity about his situation. The beginning of the story must give a clue as to what the story is about. Action takes place throughout the story and moves the dialogue from one situation to another.
- *Suspense.*—Suspense is characteristic of the second part of the story. The writer of the story must present step-by-step facts in preparation for a climax.
- *Climax.*—The climax is the high point; it carries the truths of the story.
- *Conclusion.*—The ending moves the listener from the climax of the story in an effort to put his mind at rest.

When selecting appropriate stories for preschoolers, use the following checklist:
1. Has a simple, well-developed plot (the plan of the story). This plot may be centered in one main sequence of events and structured so that a child can anticipate to some degree the outcome of events.
2. Contains action throughout the story.
3. Provides a slight surprise element which adds excitement and makes the children wonder what will happen.
4. Utilizes direct conversation among characters.
5. Uses repetition, rhyme, and catchphrases to add interest.
6. Contains situations involving familiar happenings that will enable the fours and fives to relate to the story. These situations would not be the same for all children. The storyteller needs to consider the background and experiences of individual children in his group.
7. Has a simple and satisfying climax which needs to be reached.
8. Contains one main character with whom the children can easily

identify. Too many characters can be confusing to preschoolers.

9. Utilizes a variety of cultural and racial backgrounds. Such stories should present a realistic picture, not stereotypes of racial or ethnic groups.
10. Has carefully chosen, colorful, and understandable language.
11. Communicates acts of kindness and helpfulness by Jesus in difficult situations.

When Can Story Conversation and Stories Enrich a Child's Experience?

During a session with preschoolers, teachers have many opportunities to use story conversation and stories to enrich the experiences of the children. Young children can listen when they are participating in an activity or quietly looking at a nature item. Teachers should watch for moments when a child's experience can be enriched with appropriate story conversation or a story.

Teachers in a baby or creeper department can use story conversation in the following or similiar situations:

● *Teaching Episode A.*—A teacher shows the picture of Baby Jesus and Mary to the child and says: "The baby's name is Jesus. God made the baby. God made Amy."

● *Teaching Episode B.*—At another time a teacher could say: "The mother is holding the baby. The mother loves the baby. Mary loves Jesus. Mother loves Matthew."

The following story conversation can take place in a toddler department:

● *Teaching Episode A.*—A flower offers opportunities for teachers to say to a young child: "God made the flower. God made the sun. The sun helps the flower grow. Thank you, God, for the flowers."

● *Teaching Episode B.*—Show the picture "Jesus and the Children" from *Read-to-Me Bible Story Pictures, Set 1,* No. 12 to a toddler. Use conversational statements such as: "The Bible tells us about friends. See Jesus and the children. They were friends. Thank you, God, for friends."

Two-year-olds are very active and have a short attention span. Teachers need to spend short periods of time with twos before they loose interest. When teaching preschoolers workers can use the same three rules that apply to an after-dinner speaker: "Be bright, be brief, and be gone." Preschool teachers can change the last rule and say, "before the boys and girls are gone." Following are some examples of possible story conversations with two-year-olds:

● *Teaching Episode A.*—As a two-year-old is looking at a picture of a church, a teacher can say: "There is a story in our Bible about a little boy who liked to go to church. His name is Samuel."

● *Teaching Episode B.*—As a child works in the homeliving area, a teacher can say: "Jesus came to visit Mary and Martha. Martha cooked good food for Jesus. Mary listened to Jesus talk about God. Jesus visited Mary and Martha many times. Mary and Martha loved

Jesus."

Threes, fours, and fives have matured enough to participate in group time which includes a story. Story conversation and stories can be used many times during a session with three-year-olds. Watch for opportunities to enrich the learning experiences of one child or several children as they work in small groups. Following are some situations when a story or story conversation can be used with older preschoolers:

- *Teaching Episode A.*—As preschoolers are building with blocks, the teacher could tell the story "Day and Night." Talk about the carpenters who built the child's house. Encourage conversation about what people do in the daytime and in the nighttime. Say: "I thank God for daytime when we can play with our friends. I thank God for nighttime when we can rest."
- *Teaching Episode B.*—As boys and girls taste raw fruits and vegetables, tell the story of Daniel and how he chose good food to help him grow.
- *Teaching Episode C.*—As a child works a church puzzle, use conversation about Jesus going to church when he was a baby.
- *Teaching Episode D.*—As a preschooler is rocking a doll, use story conversation about baby Obed and his mother.
- *Teaching Episode E.*—When an older preschooler places his money in the offering basket, talk to him about the woman who brought her money to church.

Use stories or Bible story conversation at some of the following times:
- While changing a baby's diaper (story conversation),
- While rocking a baby (story conversation),
- During extended sessions,
- During rest/listening time,
- During snack time,
- Before a field trip,
- During a visit to the sanctuary,
- On a nature walk,
- While waiting for parents,
- On the playground,
- During group time and activities.

Where Can Appropriate Stories for Preschoolers Be Found?

There are many books which can be purchased for young children. Some books are very good, while other books teach concepts, principles, and values which are not suitable for preschoolers. All books should be carefully read before using them with preschoolers.

Some resources which contain story conversation, Bible stories, and present-day stories are listed below:
- *Preschool Bible Teacher A.*—for directors and teachers of babies, creepers, and toddlers;
- *Preschool Bible Teacher B.* —for directors and teachers of twos and threes;

48

- *Preschool Bible Teacher C.*—for directors and teachers of fours and fives;
- *Bible Story Time Teacher.*—for directors and teachers;
- *Beginning.*—(a quarterly home book) for parents of babies, creepers, and toddlers;
- *Living.*—(a quarterly home piece) for use with twos and threes;
- *Growing.*—(a quarterly home piece) for use with fours and fives;
- *Bible Story Time Younger Pupil.*—(four page weekly home leaflet) for parents of babies, toddlers, and twos;
- *Bible Story Time Older Pupil.*—(four page weekly home leaflet) for parents of threes, fours, and fives;
- **Look and Listen, Music Time,** and **Share.**—(individual leisure-reading leaflets) for use with fours and fives;
- *Vacation Bible School* (Church Series).—(teacher's guides, resource kits, and home books) for VBS directors and teachers;
- *Mission Vacation Bible School.*—(teacher's guides, home books, and resource kits) for directors and teachers in Mission Vacation Bible Schools.

There are a number of good storybooks that have been available for many years; however, some of the stories in the books may be too long and involved for preschoolers. The following storybooks may be available at a church library or a public library:

The Bible Story Book (1963) by Bethann VanNess, Nashville: Broadman Press.

Told Under the Blue Umbrella (1962) Association for Childhood Education International, New York: The Macmillan Co.

How Should Teachers Prepare and Present Stories to Preschoolers?

Some teachers say it is hard for them to tell a story. Often these persons feel they should memorize the story and tell it verbatim. Other teachers say, "I have trouble using story conversation with preschoolers." If you are in one of the categories listed above, the tips on preparing and presenting a story can help you develop the skills necessary to feel comfortable using a story with twos, threes, fours, and fives.

A good storyteller does not need dramatic training, but he must have time, concentration, and lots of practice. The rewards of telling a story are mutually satisfying for the teacher and the children. Once this practice is begun, the teacher will immediately realize the difference that telling a story can make in his enthusiasm and in the response of the children. This teacher will never go back to just reading stories.

Tips on Preparing to Tell Stories

What a teacher needs most of all as he prepares to tell stories to preschoolers is enthusiasm for the art of storytelling and a love for the stories he tells. He should make "friends" with his stories!

The Bible story materials that are written for a given session with

preschoolers will be more effective if they are told to the children. A teacher should prepare a story carefully so that he can tell the facts accurately, mention the incidents in proper order, tell the story without notes, and continue without pausing to think what happens next, though he may have an interruption.

Most teachers enjoy telling a story when they are adequately prepared. Consider the following suggestions as you prepare your story:

- Prepare yourself mentally and emotionally through prayer.
- Study the Bible background material. Watch for its message to you as a person.
- Set as your goal the communication of appropriate portions of this Bible message to the children.
- Read the story several times.
- Find the four parts of the story: the beginning or introduction, suspence, climax, and conclusion.
- Learn the story through a series of mental pictures. Read the story slowly, forming a picture in your mind of each character and event. Close the book and think through the story in terms of pictures.
- Learn to pronounce correctly the names of the characters mentioned in the story for preschoolers.
- Decide on a good beginning to gain the attention of the children. Avoid unnecessary descriptions and explanations.
- Make changes in words if they will make the story more understandable.
- Recall the sequence of events. Think about how the people involved in the situation must have thought, felt, and spoken.
- Memorize key passages of description or conversation.
- Tell the story over and over until it becomes a part of you.
- Practice telling the story in front of a mirror.
- Study the story while you do something else that requires a minimum of concentration.

Tips on Presenting Story Conversation and Stories
Some teachers and parents think story conversation is used only with babies, creepers, and toddlers. Teaching through conversation can be effective with all preschoolers. Story conversation is usually a few lines of a story woven into natural conversation. This type of teaching can be used with preschoolers whenever a teacher finds an opportunity.

Children are sensitive to facial expressions, especially to the people whom they recognize as authorities. If they have grown to love and respect the person who is telling the story, they can give their undivided attention to the storyteller's face.

As a teacher looks into the children's eyes when telling the story, he gets much encouragement from the facial expressions of the children. Teachers receive positive feedback as the eyes of preschoolers reveal the look of awe and wonder at something they have grasped for the first time. This is especially true when the content is some biblical truth they have learned. These moments with boys and girls are worth any amount of time and effort a teacher has to spend in preparation to tell the story well enough to gain and hold the interest of preschoolers.

Often children want to crowd around the teacher as he tells the story. Before beginning the story, arrange for the children to sit in comfortable positions on the floor or in chairs. The physical setting in which a story is told is important. The children and the storyteller should be comfortable.

Below are some ways to improve storytelling:

• Before starting a story, make sure children have not been sitting too long. Give them an opportunity to stretch their muscles.

• Beware of conspicuous dress or jewelry.

• Get as close to your audience as possible.

• Sit on the eye level of the children.

• Look directly at the children. Include all children in the group, not just those nearest you.

• When telling a Bible story, open the Bible to the correct story reference and keep it open as you tell the story.

• Tell the story in a soft, natural conversational manner, but speak loudly enough for all of the children to hear. The quality of the voice has much to do with how pleasing the story is to the listener. Do not affect a "honeyed" tone just because you are talking to children.

• Do not let your voice trail at the end of a sentence.

• Use timing effectively. Vary the tempo. As action increases and things begin to happen, increase the story's tempo. Before a moment of question, surprise, or awe, a pause is effective.

• Try consciously to reduce use of connecting sounds like *or, er,* and *a.* Be silent if you are thinking about what to say next. A pause can be an effective technique in telling a story.

• If you think the children will not understand the meaning of an important word, show a picture or an object which will help them understand the word before telling the story.

• Use as much conversation between characters of the story as is reasonably possible.

• If a child becomes inattentive during the story, arouse his curiosity by lowering your voice to a whisper or by using his name. Say, "John, a boy shared his lunch with Jesus."

• Weave forgotten incidents into the story. Do not say, "Oh, I forgot to tell you."

• If during the story a child interrupts to relate an incident, he should be encouraged to wait until the story is finished to share the information with the group. Occasionally, such a contribution is valuable, but many times such interruptions can break the train of thought and ruin a good story.

• Keep the story within the limits of a preschooler's attention span. Shorten the story if necessary.

• Following the story, children may have a few questions or comments. Take time to answer their questions; then ask a few questions to help the children think.

Your greatest compliment is when a child says, "I like that story; tell it again."

Summary

Listening to a good story is an important developmental experience for a child. Through vicarious experiences with stories, a child can see life about him in word pictures, which can bring satisfying interpretations. A child can often acquire a better understanding of himself and others as he listens to stories about children having experiences which are similar to those he is experiencing. Stories can provide a child with the opportunity to increase his awareness of the beauty around him, thus, sharpening his aesthetic sense. Intellectual curiosity can be stimulated as the child's knowledge increases about matters beyond his environment.

When stories are selected with preschoolers in mind, thought should be given to how the children think, feel, and hear. Preschoolers have a limited vocabulary. They believe what adults say to them. Adults understand that words have more than one meaning, but preschoolers do not. The wrong kind of story can be frightening and confusing to children. Preschoolers must sometimes feel similar to an adult in a foreign country without the ability to communicate his needs because of the language barrier. Care should be taken so that children are not burdened with too much information, too soon.

Consider some of the following questions when choosing stories:

● Will the story help preschoolers grow in their feelings of self worth?
● Will the story help the children grow in their awareness of God's love for them?
● Will the story stimulate the imagination and curiosity of the boys and girls?
● Will the story help develop appropriate attitudes toward others?
● Will the story help children grow in their awareness of Jesus as a loving person?
● Will the story create interest and enjoyment for the children?
● Will the story help the children grow toward the long-range goals and objectives you have set for your group or for individual preschoolers?
● Will the story and story conversation be used in the same way with all ages of preschoolers?
● Will the length of the stories determine the ages for which they are recommended? Why?

Personal Learning Activities

1. Refer to *Preschool Bible Teacher A**. Underline recommended story conversations for use with babies, creepers, and toddlers. Write several appropriate story conversations to be used with the preschoolers. Use the story conversation with boys and girls. Evaluate the preschoolers' responses and your feelings as you talked to the children.
2. Refer to *Preschool Bible Teacher B**. Find several Bible stories

which are suggested for use with twos and threes. Write a short story suitable for a three-year-old. Tell the story to a child. How did he respond? In the future, how will you change the way the story is told?
3. Refer to *Preschool Bible Teacher C***. Circle several Bible stories which are recommended for four- and five-year-olds. Use the stories with four- and five-year-olds. How did they respond?
4. Read a present-day story and list its teaching value.
5. Use a cassette player to record your voice as you tell a story. Were you pleased with your voice quality? If not, practice telling the story until you are pleased with your presentation.
6. Refer to *Start*. Circle several stories recommended for use with preschoolers involved in *Mission Friends*.

Materials for Further Study
Books
Bryant, Sara C. *How to Tell Stories to Children*. New York: Gale, 1973.
Hildebrand, Verna. *Introduction to Early Childhood Education*. 2nd ed. New York: The Macmillan Co., 1976.
Jacobs, L. "Telling Stories to Young Children," in *Using Literature with Young Children,* ed. Leland B. Jacobs. New York: Teachers College Press, 1965.
Ross, Raymond R. *Storyteller*. Columbus, Ohio: Merrill, 1980.
Sawyer, Ruth. Rev. ed. *The Way of the Storyteller*. New York: Viking, 1977.
Shedlock, Marie L. *The Art of the Story-teller*. New York: Dover, 1951.

Magazines
Sherman, John Lee. "Storytelling with Young Children," *Young Children,* January 1979, Journal of the National Association for the Education of Young Children, Washington, D.C., p. 20.

Recording
Sawyer, R. *Ruth, Storyteller*. Two record album. Weston Conn: Weston Woods Studios, n.d. number W W 701 and W W 702.

---

[2]Frances Dunlop Heron, *Kathy Ann Kindergartner* (New York: Abingdon Press, 1955), p. 31.

---

*Available from Baptist Book Stores.
**Available by writing Customer Service Center, 127 Ninth Avenue, North, Nashville, Tennessee 37234; or by calling toll free 1-800-458-2772.

Chapter 4—How to Teach Through the Use of Pictures

Christine Carver McCauley

Pictures have been used to convey messages to people since the Egyptians used hieroglyphic pictures to record sacred writings. Pictures communicate information to people many times during the day.

"Reading a picture" is an active experience in which a child may see new things, interpret past experiences, or consider what could happen in another situation.

Pictures can tell a story. For most children, the pictures are of greater importance than the words of a story. Many times a child asks, "Will you read a story to me?" "To read" probably means to look at the pictures and identify verbally what is seen.

Pictures are indispensable for enriching experiences for young children about the Bible, the natural world, God, Jesus, church, families, self, and others. Pictures help preschoolers grow in their awareness and wonder of the world around them.

The imagination of the teacher determines how many or how few pictures will be used during a session with preschoolers. Limit the number of pictures in view at one time to those which pertain to the Bible teaching aim.

Why Use Pictures to Teach Preschoolers?

An old Chinese proverb states, "a picture is worth ten thousand words."[3] Listed below are additional reasons why pictures should be used with preschoolers.

● Pictures give children the opportunity to recognize things that are familiar to them; thus they feel a sense of satisfaction of identifying things in their world.

● Pictures allow children to identify with situations and scenes common to their environment.

● Pictures can provide valuable substitute experiences for children when it is impossible to provide direct experiences.

● Pictures may stimulate conversations, which can give insight into the child's concept of the world around him.

● Children enjoy seeing pictures of other children doing things which they also have done. As they observe families having happy times together, they may develop a deeper understanding of their families and homes.

● An atmosphere of worship can be created, and a child can grow in his awareness of God as he observes a picture of something God has made.

• Older preschoolers can make up stories as they observe pictures. Creating original stories encourages boys and girls to develop their imaginative and creative abilities.

• Children become more aware of good food to eat, good health habits, and safety rules as they look at pictures.

• Pictures can encourage acceptable behavior as the preschoolers observe other children doing kind and helpful things.

• Pictures can help children develop a more positive attitude toward visits to a doctor or the hospital.

• Observing pictures of children taking care of pets can help older preschoolers feel a sense of responsibility for proper care of their pets.

• Pictures can help children strengthen their ability to classify and put things in sequential order.

• Children can learn colors and shapes through the use of pictures.

Who Can Learn Through the Use of Pictures?

All preschoolers can learn through the use of pictures. Pictures can reach young children on their level of understanding. Because of their limited vocabularies and short attention spans, preschoolers learn more through seeing and hearing than through just hearing. Sometimes adults do not have a total grasp of a situation until they see the item or person involved. If this is true of adults, then pictures need to be a vital part of a preschooler's learning environment.

The baby can become increasingly aware that God planned for him as a teacher talks to him about a picture of a glass of milk. As the baby pats and holds the picture, the teacher can say: "Milk, m-m-m, good milk. Thank you, God, for milk." This type of teaching is not forced on the child, and is used when the child shows interest in the picture. As songs are sung and this type of conversation is used with good pictures, the baby may associate happy feelings with the object in the picture.

Creepers and toddlers show a great deal of interest in pictures. As a teacher talks to the young child, he needs to remember to use simple words and short sentences. Story conversation can be used with creepers and toddlers as they view a picture.

Simple questions can be asked as twos and threes look at pictures. A teacher could say: "I see a picture of a boy putting on his shoes. Do you see the picture?" Questions may follow such as, "Can you put on your shoes?" This subject may lay a foundation for talking with the child about how he is growing and learning to dress himself. While viewing the picture mentioned above, singing the song "I'm Growing," p. 30,† would be enriching for the child.

Four- and five-year-olds, as well as other preschoolers, need attractive, colorful, and realistic pictures. As children observe pictures and talk to other children and the teacher about the pictures, they can increase their vocabularies, learn new concepts, and clear up misconceptions.

Pictures should be placed in various areas of the room. In a baby department, pictures should be located near or in each crib. A teacher needs to have easy access to pictures.

As a creeper, toddler, two- or three-year-old moves about the room, pictures should be accessible to him. Pictures should be placed on the floor and at various places on the wall. Children should be able to pick up pictures and handle them.

In four- and five-year departments, pictures can be placed on the wall around the room at the eye level of the children and on a picture rail.

Which Pictures Should Be Used to Teach Preschoolers?
Pictures are more than decoration in a Preschool department. Well-chosen pictures speak to children in positive ways. Preschoolers need large pictures to stimulate their curiosity, thinking, and learning. An important task for teachers is the selection of appropriate pictures to use with preschoolers. Pictures should be chosen carefully. Use the following suggestions as guidelines when you select pictures:
● Pictures should be realistic, not abstract.
● Pictures should have an uncluttered background.
● Pictures should contain familiar objects and be within the realm of the child's understanding and experience.

The *Read-to-Me Bible Story Pictures* are full-color enlargements of the pictures in the *Read-to-Me Bible* (Holman). Each picture set has twelve pictures. *Read-to-Me Bible Story Pictures, Set 1* is for babies through twos. *Read-to-Me Bible Story Pictures, Set 2* and *Set 3* are for twos through fives.

The *Natural World Pictures, Set 1* has sixteen pictures which include animals, fruits, and outdoor scenes. These pictures are for babies, creepers, and toddlers. The *Natural World Pictures, Set 2* has twenty-four pictures which include zoo animals, nature themes, and fruits and vegetables. These pictures are for twos through fives.

The *Present-Day Pictures, Set 1* has twenty pictures that preschoolers (babies-toddlers) can relate to their present-day experiences. These pictures include activities such as rolling a ball and going to the park; and familiar objects such as a doll, car, and book. The *Present-Day Pictures, Set 2* has twelve pictures that preschoolers (twos-fives) can enjoy. These pictures include places a preschooler may go such as the mall, airport, park, or a farm. There are also pictures of boats, wagons, a school bus, and a bicycle.

The *People-Around-Me Pictures* has twenty-four pictures of people preschoolers know such as family members, and helpers in the community. These pictures are for twos through fives.

The *Preschoolers-at-Church Pictures* has twenty-four pictures of church-related activities for preschoolers such as singing, cooking, and playing dress-up. These pictures are for twos through fives.

Preschoolers need pictures in the department that they can under-stand and that present additional information so they can relate the

pictures to firsthand experiences. These pictures reinforce the child's firsthand experiences. Walls in the departments should not have painted murals or nursery rhyme characters because these pictures are distracting to preschoolers. Of all places, the child needs to be exposed to reality at church. In most cases, the wall murals are only decoration for the children's parents. Pictures should not be permanently attached to walls of a Preschool department. Place pictures on the eye level of the child. What preschoolers want to see, they also want to touch. Children should be allowed to touch and handle pictures.

Pictures used during a session in Preschool departments should be correlated with the curriculum emphasis for that session. The teacher's guides in Preschool Bible Teacher materials list suggested pictures to use during each session. Some pictures can be used for more than one session, but pictures should be changed frequently.

When Can Pictures Be Used to Teach Preschoolers?

Pictures can serve as a valuable substitute for firsthand experiences. When a preschooler wants to see, it usually means he wants to touch, taste, smell, and hear. A preschooler learns best through the use of these senses. Many opportunities should be given to preschoolers to use all of their senses.

Preschoolers need firsthand experiences so they can have "things" to talk about and can build language facility, vocabularies, and concepts. It is not always possible, however, to provide children with the needed firsthand experiences. In these situations, pictures can serve as a valuable substitute for firsthand experiences; however, pictures are more meaningful after firsthand experiences.

As preschoolers observe and handle pictures, they may engage in conversation with other boys and girls. As they listen to other children, they gain valuable insight into how other boys and girls view the world around them. Due to lack of experiences and understanding, children can form misconceptions, but the alert teacher can tactfully share the correct information with them.

Pictures in a department room can foster feelings such as friendliness, happiness, and thankfulness. Other pictures can suggest desirable conduct to children. Use several pictures that show children being kind to others, helping at home, and being kind to animals.

Pictures can be used in activities. For instance, put a picture in the block area that may lead preschoolers (threes, fours, or fives) to build a structure that will be unit-related. This activity can lead into natural conversation which accomplishes the Bible teaching aim. Pictures can enrich a storytelling experience. Show a picture after telling the story. Help children recall the story as the content of the picture is discussed. Clarify any misconceptions children may have about the story or picture.

Using an instant-print camera, move around the room and take pictures of children participating in different activities. Match Bible thoughts to the pictures. Allow each preschooler to take home the pictures depicting his involvement in the activities.

Following are some suggested ways to use pictures with babies, creepers, and toddlers:

Teachers can talk and sing to babies as they use Picture 6, "Rocking in the Boat," from *Present-Day Pictures, Set 1,* to help babies relate to these firsthand experiences.

In the creeper department, Picture 12, "Church," and Picture 4, "Eating Crackers," from *Present-Day Pictures, Set 1* can be used to enrich the conversations with creepers about church.

Toddlers can be stimulated through conversation and songs about the church as they observe and handle Picture 9, "Doll," and "Church," Picture 12, *Present-Day Pictures, Set 1.*

Show a picture of Jesus to a baby, creeper, or toddler and sing the song "Jesus, Jesus," p. 16†. At another time, show a picture of a flower or sunshine to fours and fives and sing the song "God Loves Me," p. 4†, substituting the names of different things in the picture for the list of things God made.

Middle and older preschoolers can participate in musical activities as they view pictures. Twos may be able to participate in some of the following activities:

● Place around the room pictures of family activities. Sing a song about families. Then ask one or two children in your area to find pictures about activities in which they participate at home.

● Sing a song and let a child choose from a group of pictures one that matches the song.

● Play appropriate music as the preschoolers walk around and look at the pictures which have been placed in various parts of the room. After the walk, ask a child to go and stand by a specific picture such as "a picture of a child helping." To vary this learning opportunity with older preschoolers, ask a child to choose a picture and tell about the picture.

Pictures are valuable teaching aids to increase a preschooler's knowledge of the Bible. Use the following suggestions to enhance learning experiences of three- to five-year-olds:

● Read a Bible thought and let a four- or five-year-old choose from a group of pictures one he thinks matches the thought.

● Ask a child to say a Bible thought and find a picture which makes him think of that thought.

● Use simple terms to explain customs of Bible days while children look at a Bible picture.

● Arrange a series of pictures of different scenes in a Bible story. Let the children recall the story by telling about the pictures.

● From out-of-date literature, cut pictures of Jesus as a baby, Jesus helping the blind man, and Jesus loving the children. Mount these pictures on construction paper and place them in the Bible where the appropriate story is printed.

● Place several Bible pictures in different areas of the room. Whisper to a child a clue to one of the pictures. Ask him to stand by the picture. When all pictures have been chosen, let each four- or five-year-old tell about his picture.

● Show a picture of children playing together happily and say, "The Bible tells us to be kind."

Four- and five-year-olds find guessing games interesting. Following are some games children enjoy:

● "What's Missing?" Choose pictures in categories such as *family*, *church*, or *community workers*. Let the older preschoolers see four or five pictures from one of these categories. Direct the children to close their eyes and ask a preschooler to hide one of the pictures. The other children guess which picture is missing.

● "What's Behind the Windows?" Choose a large colorful picture. Paste the picture on a piece of construction paper. Lay over the picture a second piece of construction paper the same size. Attach the two pieces at the top with tape. In the top piece of paper, cut small "windows" or flap-type holes at strategic points over the picture. Number the flaps in the order in which you want fours and fives to peek into the windows. Invite one child to look behind flap number one and tell what he sees. The children take turns opening the flaps until they guess what is behind all of the windows.

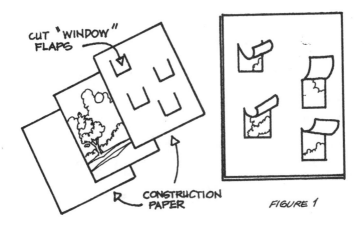

CUT "WINDOW" FLAPS

CONSTRUCTION PAPER

FIGURE 1

File folders are excellent formats for matching and classifying games, and the folders require little storage space. The following games can be made to use with fours and fives:

Cut pictures from magazines of a room in a house or draw a picture of a room. Paste the picture on one side of a file folder. Cut pictures of activities that take place in that room and the furniture that is used. See Figure 2, page 62.

FIGURE 2

Children can place furniture in the correct rooms; then they select pictures of activities that take place in these rooms.

To store pictures, paste an envelope on the front of the file folder. A cardboard box can be used to store the file folders.

To a young child everything is alive. To help children understand what is alive and what is not, cut out one set of pictures of things which are alive and another set of things which are not alive. Paste on one side of a file folder pictures of things that are alive, and on the other side of the folder paste pictures of things that are not alive. Allow the children to use the second set of pictures to match those on the file folder. As the children work, talk to them about the differences in living and nonliving things.

Where Can Appropriate Pictures for Preschoolers Be Found?

Teachers must continually watch for suitable pictures to use with preschoolers. The following pictures and materials can be purchased from Materials Services Department, 127 Ninth Avenue, North, Nashville, Tennessee 37234:

- *Read-to-Me Bible Story Pictures, Set 1, 2,* and *3* for use with birth through fives;
- *Natural World Pictures, Set 1* and *2* for use with birth through fives;
- *Present-Day Pictures, Set 1* and *2* for use with birth through fives;
- *Preschoolers-at-Church Pictures* for twos through fives;
- *People-Around-Me Pictures* for twos through fives
- *Preschool Pictures A, Set 3*

The following magazines and home books contain excellent pictures for use with preschoolers: *Beginning, Living, Growing, Living with Preschoolers, Look and listen, Music Time, Share, Bible Story Time Younger Pupil,* and *Bible Story Time Older Pupil.*

How Can Pictures Be Mounted and Filed?

Every Preschool department should have a large selection of good pictures and a well-organized picture file. The use of pictures with preschoolers gives the boys and girls ideas and helps them experience feelings about their immediate environment and the natural world.

Cover the pictures with clear contact plastic to prevent them from being torn and soiled. Protect pictures because some cannot be replaced and others are costly to replace.

Try the following suggestion on mounting and covering pictures:

• Cut a piece of corrugated cardboard, tagboard, or sturdy poster board to the exact size of the recommended picture to be covered.

• Cut a piece of clear contact plastic three or four inches larger than the picture.

• Carefully peel the paper from the contact plastic.

• Lay the plastic with sticky side up on a flat, smooth surface.

• Bend the picture into the shape of a U with the picture turned facedown over the plastic. Do not crease the picture.

• Gently lower the picture to touch the plastic; then unbend the picture onto the plastic.

• Rub the picture with the edge of a ruler to release air bubbles.

• Cut the corners of the plastic as shown below:

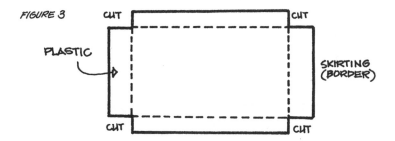

• Place the backing exactly on top of the picture which is facedown. If the backing slips, place a small amount of rubber cement in the middle of the picture; then add the backing.

• Carefully fold the plastic border on the end opposite you by pulling the plastic tightly toward you. Press the plastic to the backing. Smooth out air bubbles with a ruler.

• Turn the picture to repeat the overlapping on the other end.

• Turn the picture to overlap one side; then repeat the process to securely fit the remaining side over the first side.

Picture holders can be made for use with older preschoolers. Cut heavy cardboard the size of the picture. Cut four 6 by 4-inch construction paper rectangles for each holder. Place a rectangle diagonally across one corner. Turn the cardboard over, keeping the construction paper in position on the front. Fold the rectangle over the back of the cardboard and tape it. This makes a triangular pocket on the front. Repeat this procedure at each corner. Slip the picture under each corner pocket to hold it in place. The picture can be used on a picture rail, or propped against a wall or piece of equipment for the children to see and handle.[4]

There are several types of picture files from which to choose. Here are a few suggestions:
• Purchase from the Baptist Book Stores a Teaching Picture File and Cabinet (Item 4309-13) for use in departments for older preschoolers.
• *Make Your Own Preschool Furniture* (Item 9143-0). The instructions for making Preschool furniture, including a picture file, are available by writing Customer Service Center, 127 Ninth Avenue, North, Nashville, Tennessee 37234; or by calling toll free 1-800-458-2772.
• Select a sturdy cardboard box at least 12 inches deep, 15 inches long, and 10 to 14 inches wide. Cover the box with attractive contact plastic.

File all picture sets by sets. Other pictures can be filed under curriculum subjects such as *Bible, church, family, self, others, natural world, God,* and *Jesus.*

Bible pictures can be filed under *Old Testament* and *New Testament* or by Bible characters.

Other files can be set up such as pictures of community workers, farm animals, senses, seasons, transportation, children of other lands, pets, construction, and others. These pictures can be obtained from magazines and stored by subjects in manila folders.

Summary
Two kinds of pictures are used with preschoolers: Bible pictures and present-day pictures. Bible pictures portray Bible scenes on the child's level of understanding. Present-day pictures translate biblical truths into the everyday experiences of children.

Pictures may foster a mood of quietness, thankfulness, and moments of awe and wonder. These moments are fleeting with preschoolers. A teacher must be alert for teachable moments.

Personal Learning Activities
1. Evaluate your last session with preschoolers. Think of situations in which a picture or pictures could have been used to enrich the experiences of the children in your department.
2. Make a new picture game to use with the preschoolers whom you teach.
3. Start a picture file or update your old one.
4. Cover with clear contact plastic all teaching pictures that have not already been mounted.
5. Select a picture from *Preschool Pictures A, Preschool Pictures B,* or *Preschool Pictures C.* Study the picture carefully. List all the things you see in the picture. How do you think a preschooler would interpret what you see?

Materials for Further Study
Almay, Mildred, ed. *Early Childhood Play.* New York: Selected Academic Readings, 1968.

Holt, John. *How Children Learn.* New York: Dell, 1970.
Hymes, James L., Jr. *A Child Development Point of View.* New York: Prentice Hall, 1955.
Isaacs, Susan. *Intellectual Growth in Young Children.* New York: Shocken, 1966.

---

[3]Pauline Hargis, *Teaching the Beginner Child* (Nashville: Convention Press, 1948), p. 63.
[4]*Guide C for Preschool Teachers,* October—December, 1980, p. 95.

---

*Available from Baptist Book Stores.
**Available by writing Customer Service Center, 127 Ninth Avenue, North, Nashville, Tennessee 37234; or by calling toll free 1-800-458-2772.

Chapter 5—How to Teach Through the Use of Art Materials

Christine Carver McCauley

The value of art activities for the young child lies in the process rather than in the finished product. Art experiences offer him more opportunity for self-expression and a sense of accomplishment than any other task he undertakes. The feeling that "I did this myself," and "I had fun doing it" can help build the child's self-confidence. One child may cover every inch of his paper with red paint, while another may cover only a small portion of his paper, but each child will feel pleasure and a sense of accomplishment from his creation. The teacher should encourage this feeling by praising the child's product for itself, never comparing the item with a model he has chosen or with someone else's work.

Why Use Art Activities to Teach Preschoolers?

"He always wanted to say things, but no one understood. So he drew." These lines have an important message to teachers of preschoolers. Art for a child is a means of self-expression. He uses art to express what he does, sees, feels, thinks, and talks about. Art activities provide the preschooler with opportunities to explore and experiment, to express ideas and feelings about himself and the world around him. These experiences strengthen his ability to imagine and to observe, and increase his sensitivity to himself and others. Art experiences for the young child are basic to developing a happy, wholesome, and creative personality.

Art experiences have therapeutic value. Through art, a child can express many of his feelings. Helping a child turn his feelings into creative channels gives him an outlet he can use throughout his life.

Children grow socially as they learn the importance of working together. As children interact with each other, group leadership qualities develop, and the children grow in self-control. Social development also takes place as preschoolers take turns with materials and assume responsibility for cleaning up or returning materials after they use them.

Intellectual growth takes place as the child thinks of ways of using art materials. Concepts are developed as the child learns new terms such as *colors, slick, soft, hard,* and *rough.* He learns to solve problems and gains confidence in his ability to use materials creatively.

There are many opportunities for physical growth and motor coordination. As a child uses his fingers to finger-paint, draw with crayons, manipulate clay, paint, paste, cut, and work with wood, he is developing muscular control. Selecting shapes, choosing colors, and determining which sizes to use offer a child opportunities for visual discrimination.

Another important value of using art materials with young children is that there is no single predetermined method of using art materials. Each child can achieve successful and satisfying experiences. The children's work should never be compared. When children experience achievements, a feeling of personal worth develops.

Spiritual enrichment can take place as an older preschooler paints or draws things that God made with which he is familiar. As children express themselves through art materials, sensitive teachers can make the experiences meaningful through appropriate conversation and songs about God. Threes, fours, and fives need to hear that God loves them and that he created beauty for people to enjoy.

Who Can Benefit Through the Use of Art Materials?

At what age does the ability to express self through art begin for a child? There are differing opinions regarding this question. Some people believe art begins when a baby notices color and shape. Others agree that art may begin before a child is handed a crayon or paintbrush. A child may sit and draw with his hands in the air. His movements are spontaneous and without thought, but given a crayon and a piece of paper, the child may cover every inch or may cover only one area of the paper.

The general opinion seems to be that the use of art for a child begins around the age of two. This guideline does not mean that we should deprive younger children of the enjoyment of looking at the beauty of a red rose or other flowers, at color and shape, or at a pretty picture. Exposure to these items can help preschoolers grow in their awareness of beauty.

When a child first uses a crayon, he will start making marks on paper that appear to be uncontrolled and meaningless. To a child these scribbles provide a very important outlet.

Where Are Preschoolers in Their Ability to Use Creative Expression?

Rhoda Kellogg elaborates in her book, *The Psychology of Children's Art,* that she has discovered twenty basic scribbles of two-year-olds and seventeen placements that are common among children the world over. She points out that at first glance, scribbles may look like tangles of spaghetti, lines without form or distinction, but actually some scribbles are most complex. None of the scribbles are senseless. Her research has been carried out over a period of twenty years.[5]

Scribbling to a young child means enjoyment, happiness, and the coordination of motion. During a session at our church, a four-year-old had spent a lot of time drawing with crayons. When a teacher looked at his drawing, it appeared that he had included the twenty basic scribbles pictured in the book by Rhoda Kellogg. The child was asked if he would let some other teachers see his drawing. He willingly agreed to share the drawing. At the end of the session, the father saw the drawing. His response was, "I hope Kenny will learn to draw one day." The teacher said, "Kenny's drawing represents the twenty basic scribbles which are a part of the natural process all children go through before they draw recognizable pictures." The father was then interested in examining the drawing. He turned to Kenny and praised him for his work. Kenny, who is shy and talks very little, smiled happily at his father and his teacher. Whenever the teacher sees Kenny, he receives that same kind of smile.

Adults in a child's life need to understand the development of art expression in children. A preschooler should not be expected to draw recognizable objects to please adults. If a preschooler is encouraged to use art materials which are beyond his level of development, he may become frustrated, loose confidence in himself, and refuse to use art materials.

There is a pattern of developmental levels through which a child's artistic expression evolves. Children go through at least three stages of development; however, these stages are identified by several different names. These stages can simply be labeled *scribbling, shapes* and *design,* and *pictorial.* All children pass through the same stages of development; it is a natural course of learning to draw. The stages will vary among children. In one age group, there could be children in all three stages.

The scribbling stage usually occurs from two to four years of age. Children should have finished the scribbling stage when they are between four and five years of age. Some children appear to have missed the scribbling stage and begin to draw recognizable figures. Usually, these children go through scribbling at one point, but this stage is not recognized as such.

Around the age of three, a child has developed more muscular control and is gradually developing the ability to make shapes. At the age of three, a child uses shapes to represent things in his environment. Adults may not recognize what these shapes represent, but they have symbolic meaning for the child.

Recently, a teacher had a firsthand experience with a three-year-old who explained her drawing to the teacher. She identified two circles with faces as tigers; rabbits had triangle ears and oblong bodies; her cat had a circle head and an oval body. Sarah's drawing indicates that she is on a level where she can think of something from her own experience, concentrate on the experience, and then reproduce it on paper. Sarah's confidence and her ability to explain her drawing made it obvious that she has established a relationship between her own experiences and her creative expression.

A child's thought process, the ability to think and concentrate on something, is an important part of the initial step in creative activities. Children at this level are not trying to draw likenesses, but only to place things in a way that looks right and pleasing to them. The child who feels free to use basic shapes which please him will continue to be creative.

Between the ages of four and five, children reach the pictorial stage in their development. Their drawings represent things that hold emotional attachment for them. The most prominent figures in their drawings usually have the greatest emotional appeal for them. At this age they can draw recognizable pictures, but are not concerned with proportion or spatial relationships.

> **Every great artist began his career with scribbling.**

How Is a Creative Environment Prepared for Preschoolers?

Children need an environment that is challenging and stimulating, and one which offers opportunities for the beginnings of appreciation of beauty. To help create such an environment, the following suggestions may prove helpful:

● Allocate enough space to enable children to move freely and to work alone or in a small group.

● Place art materials on low, open shelves or within easy reach of children.

● Choose art materials and activities which permit children to have satisfying experiences. As plans are made, consider the developmental levels of the preschoolers in your department.

● Make allowance for the short attention span of preschoolers by offering a choice of activities.

● Determine if art materials are safe. The senses of taste and feel are two of the avenues of learning for young children.

● Locate the art area near a sink or a pan of water with sponges and paper towels.

● Station the art area away from activity traffic and in an area with adequate lighting.

● Use a low clothesline, a folding clothes rack, or the floor for drying paintings. Protect the floor with newspaper or plastic.

● Guide children to work at tables, on the floor, inside the room, or out-of-doors.

● Encourage the child to paint on a flat surface. An easel is not necessary for children to enjoy painting.

Materials needed for art activities

● Manila, newsprint, and construction paper (12 by 18 ins.);

● Newsprint for the easel (18 by 24 ins.);

● Jumbo crayons (flat on one side, chunky for twos and threes);

● Tempera paint (powder or liquid—red, yellow, and blue) may be purchased at school supply or Baptist Book Stores;

● Blunt-pointed scissors (left- and right-handed);

● Colored chalk, collage materials, assorted sizes of paintbrushes, modeling clay, and woodworking materials.

Liquid starch can be used for a paint extender. Less tempera powder is needed if mixed with liquid starch instead of water. Other uses for liquid starch are finger painting, pasting lightweight materials on paper, and using liquid starch with colored chalk to keep it from smearing.

This is not a complete list, but only some of the materials needed in departments for older preschoolers.

> A child uses creative materials to express himself—not to make pictures.

Which Art Activities Can Be Used with Preschoolers?

Creative expression with tempera paint

Young children can have successful and satisfying experiences using tempera paint. This media offers an opportunity to experiment and explore with color and movement. Painting serves as an emotional outlet.

Mixing tempera paints

To mix tempera paint, put equal parts of tempera powder and water in an unbreakable container such as yogurt, cottage cheese, or another plastic container. Stir the paint until the mixture is smooth. If the paint is too thick, add more water. Paint should be the consistency of thick gravy. Add a dash of liquid soap (not detergent) to the paint. The liquid soap makes it easier to wash paint out of clothing. Alum may be added as a preservative, and a few drops of glycerin or oil of wintergreen will keep the paint mixture fresh. Condensed milk gives a glossy effect to the paint.

Red, yellow, and blue tempera paints, which are the primary colors, can be mixed to create any color. Below are some colors that can be mixed:

- Equal parts of the primary colors make black.
- Unequal parts of the primary colors make brown.
- Equal parts of red and yellow make orange.
- Equal parts of red and blue make purple.
- Equal parts of blue and yellow make green.

Making Painting Smocks

Children should be well covered before they are allowed to paint. Painting smocks may be made from men's shirts. Cut off the sleeves of the shirt. The smocks should be open in the back. Fasten one button or clip the shirt together with two spring-type clothespins.

Another possible smock can be made from a large trash bag. Cut from the closed end a hole large enough for the child's neck. Cut armholes from the sides of the bag. Cut the bag from the neckline to the bottom. The smock should open in the back. Clip the sides together with spring-type clothespins. Plastic aprons can be purchased from a school supply company or Baptist Book Stores.

Painting with tempera paint (2-5)

Children can paint with different size brushes on a table, floor, or at an easel. Some educators recommend allowing children to work on flat surfaces instead of an easel. If an easel is used, clip several layers of newspaper to the easel before adding the newsprint. This eliminates cleaning paint from the easel each time it is used.

When two-year-olds have their first experience with paint, provide just one color. As children grow in their painting skills, add other colors. Encourage children to replace brushes in the same color paint which they are using.

Provide a pan of water, a sponge, and paper towels for twos and threes to use while painting and cleaning up. If running water is not nearby, provide a pan of water, a sponge, soap, and paper towels for fours and fives. Use appropriate conversation to help children think of colors of paint they are using. Say: "Charlie, you are using the blue paint in an interesting way. The paint reminds me of the sky." Sing the song "God Gave Me Eyes."

Washing paintbrushes is usually an experience older preschoolers enjoy if there is one teacher available to guide the children. Store brushes, bristle end up, to dry.

Squeeze-bottle painting (3-5)

Pour liquid tempera paint into plastic squeeze bottles such as detergent, mustard, and catsup bottles. Children can squeeze paint from the bottles in thick or thin lines, blobs, or other designs.

Blob painting (3-5)

Pour liquid tempera paint into bowls or similar containers. Add a spoon. A child may spoon small amounts onto construction paper. Place waxed paper over the paint. The child may spread the paint around and to the edges of the paper. Allow the paint to dry completely. Peel the waxed paper off. Some of the wax will stick to the paint, giving the picture a glossy effect.

Blot painting (3-5)

Fold a sheet of manila paper or newsprint in half. Spoon tempera paint along the crease. Fold the paper and press. Open the paper to see the design and color combinations. Encourage children to use their imaginations by asking questions such as: "What does that shape remind you of?" "What colors did you use to get that color of paint?"

Golf ball or marble art (3-5)

Secure a box about 2 inches deep, 12 inches wide, and 18 inches long. Place a sheet of manila paper in the box. Pour a small amount of liquid tempera paint into several pie tins; add golf balls. Spoon the golf balls onto paper. Pick up the box and tilt it from side to side. As the golf balls roll back and forth, they create interesting designs. Marbles may be substituted for golf balls, but for younger children, golf balls are easier to use.

Sponge painting (3-5)
Cut sponges into various shapes and designs. Attach a spring-type clothespin to each sponge. Provide several containers of liquid tempera paint. Children enjoy dipping sponges into paint and stamping shapes on paper. They also enjoy rubbing the sponges across the paper.

Roller paint (2-5)
There are several types of rollers that can be used for painting, such as small rollers used to paint the corners of a room. These can be bought at a hardware store or paint store. As an alternative, glue string in interesting designs onto a rolling pin or tin cans and let the glue dry. The child can dip the rollers in liquid tempera paint and press the rollers on paper for interesting designs.

Roll-on painting (3-5)
Remove the plastic ring that holds the ball of a roll-on deodorant bottle and then remove the ball. On some deodorant bottles the ball and ring can be removed together. All deodorant bottles are not made with removeable tops. Fill the bottle with tempera paint which has been mixed with water, not starch. Starch will cause the ball to stick and it will not roll easily. Children enjoy rolling paint onto paper to make designs or pictures. Older preschoolers should have a choice of three or four colors.

The more spontaneously a child draws, the less chance there is for him to become inhibited.

Wheel painting (3-5)
Find toy cars, airplanes, or tractors with attractive designs on the wheels. Pour liquid tempera into two or three different containers that will accommodate the wheels of the toys. Children can run the toys over the paper for interesting designs from the wheels of the toys.

Finger painting (2-5)
Finger painting is one of the most tension-relieving and enjoyable creative experiences for preschoolers. The direct sensory experience is vital for children. Finger painting is an experience in itself; the end result is not important. This activity can be more successful if the preschooler

stands. Standing enables the child to use his large arm muscles more freely, and it also enables him to reach the entire painting area. Smocks will protect the child's clothing during his finger painting experience.

Commercial finger paint is delightful; however, it is more expensive than some other materials that can be used. Some of the following ingredients can be mixed and used in finger painting: hand lotion, liquid starch, soap flakes (beaten with an electric mixer to the consistency of cream), cooked thick starch, and finger paint powder. (This powder comes in different colors.) Children can paint directly on a plastic table-top, on an oilcloth, in serving trays, on cookie sheets, or on glazed paper.

Provide plenty of elbow room and plenty of time for the preschoolers to enjoy finger painting. Two to four children can enjoy this activity at one time. As children enjoy finger painting, talk with them about how the paint feels. Say, "Aren't you glad God gave us hands to feel?" Ask, "Does the paint feel smooth or rough, soft or hard?" After a child has finished painting, pick up his design or picture by placing a sheet of paper directly over the painting. Rub the paper until the painting is transferred to the glazed paper. This piece of art is called a *monoprint*.

Corrugated-paper painting   (3-5)

Paint on corrugated paper and watch the paint mix in the grooves to make new colors. Provide red, yellow, and blue liquid paint and brushes. As the children paint the paper, ask, "What new colors do you see?"

Gadget painting   (2-5)

Look around your house and church to find gadgets that can be used for painting. Rubber shower heads, spools, bottle caps, cookie cutters, potato mashers, and hair curlers are just a few gadgets that can be used. A child dips the gadget into liquid paint and stamps it onto the paper.

String painting   (3-5)

Attach a spring-type clothespin to a twelve-inch string, and dip the string into liquid paint. A preschooler can let the string fall onto the paper in any pattern he chooses. The string can be pulled in circles or criss-crossed on the paper. Different sizes of string can be used for interesting designs.

Chalk and starch   (3-5)

Brush liquid starch (or water) across the entire surface of a sheet of paper. While the paper is still wet, a child may draw a picture with colored chalk. (White chalk can be used on dark paper.)

Glue design (3-5)

Add tempera paint powder to squeeze bottles of white glue. The preschooler can squeeze the glue onto paper to make a picture or a design.

Making collages (3-5)

A collage is a variety of materials glued to paper or wood. Through the use of collage materials, a child can learn about textures, balance, colors, likeness and difference. A variety of materials (large enough for small fingers to handle) can be used such as lace, rickrack, cotton, silk pieces, yarn, suede, and netting.

Collage materials should be placed in several containers, not thrown together in one big box. Preschoolers have a tendency to use too much glue. Paste is much more appropriate for their use. The children can use their senses of touch and smell to experience paste.

Tissue paper collage (3-5)

Tear or cut several colors of variegated tissue paper into various shapes and sizes. Brush liquid starch onto construction or manila paper; add tissue paper. Then brush more starch over the tissue paper. Overlay tissue paper for interesting effects.

Cutting and pasting (3-5)

Children enjoy experimenting with cutting and pasting. When children first begin, they tend to heap the cut pieces of paper together with lots and lots of paste. They may decide to paste the pieces over the edges of the large piece of paper they are using, but they are learning and experimenting. Teachers should not submit to the temptation to change the position of the preschooler's cut pieces of paper or "advise" him to do so.

To master the skill of cutting with scissors, good coordination and strong finger muscles are required. Cutting is very important in developing dexterity and muscular control. There are some three-year-olds who can use scissors and some fives who are still having difficulty using scissors. Cutting can be very frustrating for young children. Do not expect more than they can produce; using scissors takes lots of practice. When cutting out pictures, draw a heavy line around the picture. Children will find it much easier to cut on the line than on the picture. Provide left-handed as well as right-handed scissors.

As preschoolers begin to use paste, they will have difficulty managing the medium. Three-year-olds usually put big lumps of paste on the paper, and many times they will put paste on both sides of whatever they are pasting down. Threes and fours find it easier to use their fingers to spread paste. Older fours and fives can use craft sticks for pasting. Liquid starch can be used by children to paste items on lightweight materials.

74

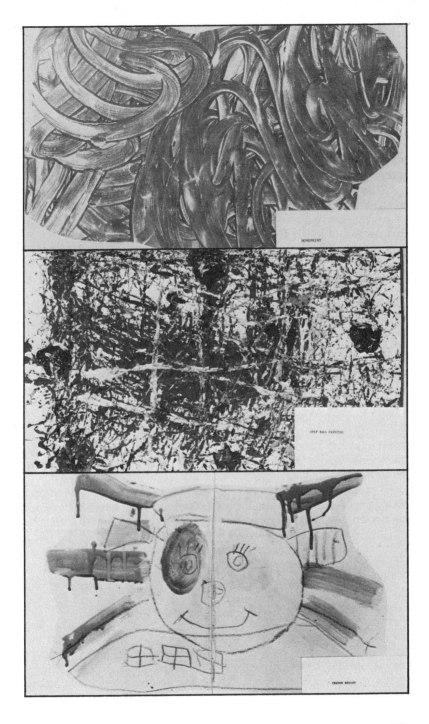

MONOPRINT

GOLF BALL PAINTING

CRAYON RESIST

> **Preschool teachers should not interfere with a child's art work. Interference by the teacher will negatively influence the child's self-confidence.**

Using crayons (T-5)

When children make their first exploration with crayons, they do so in imitation of what they see others doing. However, they soon become aware that they are making something appear on paper where there was only blank space.

When does a baby make his first mark with a crayon? A one-year-old (or younger) can grasp the crayon, wave it about, and be shown how to make the end of the crayon mark on paper. Guidance in this repetition helps a child learn quickly and start scribbling.

Toddlers and twos can get into the business of scribbling quickly. Children need to scribble because this is one of the first nonverbal means of expressing themselves. Through scribbling, a child is acquiring muscular control needed for the next stage of development.

When jumbo crayons are provided, they aid in the use of large muscles. Provide large sheets of paper for crayon work. Some teachers remove the coverings on crayons to encourage using the sides for coloring large areas and for crayon rubbings. For general use, children need new crayons with covers. Provide as many as eight colors for children to use. The regular size of crayon recommended for fives is ⅝ inch diameter. The child should be given the choice of several kinds and sizes of crayons to use.[6] Crayon is the most popular and most easily available art material. Crayons are also versatile tools for creative expression. Because of the availability of crayons and paper, too often these are the only creative materials offered to some preschoolers. Even the most popular art medium can be overused. Crayons do not have to be "just coloring"; there are many creative ways to use them. Following are some suggestions that boys and girls will find interesting:

- *Texture Board* (3-5).—Texture boards can be made by cutting cardboard into 12 by 18-inch pieces and covering the boards with different types of textured materials. Different types of screen wire, rubber drain mats, corrugated paper, rough sandpaper, burlap, and other textured materials can be used. Put textured material on cardboard and bind together all edges with masking tape or plastic tape. Place a piece of paper over the texture board and rub the side of a crayon over the paper. Look at the unusual designs made from the texture. Help children think of concepts such as rough, smooth, hard, and soft as they use the texture boards.
- *Crayon Resist* (3-5).—A child draws a picture or design with crayons on manila paper. The entire paper should then be covered with thinned tempera paint, brushing in one direction. The paint will be absorbed by the uncolored paper, but will be resisted by the wax of the crayon.

76

• *About Coloring Books.*—When some people think of crayons, they immediately think of coloring books. Coloring books are as much a part of our culture as peanut butter. One is for a quick snack, and the other is for peace and quiet. I have heard many adults say, "But children love coloring books." Preschoolers do not discriminate between things that are good for them or things that are detrimental. When coloring-within-lines, preschoolers are regimented into an activity that makes no provision for their differences as individuals. Once conditioned to patterns, children expect them at all times. When they are given unstructured materials, they are completely lost and without confidence to use their imaginations independently.

Woodworking (3-5)
Preschoolers feel very important when they have opportunities to use carpentry tools and materials. As they become skilled in doing so, their feelings of accomplishment boost their self-confidence and self-esteem. For introductory experiences, provide only a hammer, nails, and pieces of soft pine wood that can be nailed together. Provide help in learning to use the hammer if help is needed or wanted. Certain rules should accompany the use of tools.
1. Tools are used only in the carpentry area, unless an adult has made other arrangements.
2. Only two children at a time may work in the carpentry area.
3. Tools are for woodworking and are not to be used for any other kind of play activities. Children can drive nails in a tree stump or use a saw on the stump.

When Do Teachers Play Important Roles in Art Activities?
The role of teachers in art activities is to create an environment where children can assume responsibility in the care of materials, can feel secure enough to think, and are able to select and make decisions in their use of art materials.

Interfere in the activity as little as possible; give children the freedom to express their individual feelings. This freedom does not mean that a child is allowed to damage property or do things to hurt himself or someone else. Appropriate guidance is given as needed.

Models for children to copy can be detrimental to their creative ability. Expecting children to reproduce something that is not within their capability can cause children to dislike art; then they may refuse to participate in any type of art activity.

A new art idea, no matter how good it sounds, should be tried by the teacher before using the activity with preschoolers. This particular activity may not be suitable for your group of children.

Place more emphasis on the process the preschooler uses than the finished product. Well-timed comments as a child works are invaluable to his self-esteem.

Children do not like to be rushed. Allow plenty of time and opportunity for preschoolers to use art materials so that they can have satisfying experiences.

Some children may not enjoy using art materials. Encourage and invite the boys and girls to use art materials, but do not insist on their involvement. When they feel comfortable, the children will participate. Grant the child who is uncertain about being involved in the activity the right to refuse. A preschooler can benefit from the opportunity to stand and watch. Observing others is a valid way to learn.

As children experiment with art materials, carefully phrased statements should be made to help them grow in their feelings of self-worth. Some positive statements can be made such as: "Thank you, Sara, for remembering to wipe your paintbrush inside the jar," or "John, you put on your paint smock all by yourself. You have grown!" or "Sue, sharing the red crayon with Tom was kind of you. It reminds me of the Bible thought "Be ready to share" (1 Tim. 6:18).

Limit "I like" comments; otherwise, a child may get the feeling that he must do everything to please the teacher instead of what he likes to do.

A child simply does not see the world through the eyes of an adult. As he creates, a child is not concerned with color or proportions. His tree may be purple, and his people may be too big for his house. If adults criticize him, however, they interfere with the child's emotional attachment for things which he exaggerates.

Viktor Lowenfeld points out in his book *Your Child and His Art,* that if a child cannot express himself through art, it is usually due to these three causes:

1. A child has been told his drawing was "not good enough" or was told "how to draw."

2. The child was unable to recall enough attributes of the object which he intended to draw, or he may have had nothing in mind.

3. The preschooler has become conditioned to tracing and copying.

Teachers need to be selective in art materials they choose for preschoolers. Materials that are made available to children should be within their ability to use the items creatively and should help preschoolers grow in self-confidence. Materials can encourage a child's spontaneous expression without a great deal of teacher guidance. Avoid the "craft-type" materials; these items are generally not materials for self-expression.

Summary

Children have opportunities to grow socially, physically, emotionally, intellectually, and spiritually as they express themselves through the use of art materials. Children will feel free to experiment and to experience different ways of expressing their feelings and ideas in a quality learning environment. In this type of environment, children can grow in the important developmental areas listed above.

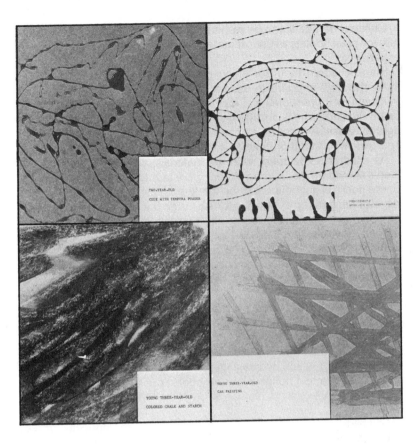

TWO-YEAR-OLD
GLUE WITH TEMPERA POWDER

YOUNG THREE-YEAR-OLD

YOUNG THREE-YEAR-OLD
COLORED CHALK AND STARCH

YOUNG THREE-YEAR-OLD
CAR PAINTING

As teachers plan art activities for preschoolers, consideration needs to be given to those areas which deal with a child's feelings and self-concept. Since preschoolers have limited speech, their need to find self-expression is of vital importance to help them grow. Art can provide satisfying and acceptable outlets for a child's feelings. He can release feelings of frustration and hostility in acceptable ways as he finger-paints, pounds clay, and engages in other more physical art activities.

As teachers show genuine appreciation for the creative efforts of preschoolers, the children grow in self-confidence and develop feelings of self-worth. How children feel about themselves during the Preschool years can determine whether they become creative, constructive adults. Every session at church should provide preschoolers with opportunities to be successful and feel good about themselves. Through these experiences, a foundation is laid for developing a positive self-concept.

Teachers need to allow preschoolers to help with cleaning up after art activities. Twos and threes as well as fours and fives can use a sponge or paper towels to wipe up paint and wash paintbrushes. Allow enough time for cleaning up. We do children an injustice by not giving them an opportunity to help. As children accept the responsibility of cleaning up and are praised for their efforts, they grow in self-confidence.

Personal Learning Activities

1. Observe a two-year-old participating in an art activity. Answer these questions as you observe the child: Did he feel good about his experience? Was the activity too difficult for him? Plan an activity which you feel most twos can enjoy.
2. Finger-paint and list your feelings as you participate in the activity.
3. Try a new art idea; list the areas in which preschoolers can benefit from the experience.
4. Evaluate art activities that you have used with preschoolers during the previous quarter.
5. List preschoolers who could benefit from more participation in art activities. Think of ways to encourage these preschoolers to become involved in art activities.

Materials for Further Study
Books

Hendrick, Joanne. *The Whole Child.* 2nd ed. St. Louis: The C.V. Mosby Co., 1980.

Hildebrand, Verna. *Introduction to Early Childhood Education,* (Chp. 7). 2nd ed. New York: The Macmillan Co., 1976.

Kellogg, Rhoda, and Scott O'Dell. *The Psychology of Children's Art.* San Diego: CRM Books—Random House Publication, 1967.

Leeper, Sarah H., et. al. *Good Schools for Young Children.* 4th ed. New York: The Macmillan Co., 1979.

Lowenfeld, Viktor, and W. Lambert Brittan. *Creative and Mental Growth.* 4th ed. New York: The Macmillan Co., 1975.

Lowenfeld, Viktor. *Your Child and His Art.* New York: The Macmillan Co., 1954.

Filmstrip

Little Boy, The. Instructional Media Division, Utah State Board of Education, Salt Lake City, Utah.

---

[5]Rhoda Kellogg, *The Psychology of Children's Art* (San Diego: CRM Books, 1967), p. 19.

[6]Sybil Waldrop and Alma May Scarborough. *Dimensions,* "Using Crayons," (Little Rock: SACUS, 1981), p. 144.

[7]Viktor Lowenfeld, *Your Child and His Art* (New York: Macmillan, 1954), p. 31.

---

*Available from Baptist Book Stores.

**Available by writing Customer Service Center, 127 Ninth Avenue, North, Nashville, Tennessee 37234; or by calling toll free 1-800-458-2772.

Chapter 6—How to Teach Through the Use of Blocks

Patsy Driggers

"Walking, walking" can be heard by Michelle as she walks on Block-busters for the first time, holding a teacher's hand. The toddler is mimicking words she has heard her teacher sing.

"I'll have to solve that problem," can be heard by a five-year-old as the roof falls in on the house he is building.

Are statements similar to these heard in your department? As you study this chapter, underline the ideas or activities you could use with the children you teach.

Why Are Blocks Used with Preschoolers?

Block play is a fun way for preschoolers to learn. In fact, because block building is enjoyed by most preschoolers, the learning is enhanced. Playing with blocks involves the whole child: muscles and senses, intellect and emotion, individual growth and social interaction. As children build with blocks, much imaginative play is evident. This imaginative activity results in learning. Actually block building is a lifetime activity—arranging supplies on shelves, handling various forms, and even placing brick around a flower bed.

"Next to water, sand, and mud, the most valuable play material for young children is likely to be blocks."[8] Is this a new thought for you?

You have probably quoted Luke 2:52 many times. One translation of the Scripture reads, "And Jesus grew, both in body and in wisdom, gaining favor with God and man."[9] Consider the areas in which Jesus grew. How many of these areas of growth can take place in the lives of preschoolers as they are involved in block activities?

We probably think first of all the *physical* opportunities afforded with blocks. Close observation will reveal bending, stretching, lifting, carrying, reaching, pushing, placing, and balancing, which require the use of muscles. Eye-hand coordination is also increased through block activities. Kevin (two and a half years old) was trying to balance an eleven-inch unit block on two other blocks of the same size. The look on Kevin's face was a clue of his intense interest and effort.

Block building can play an important role in developing a child's *self-concept*. Almost every child can build something which provides personal satisfaction as he sees results quickly. Because the construction is his creation, he feels important. Even the simplest structure is acceptable. If the preschooler makes a mistake, he can try again. "I can fix it," one five-year-old was heard to say as his structure fell. For the shy child, blocks offer an acceptable way for him to express himself. For the aggressive child, blocks offer a way to relieve tension.

Social interaction can be seen to emerge even as children under three build side-by-side (parallel play). The brief encounters of toddlers and two-year-olds are steps toward dramatic play by older preschoolers. Dramatic play comes forth when a child creates the environment for his play, rather than finding it. In order for this to take place, the child must have had many opportunities to use blocks freely and with time to try out ideas.

A teacher does not have to be talking for a child to learn. In fact, at times, listening may provide the best teaching. Block activities offer opportunities for listening to the children in your department. As an experiment, consciously try for a specified length of time to listen twice as much as you talk. This discipline is not easy. There will, however, be opportunities to use Bible thoughts and songs to reinforce actions by the child. Here are a few Bible thoughts which are suggested in Preschool Bible Teacher and Bible Story Time materials:**

"God made the cows" (Gen. 1:25).
"Help one another" (Gal. 5:13).
"I like to go to church" (Ps. 122:1).
"Be kind to each other" (Eph. 4:32).
"Jesus went to church" (Mark 11:15).
"Sing thanks to God" (Ps. 147:7).
"Work with your hands" (1 Thess. 4:11).
"God loves us" (1 John 4:10).
"We are helpers" (2 Cor. 1:24).

Preschoolers remember more of what we sing to them than what we say to them. How could you use the adapted songs listed below to enrich or guide experiences with blocks?

"I Like to Go to Church," p. 27†
  "Billy likes to come to church;
  He likes to come to church.
  He likes to build with blocks at church;
  Billy likes to come to church."
"Stack the Blocks," p. 81†
  "Stack, stack, stack the blocks,
  It's fun to stack the blocks.
  Stack, stack, stack, the blocks,
  It's fun to stack the blocks."
"I Can Help," p. 36†
  "Jeffrey can help pick up the toys,
  He can help, he can help;
  Jeffrey can help pick up the blocks,
  He can help his teacher."

Other songs you may enjoy using in the block area are "I'm Growing," p. 30,† "It's Fun to Work," p. 83,† "I Am Happy," p. 38,† and "I Can Be a Helper," p. 10††.

Portions of Bible stories may also be recalled by the teacher in the block area. These stories are printed in the teacher's guide of Preschool Bible Teacher and Bible Story Time materials,** and if studied they can be recalled easily.

Who Can Learn Through the Use of Blocks?
Babies can begin to learn from block activities as they pat and move a covered cardboard block while in bed. This is the first step to later moving the block on the floor when the child can sit alone. He will also be attracted to a covered shoe box, or to milk cartons stuffed with paper and securely sealed with tape. The baby needs many opportunities, lots of time, and introduction to various sizes of blocks.

Long before the baby can speak, accompany your own actions or the baby's actions with the appropriate words. Say "up" when you stack blocks for the baby. Say "down" when he pushes them over. Praise him as he makes appropriate sounds.

As early as twelve to eighteen months, the child may be introduced to several of the small wooden building blocks. A few blocks of different sizes help as he tries to add one block on top of another block. For a first-time experience, a teacher may stack two or three blocks. This would be an activity you could use with the child as you visit in the home as well as at church.

Cardboard blocks are used by toddlers when practicing stacking, walking, sitting, and standing skills. A two-year-old will enjoy cardboard blocks, but he may build more creatively with wooden building blocks.

When introducing building blocks, begin with two or three shapes and add other shapes as children develop. This provision will encourage creativity. Continue to add to the shape and the number of blocks through the Preschool years. The child's world expands as he takes on the role of those he knows in his block-built environment.

How Do Teachers Guide Experiences with Blocks?
The teacher's first role in guiding block activities is to create the learning environment for playing with blocks. This may include:
- Making or securing blocks suitable to the age of the child;
- Stacking cardboard blocks two or three blocks high in an area accessible to the creeper, toddler, or two-year-old;
- Arranging wooden blocks on shelves by sizes for the two-, three-, four-, or five-year-old;
- Selecting and placing appropriate accessories and pictures in the block area;
- Providing plenty of space for buildings;
- Being ready before the first child arrives.

The teacher's presence in or near the block area indicates his interest in what is happening. Children usually come to the area and begin to build if a teacher is nearby. The part a teacher plays will depend on the age and experience of the child.

For a toddler's first introduction to cardboard blocks, the teacher may sing, "Billy likes to come to church, he likes to come to church; he likes to walk on blocks at church, he likes to come to church." Walking on Blockbusters for the toddler calls for balance and coordination—skills a teacher can help the child develop. At times it is fun for the teacher to sit on the Blockbusters with the children and enjoy talking, singing, and just being together.

Listen to conversation as the boys and girls build with blocks. Be sensitive about interrupting conversation. Listening is more important than talking.

Occasionally a teacher may be in the block area and the children still not use the blocks. Gestalt's psychology on the unfinished task may be helpful. Place two blocks at right angles on the floor. This procedure usually starts some sort of activity by the children.[10] The teacher's attitude is an important factor in encouraging activity.

Safety with blocks is certainly a priority for teachers with preschoolers. Being nearby to hold a toddler's hand, or intervening before one toddler pushes another child off a cardboard block can prevent an unnecessary accident. At some point, rules usually have to emerge.

Here are some possible guidance suggestions:

- Build on the floor.
- Build no higher than your chin.
- Build in this area (block).
- Walk on the floor rather than on these blocks (wooden unit).
- Build with the blocks rather than throwing them, pushing them, or kicking them.
- Build far enough from the shelf to allow others to get blocks (two to three feet).
- Keep your hand on the car as you are making it go fast.

Do not tell a child what to build. A teacher who builds with blocks creates the same disadvantage that a teacher in the art area creates when making models to be copied in clay and art.

If a teacher should make building suggestions, the final product will not be the child's thinking. "That is something you can try," may encourage a child to think. The child builds something he has experienced. Pictures and accessories placed in the area may lead the child to build something related to the unit. Do not, however, feel you have not taught effectively if the child doesn't build something related to the unit.

The number of blocks and the size of the area will determine the number of children who can build purposefully; as a general rule, three to four children would be the limit. At times, a teacher in the block area can move furniture to accommodate the children or direct additional children to another area.

Overcrowding the area can lead to disagreements and difficulties in taking turns. If there is no room for a child to play, start a list of children who want to play. Say: "You may choose to work a puzzle or listen to a new recording. I will write your name on this wall chart. When there is space for you to use the blocks, I will call you."

When conflict develops between two children while playing with blocks, try to let the children solve the problem themselves. If there is a possibility of a child getting hurt, of course, the teacher must intervene. If the problem remains on the verbal level, however, many times the children can come to a suitable solution.

Scattered blocks will usually not attract a child to the area. The teacher of younger preschoolers will be "straightening" the blocks throughout the session.

A part of guidance is getting the children involved in cleanup or transition. A serious block builder will need to be reminded several times to finish because it will soon be time to put the blocks away. Just because a child was last to work with blocks may not necessarily mean he puts them away. Cleanup in another area may be more interesting to the child.

Blocks often get knocked down. This occurrence is acceptable, but a teacher needs to encourage children to take down the structure piece by piece. The teacher can work with the children in putting the blocks away.

At times, the teacher initiates putting the blocks away. This may be done by asking a child to find all the blocks of a certain size and putting them together on the shelf. A statement such as, "Keith, you and Bob can put the long blocks on this shelf" may give a positive approach for the child who does not know how to help. This gives the teacher the opportunity to use such words as *smaller, larger, bigger, longer, higher,* and *shorter than.* With older preschoolers, very little guidance will be needed. At times, arranging blocks on the shelves can be as meaningful to the child as building on the floor.

Occasionally older preschoolers may build a structure that will be left in place. During group time, the builders can talk about and show what they built. At times, parents may wish to see what their child has built. When the structure remains from one session to another, it would be advisable to label it with instructions. Leaving the structure would be possible during Vacation Bible School, kindergarten, from Sunday School to Discipleship Training, Mission Friends, and Preschool choir if the same children use the room. The structure could also be preserved with a drawing or a photograph by a teacher. A child's self-esteem is heightened when a teacher takes seriously what the preschooler has built.

When Are Blocks Used?

Children may choose to begin building with blocks upon arrival in the department room. Block play will be more purposeful if activities are scheduled during a long uninterrupted length of time. Two- and three-year-olds may move to every area during the time for activities, while fours and fives may choose only one or two areas. Activities for toddlers through twos will be approximately one hour to one hour and fifteen minutes. For threes, fours, and fives, activities may be from forty-five minutes to an hour, depending on the length of the session.

There may be more than one time for activities, depending on the length of the session. For example, there will be activities during Sunday School or Discipleship Training, and another time for activities during the extended session. Vacation Bible School, kindergarten, day care, Preschool choir, and Mission Friends may also have two scheduled times for activities.

What Materials Are Needed for Block Activities?

The block may be as simple as a milk carton stuffed with paper and securely fastened with tape; a cardboard block; a wooden unit building block; or, when space permits, a large hollow block.

Blockbusters (the brand name of one kind of cardboard block) are more frequently used with children under three; however, they may be used with all ages. Blockbusters may be purchased from Baptist Book Stores or other companies specializing in teaching materials for the young child. As a rule, twelve Blockbusters are packaged flat and have to be assembled. With proper use, Blockbusters will last many years in a Preschool department. These blocks are strong enough to support the weight of a teacher.

Twelve Blockbusters will be a sufficient number for younger toddlers to manipulate; however, the number of blocks in a department needs to be increased as the children's stacking and building skills improve. With two-year-olds, you will probably need twelve blocks, or one set of Blockbusters. A church with a day-care center may need two sets of Blockbusters for two-year-olds. Remember, it is usually best not to combine Blockbusters with wooden unit blocks.

Cardboard blocks may be made by stuffing milk cartons, shoe boxes, or baby food boxes with crumpled paper and sealing the containers with tape. These blocks are made more colorful and durable when covered with contact plastic.

The wooden unit building blocks may be used with children three through five years of age. The wooden blocks are optional for two-year-olds. Hardwood, usually elm or maple, is suggested for unit building blocks because of their durability. Soft wood blocks splinter and topple easily. Blocks should be left their natural color. Wooden building blocks in a variety of sizes and shapes can be purchased in sets from Baptist Book Stores or school supply firms. Another source is Childcraft Education Corporation, 20 Kilmer Road, Edison, New Jersey 08817.

Hollow wooden blocks are primarily used for kindergartens and day-care centers. They may be used in the department room and on the playground. These blocks provide many opportunities for learning experiences. One caution is that there must be available storage areas and space to build with the blocks, so that the hollow wooden blocks do not have to be mixed with the unit building blocks.

Wooden blocks may be made from lumber using specifications given in Figure 4, page 87. You will need a source for hardwood lumber and power tools. Cut the wood carefully, because variation in the angle of cutting can make the block useless in building. The chief requirement in making wooden blocks is that the measurements of the larger blocks must be exact multiples of the smallest blocks.

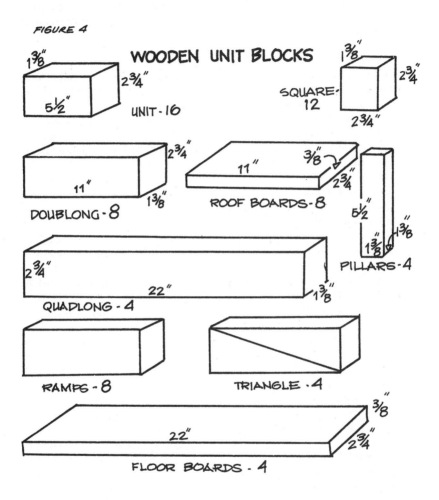

If you are using two-by-four lumber, get units of three and one-half-inch times three and three-fourths-inch, cut the lumber into various lengths that will be multiples of three and one-half-inch: three and one-half-inch, seven-inch, and fourteen-inch. A set of unit blocks for three or four children would include about 100 to 150 blocks of various sizes and shapes.

The wooden blocks are stored by sizes on movable, closed-backed shelves, and are placed so that the children can take the blocks out and put them away. The shelves should allow the child to see the various lengths as well as the shapes of blocks. Crates may be used until shelves are available. Boxes for blocks are not suggested. The children have a tendency to throw blocks in a box rather than place them inside a box.

Blockbusters are stacked on the floor. There seems to be more possibility for younger preschoolers to use Blockbusters if the blocks are not stacked in a corner.

At times, because of the acoustics of the room, the temperature at the floor level, or because one department is located on the second floor over another department, it is advisable to have carpet on the floor in the block area. The carpet should be large enough not to confine building. The floor covering should be a very flat surface because it is easier to build with blocks on a smooth surface. Building with blocks will be frustrating to the children if the pile of the carpet does not give them a firm building base.

Accessories can make block play even more meaningful and will greatly enhance dramatic play. Block accessories are often suggested in units of the teacher's guides of Bible Story Time and Preschool Bible Teacher materials.** The accessories may be purchased, made from magazine pictures, or hand-drawn. Stand-up figures and other accessories are often contained in the resource kits of the Bible Story Time and Preschool Bible Teacher materials. Homemade accessories will be made durable if mounted on cardboard and covered with clear contact plastic. Accessories will store more easily if they are not permanently attached to a stand—a tissue roll, a cardboard cylinder, a large spool, a piece of polystyrene foam, a one and one-half to three-inch thick piece of foam rubber, or a small block.

When selecting block accessories, keep in mind the same principles used with puzzles and pictures. Avoid toys with faces painted on the front of them such as a train with the lights serving as the eyes and the remainder of the face painted on the item; these features are not realistic and could confuse the literal-minded preschooler.

Accessories may include human and animal figures. These standup figures may be made from wood, plastic, rubber, or cardboard. Other accessories include interconnecting trains, trucks, cars, wagons, planes, boats, buses, street signs, and miniature church furniture.

Accessories may also include objects such as a fire fighter's hat, a doll, some flowers, or a small basket. The Bible and mounted pictures will be used in the area for most sessions. Containers such as oatmeal boxes, empty coffee cans, and several plastic or metal frozen juice cans can add interest to the block area. Boxes will also be added from time to time.

Keep the block area uncluttered and interesting. When you add additional items to the area, you may need to remove things used during previous sessions. In fact, it is a good plan to put away all accessories used in the block area at the end of each session.

Floor scenes can add variety for older preschoolers. The scenes may be made on a discarded window shade or a piece of poster board. At times these scenes may be included in Preschool Bible Teacher and Bible Story Time materials resource kits.** Streets may be outlined on the floor with masking tape.

Change accessories often and use only those which enrich the unit. Too many accessories will limit block building. The children will play with the accessories rather than the blocks.

For five-year-olds you may also add:

- Samples of tiles or rugs that can be used for floor coverings,
- Pebbles and small stones which can be "cargo" for trains or trucks,
- Lumber scraps which serve as flat roofs,
- Thin pieces of rubber tubing attached to a cylinder block to make a simple gas pump, and
- Signs written for the buildings which the children construct.

Remember that accessories are to enhance and enrich the block area. When the accessory becomes the major interest, its value needs to be reconsidered. For example, occasionally a toy garage with small cars will be brought from someone's home and used in the block area. With this accessory, very little block involvement usually takes place. This item and others like it should probably be reevaluated for use in the block area.

Where May Blocks Be Used?

Blocks may be used in the bed with a baby, on the floor with a creeper or toddler, and in a special area of the department with twos through fives. Some blocks may be used on the sidewalk or on the playground.

Blocks and block accessories are one of the most expensive items in the room, so they should not be treated carelessly. After each session, they should be returned to a storage area.

The placement in the department will depend on the amount of space and the number of blocks. When arranging a department for twos through fives, some teachers select the area for blocks first. The block area should be away from crosstraffic of entrance doors or the bathroom. Conflict can occur when children are crowded. Provide room for the children to have space to build and move about.

In a creeper or toddler department cardboard blocks are stacked on the floor. Wooden building blocks for twos through fives are placed by sizes on closed backed shelves. As mentioned earlier, crates may be used until shelves are available.

With good care, wooden blocks should last ten years before they begin to splinter. Sanding can extend the life of a wooden block. Occasionally, oiling, waxing, or shellacking will prolong the life of a block.

The life of a Blockbuster will depend to a great extent on who is to use it. If the blocks are used only by creepers, toddlers, and twos, the Blockbusters will last many years. These blocks are not designed for the rough treatment that older preschoolers may give them. Blockbusters may be covered with clear contact plastic when they are new. That procedure, however, is expensive. Repair cardboard blocks when holes are made. A toddler has the tendency to get his finger caught in a little hole. Cardboard blocks can be repaired by placing tape inside the block. (Masking tape attached so a toddler can see it will be removed by the child.)

The age of the child and the amount of space for block building will determine how many wooden blocks to have. A two- or three-year department with an enrollment of four to six could use as few as 29 blocks, while those departments with a larger enrollment, and perhaps more space, could purposefully use sixty to seventy blocks in seven to twelve shapes. A department for fours or fives could use one hundred to one hundred fifty blocks in nineteen to twenty-seven shapes. Some five-year-olds may use as many as seventy blocks during a kindergarten session.

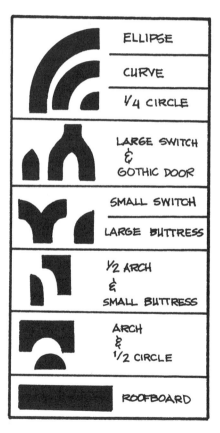

SHAPE	NAME
■	SQUARE
▬	UNIT
▬▬	DOUBLE UNIT
▬▬▬	QUADRUPLE UNIT
▮ ▮	PILLAR / HALF PILLAR
◣ ◥	SMALL TRIANGLE / LARGE TRIANGLE
▮	SMALL COLUMN / LARGE COLUMN
◢	RAMP
	ELLIPSE
	CURVE
	1/4 CIRCLE
	LARGE SWITCH & GOTHIC DOOR
	SMALL SWITCH / LARGE BUTTRESS
	1/2 ARCH & SMALL BUTTRESS
	ARCH & 1/2 CIRCLE
	ROOFBOARD

FIGURE 6

From "Unit Blocks—The Cornerstone for Learning," © 1977, 1979 Childcraft and Education Corporation, Edison, New Jersey.

Summary

Blocks can offer an exciting, challenging learning medium for pre-schoolers. Blocks will provide reasons to take turns, social contact with other children, relationships with teachers, a way to put ideas in concrete form, a way to experiment, and a way to feel successful. Some children are creative enough to seek their own mediums for expression. The environment a teacher creates both with suitable materials and his presence will greatly aid the learning that can take place with blocks.

The teacher does not need to talk all of the time he is in the block area. Listening to the children is a large part of teaching. The teacher will ask questions, recall Bible thoughts, and use songs as appropriate.

Keep the unit purpose in mind as accessories and pictures are placed in the block area. Memorize Bible thoughts and songs to use with the children. Analyze the number of blocks. Are there too many for the number and age of the children in the department? Do additional shapes and sizes of blocks need to be added? Is the block area inviting? Does the area encourage the children to build with friends? Is block building an enjoyable and meaningful way for preschoolers to learn in your department?

Personal Learning Activities

1. Draw an outline of your department room including windows and doors. Indicate where you would place the block area in light of the guidelines given in this chapter.
2. List items you would like to add to your block area.
3. If a child in the block area said to you, "Build me a house," how would you respond?
4. List three possible ways you could affirm a child who builds with blocks.
5. Select three songs listed on page 82 which can be used with block activities.
6. Recall two values for block building.
7. If you do not have blocks in your room, what could you do to add a block area to your department?

Material for Further Study

Hirsch, Elisabeth S., ed. *The Block Book*. Washington, D.C.: National Association for the Education of Young Children, 1974.

---

[8]Katherine Read Baker and Xenia F. Fane, *Understanding and Guiding Young Children* (Englewood Cliffs: Prentice-Hall, Inc., 1967), p. 189.
[9]This quotation is from the *Good News Bible*, The Bible in Today's English Version. Old Testament: Copyright © American Bible Society 1976; New Testament: Copyright © American Bible Society 1966, 1971, 1976. Used by permission.
[10]Elisabeth S. Hirsch, editor, *The Block Book* (Washington, D.C.: National Association for the Education of Young Children, 1974), pp. 93-94.

*Available from Baptist Book Stores.
**Available by writing Customer Service Center, 127 Ninth Avenue, North, Nashville, Tennessee 37234; or by calling toll free 1-800-458-2772.

Chapter 7—How to Teach Through the Use of Books

Florrie Anne Lawton

Randy reaches toward the washable book standing open in his crib. He smiles and makes random hand and arm movements as he views the picture of the dog. His teacher sings, "Thank you, God, for the dog."

In the toddler department, Karen picks up a book from the floor and looks at Mrs. Thomas who is sitting nearby on the floor. Mrs. Thomas holds out her hand to take the book while Karen snuggles next to her. Mrs. Thomas smiles as she talks with Karen about the pictures in the book. Mrs. Thomas says, "I'm so glad we can look at the book together."

Meanwhile in the five-year department, Ed and Rose are looking at a book. Sitting next to them are Kirk and Mark, looking at another book. Kirk laughs and points, "Look at the frog jump." The other children look at the book and laugh with Kirk.

Books are for looking. Books are for reading. Books are for taking turns. Books are for having fun. Books are used to provide opportunities for learning experiences. Books are for communicating ideas. Books can foster a warm, happy feeling—alone or with friends. Teachers in the Preschool departments mentioned above had specific objectives in mind as they purposefully arranged books for informal "reading" by preschoolers.

Who Can Enjoy Books?

All preschoolers learn through their senses. In thinking about how adults teach through the use of books with preschoolers, teachers recognize that the baby enjoys not only seeing the brightly colored picture or photograph, but also absorbs the feelings of the person who is sharing the book with him.

Often, the five-year-old who was introduced to books early in his development continues to experience joy in learning from books.

An important goal in the education of the preschooler is the development of a love for books. An early love of books can grow into a lifetime of enriching and pleasurable experiences.

Relating closely to this overall goal is the use of "picture reading" and storytelling to meet the emotional needs of children. Sitting close to share a book with another person can provide a child with feelings of security and of belonging.

Books may be used in many places. Sometimes a child may choose to take a favorite book outside and read as other children are playing.

You may see a child take a book to "read" to the doll in the homeliving area.

As you study this chapter, you will better understand the need of having books in each Preschool department at church as well as suggesting books for parents to use with preschoolers in the homes. Each stage of development builds on the one just before it as the child develops physically, mentally, socially, emotionally, and spiritually.

The teachers' periodical, *Preschool Bible Teacher A*,** gives suggestions for books to use with babies, creepers, and toddlers and instructions on how to use the books with these children. Look in a copy of *Preschool Bible Teacher A* and list the books suggested for this quarter.

The toddlers' language development is changing from single-word babbling or utterances to two-word phrases. Toddlers enjoy turning the pages of appropriate picture books. They can name familiar objects and point to pictures of people and objects with whom they have had experience. Babies, creepers, and toddlers catch ideas and impressions from seeing pictures and from hearing adults talk about the book. They develop feelings of love and security as teachers look at books with them.

Books help many toddlers unwind and rest. Books may help the child become more aware of his environment and give him a better understanding of his world.

*Beginning*** is a quarterly publication designed to nurture and encourage parents of babies, creepers, and toddlers. When you visit a toddler's home, sit on the floor and look at the pictures in the home book *Beginning*. This modeling would give the parents an idea of how to use *Beginning* with their child.

*Preschool Bible Teacher B*** is a helpful resource, not only to find books recommended for twos and threes, but practical suggestions on specific ways to use the books with the children.

The use of songbooks with twos and threes can be a joyful time as children turn to pictures in a book and want to know the song. Singing extends the joy of books when a teacher sings songs which are suggested in *Preschool Bible Teacher B* as an overflow of his experiences in the book area.

Books can be used to capture the interest of twos and threes. Twos and threes have short attention spans, but teachers can take advantage of teachable moments by being prepared to teach from the overflow. A wise teacher can use Bible conversation, Bible thoughts, Bible stories, and songs with boys and girls. The Bible can be on the floor or placed where there is a low bookrack in the two-, three-, four-, or five-year departments.

Teachers can encourage preschoolers to take good care of books. A teacher could say: "You really do a good job of turning the pages in these books. Our books are so pretty. Thank you for taking care of them."

Living is a quarterly publication which is designed for parents to use with twos and threes in their homes. One of the joys of using this book is that it can be taken into the child's home as a teacher goes to visit. Teachers have a wonderful opportunity to show parents how to use this book with their children.

Teachers of fours and fives in Sunday School and Discipleship Training have as their source book *Preschool Bible Teacher C.*** Suggestions are given in *Preschool Bible Teacher C* for books to use with the children during each session, in keeping with the Bible teaching aim (desired outcome) for that session. Using books with fours and fives can stimulate curiosity and help stretch the child's mind. When fours and fives are provided with the right kind of books, they become more aware of their world. Teachers in Mission Friends use books for preschoolers which are recommended in *Start*. Preschool choir leaders use books with preschoolers which are listed in *The Music Leader.*** These children should be exposed to the same type of books recommended for Sunday School and Discipleship Training sessions.

Are you teaching a combined group of preschoolers? In a church where a combination of age groups is a way of meeting needs, place the books on the floor in areas where the children will sit. The *Bible Story Time Teacher* materials describe how to use books with preschoolers in a multi-age group.

Whether in a room with all ages or under the shade of a tree, a book suggested for every group of preschoolers is the Read-to-Me Bible (Holman). Other Bibles may be used. Since our responsibility as teachers is such an important task, guiding the child to recognize that the Bible is more special than other books is extremely important. The Bible should be available to preschoolers at all times. In the younger departments a teacher needs to be nearby to give guidance in turning pages and holding the Bible.

Why Are Books Important to Preschoolers?
Through the use of books the preschooler develops

Physically
Looking at books can stimulate the development of eye muscles. Bright colors, beautiful pictures, various textures, and the printed word help the preschooler focus his eyes and assimilate information in relation to what he sees.

Visual stimulation motivates a child to reach to that which he sees. Eye-hand coordination is an important aspect of a child's motor and intellectual development. The baby can focus on a brightly colored picture in a book, attempt to grasp the picture, and pull the book to his mouth.

Mentally
The preschooler learns to think when using books. For the young child, give a name to a picture in a book. Books guide preschoolers in under-

standing the meaning of words. There is anticipation of wanting to know what will happen to the character as he listens to the story. Thinking about how the seed grows or which object is an airplane and which is the car, sets into motion thought processes. This leads to processing and storing information which at a later time can be related to another experience.

Bible thoughts, Bible conversation, Bible stories, Bible songs, and biblical concepts can be used in connection with books. A toddler can associate the Bible thought "God made the fish" (Gen. 1:21) as he views the picture of the fish in the book. The preschooler can come to realize that the Bible is a very important book. Furthermore, the older preschooler can associate the Bible stories in the child's book with stories in the Bible.

Books develop and extend a preschooler's world. For example, Kristy had no interest in butterflies until her teacher read the book *Where Does the Butterfly Go When It Rains?* by Garelick; then Kristy wanted to read other books from the library related to butterflies. Kristy's father told the teacher that he and Kristy took a walk to look for butterflies.

A teacher may be able to identify a preschooler's interests or needs as they read a book. An unhappy toddler becomes excited when he sees the picture of a fire truck in the book. He wants to read the book over and over again. A fire truck may be a toy which is added near the cardboard blocks to help meet the interests and needs of a particular toddler.

The preschooler who has positive experiences with books develops a joy in looking at books. He learns that reading is an important skill to develop. He will develop a desire to learn to read. A four- or five-year-old may imagine that he can already read. A child may imitate his teacher as he "reads" the book to a friend.

Language

The most rapid developmental period for language is during the Preschool years. The first two years of life involve listening to conversation, learning to babble, making familiar sounds, learning words for objects, and learning to put words together for expressions of desire. The ages two to four years allow the preschooler opportunities to learn basic communication skills and expand these skills. The following years allow for cultivation and establishment of language patterns. Looking at books with a teacher and with friends who love you stimulates conversation. A baby may babble as the teacher holds him, looks at a book, and talks. The beginning of language acquisition is hearing language. The two-year-old may name the objects as the teacher reads. The four-year-old may imitate the teacher as he "reads." Preschoolers learn to talk through modeling conversations.

Finally, the growth and development of the preschooler can be evaluated by the teacher(s) through the use of books. The teachers may notice that Jim enjoys books on insects and nature. More books are added about insects and nature objects. Nature walks may be planned to enhance Jim's intellectual growth. A teacher may observe that Marsha has grown socially to the degree that she is willing to share her book with Cameron. This sharing of a book is an outgrowth of learning to take turns with books earlier.

Socially
Looking at a book with a teacher or a friend is fun. Older preschoolers like to express to others the things they enjoyed about a book. The giggles of delight from preschoolers as they look at a book together indicate social development. A group of preschoolers may enjoy being with each other as they listen to the teacher read or tell a story. Preschoolers learn the "give and take" of social relationships as they learn to take turns using a book. They learn consideration for each other as they take turns conversing about their response to the book in a group. Looking at books may provide opportunities for warm times of sharing between teacher and child. Learning respect for a friend who needs to look at a book alone is also an important element of which to be aware.

Spiritually
Preschoolers can many times identify with characters in a book as they participate with others in a dramatization or imitation of the characters in a book. Young preschoolers may imitate the sounds of a dog or a cat. Older preschoolers may dramatize the story of Boy Jesus in the church.

Preschoolers can learn to thank God as the people in the story did. They may learn to give things to others as Jane, a character in a book, shared with her elderly neighbor.

Books may aid a child in developing spiritual concepts. He can begin to associate the words *Jesus, church, Bible, self,* and *God* with warm feelings of looking at the Bible with teachers at church. Older preschoolers may learn more about the *natural world, family,* and *others* as they use books and talk with their teacher.

Emotionally
A preschooler experiences a "good" book. He experiences exhilaration as he intently follows the suspense in the story. He gets excited when he sees a picture in the book with which he can identify. He likes to feel the texture of a plastic-coated book. He can identify with the happiness, sadness, or loneliness of the characters in the book. He can look at pictures of facial expressions of the characters and think about how they may feel. He learns it is OK to have some of these feelings and express them.

Guidelines for selecting books for various ages and stages
When a teacher realizes the value of using books with preschoolers, he will want to know the appropriate books to use with a particular age

group at a particular stage of development. The five-year-old would not be challenged with a washable book with pictures and large words. Neither would a baby be interested in listening to a teacher read an entire book. *Preschool Bible Teacher A, B,* and *C;*** *Bible Story Time Teacher; Start;* and *The Music Leader* give specific suggestions on which books are needed for various purposes.

First, teachers need to recognize characteristics and needs of preschoolers at various ages and stages. For help in understanding characteristics, carefully study the book *Understanding Today's Preschoolers* by Waldrop. At the same time it is important to remember that each preschooler has a unique pattern of growth. In selecting books, special consideration should be given to those preschoolers who advance at faster or slower rates than the average child. Also, preschoolers have different interests, and books need to be provided which deal with the interests of a wide variety of the children.

Second, teachers will want to observe preschoolers with books. This observation will provide clues regarding the reading interests and reading habits of preschoolers. Does the child select books about nature? Does he follow the leadership of one or two friends selecting books according to their interests? How long does he look at a book? Does he talk about his observations of the book? What is the most used book in the department? Why does the book appeal to preschoolers?

A teacher will make notes of books which a particular child enjoys. Which books could be added to the book area to challenge the different preschoolers in your department?

Basic criteria can be considered in selecting appropriate books for various ages and stages. Babies, creepers, and toddlers like books they can handle, chew, mouth, or carry around with them. The books should be durable and washable. Paperback books are not durable with this age child unless the pages of the book are covered with clear contact plastic.

Babies, creepers, and toddlers are egocentric. Egocentricity does not imply selfishness, but it means the child cannot capably assume another person's point of view. He likes books that relate to him. For example, *Baby's Playthings* and *Baby's Toys* by Provenson are books which would appeal to younger preschoolers. They enjoy books with bright colorful pictures. The pictures in books should be realistic. There should be a limited amount of print. Some books (pages) might have no print.

Two- and three-year-olds experience rapid language development. They have a keen interest in words by repeating words and rhymes. They are curious about objects, people, and animals. They are becoming more aware of the words *Jesus* and *Bible.* They begin to associate some Bible stories with the Bible. They require books that can be read at one sitting. They enjoy participating by touching, pointing, or repeating the words the teacher reads.

Stories about self, pets, everyday experiences, playthings, and home are most appealing to this age child.

Books for four- and five-year-olds should have some relationship to self, friends, home, play, community workers, animals, or emotions. Books such as *Thank You, God, for Spring* by Moncure help this age child begin to sequence time and seasons. They enjoy stories that involve the imagination such as the book *Where Does the Butterfly Go When It Rains?* by Garelick. They also enjoy stories with happy endings. They need books which can be read and discussed in one sitting. The book should be simple enough that the four-or five-year-old feels he can enjoy the book silently or discuss it with one or two of his peers. Some books for older preschoolers need to create ideas which lead to extended activities, dramatic play, pretend play, or pantomimes. (Note suggestions for extended use of books throughout this chapter.)

How Are Books Used at Various Ages and Stages?

A good way to interest preschoolers in books is to read to them frequently from the very earliest age. The youngest baby needs the opportunity to hear a teacher read or talk to him about a picture in a book. When using books with babies or creepers, the book may be propped in the crib with the book opened to an attractive picture. The teacher can stand at the crib to read or converse with the child. The teacher's conversation may be using one word such as *ball* or a simple sentence "John rolls the ball." Books may also be used while sitting on the floor with a baby or a creeper. The book may be placed upright on the floor, or the teacher may put the book flat on the floor in front of the baby or creeper who is on his stomach. The teacher will read as a baby or creeper observes. The teacher may also read a book as he rocks the baby or creeper. Books may be placed on the windowsill to be seen as the teacher and a baby or creeper stand to look out the window. A teacher may sing as he looks at pictures with babies or creepers. For example, while observing the picture of a bird, sing, "God gave Jim eyes, so he can see the bird" or "Thank you, God, for the bird."

Toddlers prefer books on the floor because these preschoolers are on the floor the majority of the session. A teacher needs to sit on the floor with the boys and girls to read a book or talk about the pictures. Books may be placed on the floor or placed in a low windowsill. A shoe bag makes an acceptable holder for books in departments which are limited in space. The bag can be hung at the child's eye level so the toddler can reach the books and place them back in the bag. See instructions for making a book bag in chapter 15, "How to Make Additional Teaching Materials."

Two- and three-year-olds like to have books read to them. They also enjoy being on the floor. Books may be placed on a low book rack, an open shelf, in a shoe bag container, or placed upright on the floor. A quiet area of the room should be identified as the book area, so one or two preschoolers may look at a book privately without too much interruption. Books may be used in other areas of the room if the book relates to the activity. For example, providing dress-up clothes for a doctor and nurse would give a child the opportunity to pretend to be these community workers. The book *Betsy and the Doctor* by Wolde may be placed in the homeliving area to reinforce the emphasis. A nature activity such as planting seed may be planned. The book *How God Gives Us Apples* by LeBar may be used in the nature area. The teacher may read the book to the small group of children who are planting seed.

Four- and five-year-olds may enjoy books individually or in small groups sitting on the floor, in a chair, or even outside. Books may be used by teachers with an individual child or in small groups while teaching in the art, block, or puzzle areas. During group time the teacher may sometimes read a book to the group. Preferably books should be read to individuals or small groups rather than to a large group.

Techniques of reading aloud

Effective oral reading is an important factor in holding preschoolers' interests. Seat preschoolers close to the teacher so they can easily see the pictures. The teacher will want to sit at eye level with the preschoolers. If the preschoolers are on the floor, the teacher should be on the floor. The book should be held at the child's eye level and moved slowly so that all preschoolers will have opportunity to see the picture. The teacher should have eye contact with the group as he reads.

Distinct articulation, voice tone, and pitch are important in reading. Conversation should be read naturally and volume should be raised with the content. Feelings and emotions can be communicated through the voice.

The teacher needs to be familiar with the story. This allows the teacher to emphasize particular passages, anticipate the timing of excitement and amusing remarks. This procedure also allows the teacher to look from the book more frequently to see the preschoolers' reactions.

The length of the reading period should vary with the age and stage of development of the individual child. The teacher should plan for short reading sessions. Preschoolers enjoy listening to books being read two or three times a day for shorter periods rather than long periods.

Rather than interrupting the continuity of a book, discussion should follow the reading of the entire book. Also, preschoolers should have an opportunity to react to a book.

Preschoolers should not be denied the opportunity to hear well-told stories.

Refer to chapter 3 for information regarding the use of stories and story conversation with preschoolers.

How Can Teachers Include the Use of Books in Other Activities?

Preschoolers should be given a choice of books to read and a choice of ways to interpret a book. Allowing an older preschooler to extend his ideas about a book gives him another way to share the delights of a book. The extension may be done through dramatic play and various other methods. The following activities are planned to increase the preschooler's enjoyment of books:

• *Dramatic Play.*—Books can become more real to preschoolers as they identify with the characters through dramatic play. Dramatic play begins very early when the toddler begins to "moo" like a cow and crawl on all fours to imitate a dog. An older preschooler can extend his imagery of a character to the extent of dramatizing the birth of Jesus. One preschooler imagines himself as Joseph, and another as Mary. Preschoolers can quickly become an airplane zooming through the air or a butterfly waving its wings. Much of the dramatic play with pre-

schoolers is spontaneous and includes simple dialogue and action. Simple props and costumes may or may not be used. A well-equipped homeliving area provides many of the necessary props and costumes to dramatize a story.

• *Music.*—Books can easily be extended through music. Singing about an object or a character in a book allows the preschooler another way to identify with the book's characters. As the teacher reads the book *Little Boy Jesus* to a two-year-old, he may sing "Jesus, Jesus, I love Jesus; Jesus, Jesus, He loves Ray," p. 16.†

Books may also be extended through the use of appropriate filmstrips, creative cooking, games, or having a visitor in the department. After reading the book *Grandmother and I* by Buckley, a grandmother may be invited to visit the four-year department.

Care of books

Children should be guided to turn pages easily and to show care for the books. If the pages become torn and are left that way, misuse of the book may be encouraged. If pages are missing or if the book cannot be repaired, it needs to be replaced. Pictures from discarded books make excellent homemade books or could be mounted for individual use.

When a book can be repaired, a plastic book-mending liquid is available in school supply houses. If the liquid is not available, another possibility would be the plastic-coated tape made especially for mending books. Clear contact plastic is available for covering entire books. This is especially important when books are being used with babies, creepers, and toddlers.

Storage of books

Who is responsible for the storage of the Preschool books in your church—the teacher, the department director, the division director, the staff Preschool director, or the librarian in your media center? The major importance doesn't lie in which person is responsible for storage of books. The critical factor is that someone knows that it is his responsibility to store books. Some churches have adopted the plan of having a research room in the Preschool area. This may mean that either a person would need to be in charge of being in the resource room when someone needs a book or plan to have a check-out system so that a person can get what is needed at any time. The procedure which is used needs to be kept in good order and checked each week.

Another possibility would be to let the media center be responsible for the books that Preschool departments will be using. At a certain time during the week when planning takes place, someone can check out books for the next unit.

Some departments have good storage areas for books in their rooms.

Summary

As you use books in various activities with preschoolers, ask yourself the following questions:

• Does the way the book is being used with a baby, creeper, or toddler allow the child to use one or more of his senses?

- Does the use of the book build upon previously learned concepts?
- Does the book activity provide for thought based on concrete experiences of twos, threes, fours, and fives?
- Do the books which you have provided give opportunities for the child to experience success at the teachable moment?
- Does the book relate to the child's experience?

Books for preschoolers are meant to be enjoyed. Nothing is more rewarding than sharing a book with a child. A teacher can guide the child in discovering joy and a sense of wonder as he looks at pictures and reads a book with a friend nearby. When children have been nurtured by an early love for books, they seem to develop more sensitive minds and imaginations.

As teachers of preschoolers, we are striving to develop persons who will continue to grow spiritually, emotionally, and intellectually.

Personal Learning Activities

1. Make a list of your strengths (strong points) in using books with preschoolers.
2. List the books that are suggested in the current quarter of *Preschool Bible Teacher A, B,* or *C; Bible Story Time Teacher; Start;* or *The Music Leader* which you need to order for your department.
3. Check with the Preschool director or division director to see how much money has been allocated for new books in the Preschool budget.
4. Browse in your church library for Preschool books. Give a list of suggested books to the librarian.
5. Look at the books in your department and read your favorite book. Decide what is being taught as this book is used with preschoolers.
6. Make an inventory of the books that are in the room where you teach. Repair the ones that are torn.
7. What books will you make? How will you use them?
8. Set up a Preschool resource center, in cooperation with the Preschool Committee or Preschool Division director in your church.

Materials for Further Study

Books.

Beaty, Janice J. *Classroom Skills for Preschool Teachers.* Columbus, Ohio: Charles E. Merrill Publishing Company, 1979.

Carlson, Ruth K. *Enrichment Ideas,* Literature for Children Series. Dubuque, Iowa: William C. Brown C., 1976.

Clark, Margaret M. *Keeping Up with Children and Books* 1963-1965, Chicago: Scott, Foresman, 1966.

Georgiou, Constantine. *Children and Their Literature.* Englewood Cliffs, N.J.: Prentice Hall, 1969.

Hildebrand, Verna. *Introduction to Early Childhood Education* (Chapter 1). 2nd ed. New York: The Macmillan Co., 1976.

Hunt, Gladys M. *Honey for a Child's Heart*. Grand Rapids, Michigan: Zondervan Publishing House, 1969.

Jacobs, Leland B., ed. *Using Literature with Young Children*. N.Y.: Teachers College Press, Columbia University, 1965.

Langford, Louise M., *Guidance of the Young Child*, 2nd ed. N.Y.: John Wiley and Sons, Inc., 1975.

Taylor, Barbara J. *A Child Goes Forth*, 5th ed. Provo, Utah: Brigham Young University Press, 1980.

Tiedt, Iris M., *Exploring Books with Children*. Boston: Houghton Mifflin Company, 1978.

Watrin, Rita, and Paul Hanley Furfey. *Learning Activities for the Young Preschool Child*, New York: D. Van Nostrand Co., 1978.

Whitehead, Robert. *Children's Literature: Strategies of Teaching*. Englewood Cliffs, N.J.: Prentice-Hall, 1968.

Sources of Catalogs

For further study and information:

Baptist Book Store, The Sunday School Board, 127 Ninth Avenue, North, Nashville, Tennessee 37234.

Childcraft Education Corporation, 20 Kilmer Road, Edison, N.J. 08817

---

*Available from Baptist Book Stores.

**Available by writing Customer Service Center, 127 Ninth Avenue, North, Nashville, Tennessee 37234; or by calling toll free 1-800-458-2772.

Chapter 8—How to Teach Through the Use of Homeliving Materials

Helen Young

The dolls, child-sized dishes, and telephones used for homeliving activities at church are usually thought of as toys. Within the limits of safety, respect for others, and care of property, a preschooler should be free to use his ideas, make and carry out his plans, and engage in imaginary activities based on previous experiences. The use of homeliving learning materials by a young child frequently leads an adult who is unaware of the essentials of foundational development to exclaim, "Why, he just plays at church!" A child is playing when he uses homeliving materials, but he is *learning through play!* Note Sybil Waldrop's comments regarding play on pages 21 to 41.

Why Are Provisions Made for Homeliving Activities?
Homeliving activities are valuable to the preschooler as he develops in many aspects of life and to a teacher as he assists a child with his developmental tasks.

The preschooler who has homeliving materials to use—
• Can acquire feelings of security because some of the materials are similar to those which are a part of his everyday environment;
• Uses his large muscles that require exercise as he moves from one position to another in an imaginary home situation;
• Becomes aware of his physical self as he looks into the mirror which helps a younger preschooler learn the names of some of the body parts and helps an older preschooler understand more about his body;
• Learns through smelling, tasting, seeing, touching, and hearing;
• Has many opportunities to make choices about which materials to use and how to use them;
• Gains some awareness of how it feels to be in the role of a community worker or a family member other than himself;
• Finds it possible to repeat at home the activities in which he participates at church because there are similar materials available.

Five-year-olds made cookies in the homeliving area. They invited the pastor to be their guest, and he enjoyed the cookies with them. Later Sammy asked his mother to let him help make cookies at home and invite his teacher. He wanted to share his cookies with her.

The teacher who uses homeliving materials with preschoolers—
• May get ideas about which materials to make available in planning future homeliving activities as he observes the children at play;

- Becomes aware of some of a child's mental, social, emotional, physical, or spiritual weaknesses and strengths as he experiences the freedom of the homeliving area;
- Picks up clues relative to desirable or undesirable experiences which the child is having with other persons.

A teacher saw a four-year-old boy pretending to be leaving home for work. He hugged the girl who was pretending to be the mother and left the homeliving area with his tools. The incident seemed so natural to both of them that the teacher was reassured that the children had parents who frequently expressed love.

Another teacher observed that a three-year-old boy put a doll in the pretend oven saying, "Burn him all up!" When he visited in the home, the teacher learned that the child had a baby brother. Resentment was less evident when the older boy was given the attention that his parents did not realize he needed.

Which Age Groups Use Homeliving Materials?

Materials similar to those used in a home are suggested for all preschoolers at church. The items may take a slightly different form, and an older preschooler will use them in ways different from those of a younger preschooler. As a child becomes older and his skills increase, a greater variety of homeliving materials should be made available to him. These are presented for his use, a few at a time, according to evident needs and the Bible teaching aim.

All preschoolers use dolls. Even a baby can be exposed to such materials as a Broadman doll,* a sturdy unbreakable mirror, and plastic lids laced together. Mobiles with faces of people on them hanging in a way that the birth through six-month-old can see the faces, not just the edges of the mobile, are suggested.

A creeper can also use an over-sized hat, cans, measuring spoons (securely fastened together), plastic cups, a toy telephone, plastic tops (securely tied together), and an unbreakable wall mirror** resting on the floor and fastened sideways to the wall so that the baby can see his body from head to toe.

A toddler can use purses, a small blanket for the doll, and hats.

A two-year-old can also use empty food boxes, plastic dishes, plastic pans, ingredients used for simple food preparation (bananas, raisins, and pears for a fruit salad), water, soap, and towels.

A three-year-old can work with child-sized mops and brooms, wooden cooking spoons, small luggage pieces, play dough, and aprons.

The four- or five-year-old can use numerous additional materials. Such as a toy cash register, play money, a discarded telephone, a flashlight, a discarded camera, clothes for the doll, strips of cloth for draped clothing, scarves, utensils for cooking (child-sized for imaginary cooking and adult-sized for actual cooking with adult supervision), ingredients for cooking "from scratch," fruits, vegetables, blunt plastic needles for use with yarn and coarse cloth, baby-care materials, plastic hats* (for community workers), real or toy items used by community workers, child-sized doctor and nurse uniforms, and appliance boxes (large enough to crawl into).

When May Preschoolers Participate in Homeliving Activities?

Teaching and learning with homeliving materials may take place with the baby, creeper, toddler, or two-year-old at any time when he is not sleeping, resting, being taken on a walk, or playing outdoors with other types of materials. Usually a child makes the choice as to which materials he uses; however, a teacher may voluntarily stimulate his interest in homeliving items. The teacher may shake a mobile to attract the child's attention or move a doll closer to the baby, saying: "Michael, look at the faces. See the faces move." "Michael, can you touch the doll?" "Thank you, God, for eyes to see (hands to touch)."

A three-, four-, or five-year-old may engage in activities with homeliving materials during activities, beginning when he enters the room and ending with group time. If he is in an extended session, he may use these materials during a second activity time. Some or all of the following materials will be available at times when homeliving materials are used: books, blocks, nature materials, puzzles, music materials, and art materials.

A child may or may not choose to use the homeliving materials during part or all of the activities. If there are more than five older preschoolers in a homeliving area, communication breaks down and turn-taking requires waiting periods. When overcrowding becomes a probability, a teacher may encourage each child in the homeliving area who is not vitally involved in the activity to become involved in another activity for a while. The child who left may or may not return later. The mentally alert child will usually want to be involved in several or all of the activity areas.

Where Are Homeliving Teaching Materials and Furniture Placed in a Room?

Materials and furniture in rooms for preschoolers are organized so that items which are used for a specific activity are placed together. How the children will use each type of material is basic when deciding where to place furniture and materials. For instance, block activities may require twenty-five square feet of floor space; therefore, the block shelf needs to be located where such space is available and not in a high traffic area. Consider how the room looks to the preschooler as he enters. A happy entry is an important step toward a desirable session for a preschooler; an unhappy entry may lead to a very undesirable session for him. If friendly teachers are present and if he sees from the door items which he can associate with gratifying experiences he has had in the recent past, entering the room without a parent may not be a problem for him. Perhaps homeliving materials will be the most inviting area to a shy preschooler, since the child is quite familiar with a homelike environment. Make the homeliving area of a room for twos, threes, fours, or fives as visible and as easily accessible from the room entrance as possible. Avoid locating this area where preschoolers will be facing it during group time; the materials and furniture may distract the children as the director is endeavoring to hold their attention. A corner or a recessed portion of a room's wall can be useful for a homeliving area.

A baby's homeliving materials are placed in his bed. The Broadman doll* is placed in the bed so that the baby can see the doll's face and so that the doll is close enough for the baby to reach. Mobiles are hung above and to the side of the bed where the baby will turn his head to see the item. The unbreakable mirror is placed where a baby can see himself. Refer to *Preschool Bible Teacher A, Bible Story Time Teacher,* or *Start* for specific suggestions regarding the use of these items with babies in your Preschool-related organization.

A creeper's dolls and plastic telephones· should be placed on the floor, perhaps near the mirror. A picture of a home situation has been mounted on cardboard, covered with clear contact plastic, and placed nearby.

A toddler's dolls may be placed in the doll bed or in the child-sized rocker with a blanket nearby. Soft plastic dishes may be placed on the floor. The full-length mirror may be mounted upright on the wall.

In two- or three-year-departments, the soft plastic dishes may be placed on the child-sized cabinet-sink. The pans may be placed on the child-sized stove (some of each may be placed inside the cabinet-sink or stove). The doll may be put into the doll bed and partially covered with doll bedclothes. The dress-up clothes may be hung on a sturdy blunt hook. Purses may be placed on the floor nearby. The empty food boxes may be placed on the cabinet-sink (some may be placed inside). A wooden cooking spoon may be on the cabinet-sink (some may be placed in a drawer). A plastic utility pan with water approximately one inch deep, a small bar of soap, and a medium-sized bath towel (or some other special materials for the current session) may be on the table.

A doll in the four- or five-year department may be dressed, and doll clothes may be in one of the drawers of the child-sized chest of drawers. Most of the dishes may be in the lower part of the cabinet-sink; most of the pans may be in the lower part of the stove. (A few of the dishes and pans may be on the counter to create interest.) Dress-up clothes may be placed in two drawers of the chest of drawers. One telephone may be on the chest of drawers and the other telephone on the cabinet-sink. A doctor's and a nurse's uniform may each be on a coat hanger or hung on a sturdy, blunt hook. A large, shallow sheet-cake pan with a stethoscope, homemade adhesive bandages, cotton balls, and empty plastic ointment tubes (or some other special materials for the current session) may be on the table.

Each age group above the toddler age uses the same furniture as the younger age groups, plus other pieces appropriate for their ages. For information on the location of homeliving furniture, see the book *BREAKTHROUGH: Preschool Sunday School Work** by Davis (chapter 6).

Perhaps as you read suggestions about homeliving teaching materials in this book and in the teacher's magazines *Bible Story Time Teacher,*** *Preschool Bible Teacher A,*** *Preschool Bible Teacher B,*** *Preschool Bible Teacher C,*** *The Music Leader,*** and *Start,**** you have said to yourself, "I can't buy all those things to use for the activities described." Teachers in one organization shouldn't try to buy all of the materials. Many churches have some plan by which teachers in various organizations obtain money for their work through the church budget. Doubtless you give through the church budget. You were elected by the church to teach; therefore, there must be some way that your teaching can be financed through the church budget. Possibly, you "have not because you ask not."

Training director, Mission Friends leader, or Preschool choir leader about how to obtain money for materials. Perhaps you will be told to submit a list of needed items to a person authorized by the church to make purchases, or you may be asked to buy your own materials and turn the sales receipts over to a church secretary who can reimburse you. By all means plan ahead. Read chapter 8 in *Basic Preschool Work* for suggestions regarding preparation of the Preschool Division budget.

If your church has several Preschool departments, items such as an electric skillet, ingredients for making play dough, community worker uniforms, and accessories can be put in a central storage area. These materials are not used for every session. When the department director and teachers make plans at weekly workers' meeting that call for the use of one of these items, they may reserve the item according to the church's system of scheduling the use of such materials.

Your church may be temporarily low on budgeted money. Teachers or parents will be glad to share their electrical appliances or cooking utensils three or four times a year. Many older preschoolers can be led to share willingly such items as community worker hats, a doll, or a small suitcase. They may bring some of these needed toys to church upon request. Most parents are glad to share fruit from their trees or vegetables from their gardens for homeliving activities.

Creative teachers can make many materials from items in the home that are usually thrown away. Soft plastic containers can be used as dishes and pans; margarine tubs make good bowls; plastic tops for large containers can serve as plates; juice cans covered with attractive contact plastic can serve as glasses; adhesive bandages can be made from masking tape and waxed paper. A telephone can be made from two baby powder cans with flat sides, if each end of a heavy cord is tied to the end of one of the cans where the powder comes out. One group of fours and fives gets much use from telephone books for a town of

17,000; these books are just the right size to be interesting and manageable for the children. More suggestions for making teaching materials from discarded items can be found in chapter 15 of this book. *Bible Story Time Teacher**; Preschool Bible Teacher A, B,* and *C**; The Music Leader**; Preschool Leadership*** and *Start**** frequently carry such suggestions.

Child-sized homeliving furniture makes a room for preschoolers attractive and is very useful in teaching toddlers twos, threes, fours, and fives. Beginning with the doll bed and the child-sized rocker, furniture is added as each of the various items becomes useful for corresponding age groups. For specific information about furniture which is suitable for each age group, see the book *BREAKTHROUGH: Preschool Sunday School Work** by Davis. If a church must decide whether to buy child-sized homeliving furniture or a good supply of items such as dolls, dishes, telephones, and cooking utensils for children, the best choice is to buy the smaller items and use makeshift furniture.

Cardboard or wooden boxes can be made into a child-sized cabinet-sink, a stove, a doll bed, a chest for dress-up and doll clothes (for fours and fives), and a table. Suggestions for making such furniture can be found in chapter 15 of this book. By using imagination, adults can add realistic touches to furniture made from boxes, such as painted-on burners for a stove and nailed-on spools for knobs. Preschoolers are very accepting of homemade items. Teaching with makeshift furniture is much easier than teaching without a variety of recommended teaching materials that stimulate a child to learn.

As soon as money becomes available, homeliving furniture is a good investment for a church. Homeliving furniture can be ordered from Baptist Book Stores or made by a competent cabinet maker according to diagrams in the program help *Make Your Own Preschool Furniture.*** The contents of this packet are useful even in making furniture from boxes, since the diagrams give dimensions and show an outline drawing of each piece of furniture.

When children of several Preschool age groups must be combined, furnish the area for the youngest preschooler, as well as for the oldest child in the group. Study the suggestions about teaching materials and furniture for each age group in *Bible Story Time Teacher;** Preschool Bible Teacher A, B,* and *C;*** and the books *BREAKTHROUGH: Preschool Sunday School Work** (chapter 6) and *The Small Sunday School at Work** (chapter 6—"Teaching Preschoolers") before deciding what to put in the room. If there are several children in the group who are younger than four years of age, do not put a chest of drawers in the room. Omission of this piece of furniture may prevent mashed fingers. Instead, hang the dress-up clothes on a blunt hook, and put doll clothes in a box or a small suitcase. A toddler in the group may need watching so that he will not tip some piece of furniture on himself or someone else or bump himself as he frequently tumbles from his unsteady stance. If babies must also be in the room, put their beds at one end of the room, and encourage the older preschoolers to stay at the other end. The older children in the group will need to be watched to prevent them giving the babies items that they could swallow or with which they could hurt themselves. As soon as possible, acquire at least one more room for preschoolers.

How Do Teachers Guide Preschoolers in Constructive Home-living Experiences?

Planning to meet some of the daily needs of a preschooler is the key to constructive experiences for the child in the homeliving area. Close relationships with a child's parents, personal conversation with preschoolers who can talk, and awareness of their individual interests are ways to learn about these needs.

Parents may share with teachers their preschoolers' current stages of development in contacts made during the week. In this way, teachers are more aware of what to expect of the preschoolers. Parents can also tell teachers about toys which these preschoolers use most often at home. Such conversations can give clues as to special materials to provide and when to make the items available to the children.

Nothing can take the place of visiting in the home when a teacher is trying to meet needs of a preschooler. Telephone conversations with a child and his parents, informal chats with parents on any occasion, and a few words at the door of the child's room from Sunday to Sunday also are ways of learning about a child's needs and interests. When each department director or teacher is alert to such opportunities and shares clues with other teachers in weekly workers' meetings, good preparation usually results. With specific information about each child's home and family, the teachers can make the homeliving activities/conversations relevant to each child.

At snack time, Doug's teacher suggested, "Let's thank God for the crackers." Upon hearing this, Doug responded: "Why are we going to thank God for the crackers? My mother bought them at the store." The teacher knew that Doug's statement was correct. He also knew that the child's question needed answering, not only with words, but with a firsthand experience. He spoke of this incident during the weekly workers' meeting. The teachers present decided that perhaps all of the children needed to know more about how God gives us food. They knew the children needed to know the role of their parents and the store in procuring food. They prepared a plot of ground for a garden. Nearly every Sunday some of the children in the department went to water the plants and to see how much the plants had grown. Cantelopes, okra, and pumpkins grew. A teacher cut open a pumpkin and let the children remove the seed; then the teacher made pumpkin pie with the meat of the pumpkin. When the teacher said, "Thank you, God, for the pumpkin," the preschoolers better understood God's part and their parents' part in providing food and why we thank him for food.

Much is being said and written about the importance of stimulating babies, creepers, and toddlers to communicate and learn. The youngest baby in a room at the church likes for someone to talk to him. No one can tell how much he comprehends. Researchers say that frequent glances at a person by a baby indicate that the baby relates well to that person. A smile from him is a real reward for a teacher! Lovingly associating a child's name with the words *mother, daddy, doll,* and *book,* in conversation and also frequently using comments about God, Jesus, and the Bible will result in happy, secure feelings for the baby at church. Teachers of babies do more than keep them from crying and see that they are dry and clean. Teachers are stimulators of love, trust, thinking, and communication, which are important needs of all preschoolers, including babies. Time is well spent in turning the mirror (or the baby) so that the baby can see himself, picking a baby up so that he can be close to a friendly person and have a change of scenery, or singing the song "Doggy, Doggy" (p. 114)††† to the child. These are important ways of beginning younger preschoolers' awareness of the homes which God planned for them.

Many Preschool teachers do not talk to the children in their departments because they do not know what to say. A helpful activity to include in weekly workers' meetings is to decide on suitable statements to make in conversation with a child. Suitable Bible thoughts and songs may also be selected and practiced at weekly workers' meetings. Talking about the simple words to use in prayers with preschoolers and the appropriate times for such prayers helps teachers make the most of their time with the children. A teacher says, "Get the puppy, Lisa," as he puts a soft rubber dog in Lisa's bed. When the task is achieved, he says, "Lisa got the puppy!" She will be more likely to pick up the puppy if she hears the director say that picking up the puppy is the thing to do. The teacher may even go farther and say, "Thank you, God, for Lisa's hands," and also sing: "Doggy, doggy, Bow- wow- wow; Doggy, doggy, Bow- wow-wow; Thank you, God. Thank you for my doggy," if he knows this is the appropriate approach.

Words used in Bible thoughts may be applied to many homeliving situations. Without question, the meanings of many words in Bible thoughts can be expanded for any preschooler. Be alert for opportunities, and use these and other such words with preschoolers as they apply to their actions in the homeliving area: *help, kind, gentle, good, love, feel, give, friends, parents, care,* and *near.* Keeping in mind the current Bible teaching aim helps a teacher expose the children to a variety of words. If a teacher depends only on taking advantage of incidental opportunities for the use of these words, he will overuse some words and not use others. A child can more easily associate Bible thoughts and Bible stories with his present-day activities if he has teachers who use some of the same words that are in Bible material in natural situations.

Teaching opportunities that are directly related to the spiritual aspects of a child's life occur when preschoolers are using homeliving materials. A Read-to-Me Bible,* a picture related to a Bible story, play

money and purses, a handmade piano keyboard taped to the homeliving table, and a songbook frequently stimulate activities that provide such opportunities. A child may turn to a picture in the Bible and ask a teacher what the picture is about. He might stop in front of a picture or pick it up for a better look. At this point a teacher needs to help the child know about or recall the Bible story to which the picture is related. An older preschooler may be told how the money he brings to church is used, as he uses the playlike bills and coins. He can have enriched imaginary experiences as a pianist when a teacher joins him by singing a Bible-related song. He might be attracted by the colorful songbook that has been placed in the homeliving area for that session. Then a teacher in that area could sing a song about God or Jesus from the book as the child listens. A prayer before a pretend meal is a well-accepted practice by many older preschoolers.

A pallet may be used instead of a bed for a doll on a Sunday when the Bible story is to be about Jesus healing the man who was let down through the roof. The pallet may lead to conversation that will help a four- or five-year-old think about the helpfulness of friends by thinking about the problems involved in letting a present-day bed down through the roof.

In his eagerness to teach Bible truths, a teacher can cause a child to develop a dislike for Bible content. If a child feels he has been interrupted with a Bible thought while he is engaged intently in working a puzzle, his facial expressions will register this feeling. If he walks away during the recall of a Bible story, the child is not interested in what is being said. If he says, "I know it," after a teacher says a Bible thought, perhaps the child is bored. In such cases, do not force him to listen. Doing so could create negative feelings about the Bible.

Preschoolers need freedom within limits, but they also need guidance that helps them stay within the limits of safety, care of property, and respect for others. Such guidance begins with a well-prepared room and continues as understanding teachers work with the children during a session. These suggestions may help:

See that each homeliving item used regularly is in a designated place each time the room is prepared for a specific group of preschoolers.

Four to six of the following unbreakable items are needed regularly by twos, threes, fours, and fives: child-sized plates, juice cups, and cereal bowls. One or two washable dolls and one or two plastic telephones are also needed by these children. More of these items encourage clutter and frustration.

While helping twos, threes, fours, and fives straighten the homeliving area at transition or near the close of a session, make definite suggestions such as, "Marcia, the stove is a good place for the pans." "Jim, this shelf is where you may put these bowls."

Remove the added materials when they no longer relate to a current focus. If they are in good condition, store the items for future use. Play dough is best used as an additional material. If it is used regularly it may too often lure children away from homeliving materials that can stimulate more profitable experiences than those that result from the use of this modeling substance.

Encourage all preschoolers to use homeliving materials in ways that such items are actually used in orderly homes. If teachers will handle these materials in similar ways and will make such comments as those that follow, the children will ordinarily use homeliving items properly. A teacher may say, "The broom is used on the floor." "The receiver goes on the telephone." "Put the doll blanket around the doll or on the bed." Such reminders frequently work, even when twos, threes, fours, and fives are misusing items.

"Bring the doll over here" will often lead a toddler or a two-year-old child to move a doll from a high traffic area, to a safer place.

Remind threes, fours, and fives to use homeliving materials only in the homeliving area, unless they are pretending to go on a trip or to make a visit. They may take some materials outside for a picnic.

Some activities include plans for twos, threes, fours, and fives to prepare food that will be eaten. See that each child who participates first washes his hands.

To avoid needless splashes and spills, during activities that require water, provide only enough to make the learning task possible.

Personally commend a child who improves in some way such as being more cooperative, constructive, gentle, or imaginative.

If voices begin to get loud and children begin to get boisterous, calmly try to interest each disruptive child in some other activity within the homeliving area or in some other part of the room.

Several different kinds of homeliving activities stimulate varied learning activities. Adding some material(s) other than the doll and dishes and placing the item(s) on the table in the homeliving area is all that is required to interest the child. Some of these types of activities include the following:

• *Dramatic play.*—Frequently children two through five play out situations similar to those situations which they have experienced. Those involved make up their own conversation and work out their own plots. One group of children followed the lead of the pretend mother as she created an imaginary situation based on the picture "A Family Goes Camping" (*People-Around-Me Pictures,* Picture 24). This picture was on the wall in the homeliving area of a room for fives. The mother pretended that the picture was a window and that through the window she saw campers who had to stay in that location for several days. The campers ran out of food, according to the dramatic play, and the mother in the homeliving area involved others in preparing food for the imaginary stranded family.

When a similar activity takes place, the teacher stays aware of what is happening and makes suggestions if the conversation lags or the plot breaks down. At the invitation of a child or if he can skillfully work himself into the plot, the teacher may temporarily take the role of some

114

person involved in the situation, but should avoid taking the lead.

Occasionally a younger preschooler engages in dramatic play with homeliving materials. He may talk to himself, as if interpreting what he is doing, or to the dolls as if they were persons.

As the experience of an older preschooler extends into the community and he has meaningful experiences with persons engaged in community services, activities with homeliving materials give these preschoolers imaginary experiences as such workers. Frequently only a representative headpiece or item of equipment is all that is required to lead threes, fours, and fives into dramatic play about community workers. One nurse says that she can remember playing nurse many times when she was as young as three. From that time on, she planned to be a nurse.

● *Food preparation.*—A two-, three-, four-, or five-year-old can learn much from food preparation. He can do some or all of these things: clean, break apart, and measure vegetables and fruits. He can stir pulverized ingredients into liquids. He can shape dough into a ball and roll it in confectioner's sugar. He can eat the food he has helped to prepare and give some of it to the children and teachers who did not help with the preparation. Such activities give experiences in using all of the senses to learn. The preschooler learns what is required in the preparation of food. He has practice in taking turns. His self-esteem increases. Imaginary food experiences can result from the use of play dough, but firsthand experiences with real food are much more meaningful. For more suggestions about food preparation, see chapter 15 of this book.

● *Helping activities.*—The older preschooler can perform routine tasks that will improve the room's environment. He can dust the windowsills, wash paint smudges, arrange a bouquet of flowers, sort clothes so that doll clothes are in one drawer and dress-up clothes are in another, and he can wipe the table with a wet sponge. Such activities give the child firsthand experiences in learning to assume responsibility and in performing jobs at church and at home.

Summary
Homeliving materials and furniture seem to contribute to a young child's feeling of security at church. Homeliving materials are of interest to a child throughout the Preschool years, if they correspond with his skill development and experiences as he grows mentally, physically, socially, and spiritually. If there must be a choice between having furniture or teaching materials for a Preschool department, teaching materials are more important than furniture. The better a teacher knows a child, his family, and his environment, the better that teacher can meet the child's individual needs. Experiences which foster spiritual development may come about frequently during a child's use of homeliving materials. How much a teacher helps a child learn from experiences depends on that teacher's willingness and ability to discover needs. The

teacher must be able to select stimulating teaching materials and have skill in identifying and using teachable moments. This process would include his ability to use meaningful comments, Bible story conversation, Bible thoughts, and songs in the homeliving activities.

Personal Learning Activities

1. Why are play experiences important for a preschooler?

2. Name two suitable homeliving materials for each of the following groups of preschoolers: babies, creepers, toddlers, twos, threes, fours, and fives.

3. Are homeliving materials in a desirable location in the room where you teach at church? If not, how could the location of the materials be improved?

4. What three words will you start using with preschoolers as they engage in homeliving activities?

Materials for Further Study

Hendrick, Joanne. *The Whole Child,* 2nd ed. St. Louis: The C. V. Mosby Company, 1980.

Uland, Zadabeth. *Bible Teaching for Preschoolers.* Nashville: Convention Press, 1984.

Reynolds, Jean, compiler. *How to Choose and Use Child Care.* Nashville: Broadman Press, 1980.

Terrell, Jerry. *Basic Preschool Work.* Nashville: Convention Press, 1981.

---

*Available from Baptist Book Stores.

**Available by writing Customer Service Center, 127 Ninth Avenue, North, Nashville, Tennessee 37234; or by calling toll free 1-800-458-2772.

***Available from Woman's Missionary Union, P.O. Box 830010, Birmingham, Alabama 35283-0010.

Chapter 9—How to Teach Through the Use of Music

Sue Raley

Sing joyfully to the Lord, you righteous;
It is fitting for the upright to praise him.
Praise the Lord with the harp;
Make music to him on the ten-stringed lyre.
Sing to him a new song;
Play skillfully, and shout for joy" (Ps. 33:1-3, NIV).[11]

Joyous singing has always accompanied the worship of God.
- Moses led the Hebrews in a song to celebrate God's deliverance at the Red Sea (Ex. 15:1-8).
- Deborah and Barak praised God in a song which recounted their victory over the Canaanites (Judg. 5).
- The Hebrews celebrated with singing, instruments, and a choir robed in fine linen when they dedicated the Temple (2 Chron. 5:11-14).
- David praised God's handiwork in a song (Ps. 8).

Few biblical experiences involving music are as joyous as the story told by Matthew when the children expressed their love for Jesus through happy songs (Matt. 21:12-16). Perhaps preschoolers were among those whose song "Hosanna to the Son of David" greeted Jesus in the temple. The praises of the children must have meant a great deal to Jesus. He loved children, as we know from Matthew 19:13-15. As they sang, he accepted their praises with special attention. Jesus' enemies criticized him for letting the children sing, but he replied, "Have you never read, 'From the lips of children and infants you have ordained praise'?" (Ps. 8:2, NIV). In effect, he was saying, "God is pleased."

Why Is Music Used as a Teaching Tool at Church?
An often-repeated conversation between a busy mother and a curious preschooler goes something like this:
Child: "Why?"
Mother: "Because."
Child: "Because why?"
Mother: "Just because."
The "why" of music as a teaching method can be answered as follows:
- *Music is enjoyable.*—The infant delights in the sounds of music

boxes, bell rattles, and lullabies. The two-year-old responds to recorded music with clapping hands and awkward marching. The four-year-old is fascinated with his newly discovered skills in tapping the sticks, beating the drum, and strumming the Autoharp. Hearing a teacher sing: "I have a good friend. John is his name," pleases a preschooler of any age.

• *Music may assist in the formation of concepts related to Bible truths.*—The young child hears and eventually sings: "Jesus, Jesus, I love Jesus. Jesus, Jesus, he loves me." A concept about Jesus is being formed. Carefully selected songs for preschoolers at church express concepts about the Bible, God, Jesus, church, family, self, others, and the natural world. As the child learns these songs during his Preschool years, the foundation for further spiritual growth is being laid.

• *Music can help preschoolers experience wonder and joy.*—Amy sees, touches, smells, and tastes a bright, red apple. She sings with her teacher: "God loves me. God loves me. God made the apple and God loves me." She then exclaims, "God made apples for *Amy*!" Amy feels good about herself and this fleeting moment of wonder and joy.

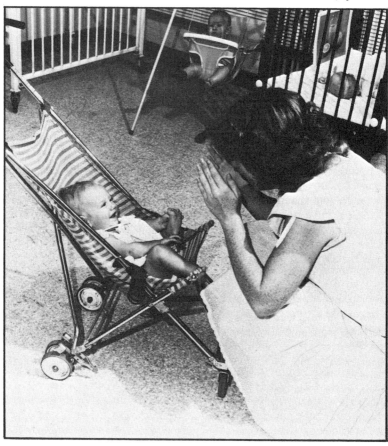

● *The child's feelings of well-being and personal worth may be nurtured through music.*—Preschoolers discover an acceptable outlet for their emotions through singing, moving, and using instruments. Four- and five-year-olds may feel successful as they make their own tunes, words, or rhythms. Participation with and acceptance by others in a musical activity helps the child feel good about himself and his relationships with those in the group.

● *Music invites active participation.*—Preschoolers have been described as "on the move." The preschooler learns and develops as he wiggles, sits, stands, jumps, rolls, and falls during his everyday life. Music encourages the active use of many of the child's developing skills: listening, verbalizing, responding to rhythms, and controlling body movements.

● *Music can be used to further other kinds of learning.*—Music seems to have a natural appeal which makes the child eager to participate in the musical experience being offered. Through his participation, he learns many kinds of things: vocabulary, concepts, motor skills, and social behavior. At the same time, he is learning to appreciate music and to be sensitive to the beauty of musical expression.

Who Can Enjoy Music? Who Can Learn Bible Concepts Through Music?

"Brian needs to ask Aunt Sue to get a longer string," the young mother commented as she walked toward Brian's bassinet. She pulled the string to activate the music box. As the music played, the string coiled into the box, stopping the music when all of the string was recoiled. As long as the music played, Brian lay contented and relaxed, but each time the music stopped, he wiggled and fretted until someone pulled the string to reactivate the music box. Brian was two weeks old when this episode occurred.

Very young babies enjoy being talked to and sung to long before they understand words. Music soothes and encourages vocalizing and social responses from babies.

Music helps comfort toddlers and provides a relaxing atmosphere when needed. As the children begin to feel more secure in a room, they are ready for play and lively songs.

Twos, threes, fours, and fives are capable of enjoying and participating in many kinds of experiences with music. Each child, at his own level of understanding, learns Bible truths through well-planned music activities provided for him at church. All methods and materials that are used with preschoolers should be child-centered. That is, the needs and abilities of each child should be kept in mind as the teacher prepares for musical experiences.

- Baby Matt is calmed by the sound of a quiet lullaby.
- Creeper Andy delights to the sound of the wind chime.
- Toddler Carrie claps her hands when she hears music on the cassette tape.
- Two-year-old Jason imitates sounds in his world—animals, machines, and people.
- Three-year-old Kristi sings while she plays, using her own words and melody.
- Four-year-old David hums the song "Jesus Loves Me" (p. 17)† while he builds with blocks.
- Five-year-old Emily sings as she strums the Autoharp to accompany herself.

Music is used informally with preschoolers from the first day they come to the church on through the Preschool years.

Which Experiences with Music Are Appropriate for Preschoolers?

Listening
The first music activity is listening, since listening is the basis of all music expression. Listening is basic to learning—learning music and learning biblical truths through music.

The very youngest babies can enjoy listening to music. They may not understand the words they hear, but they gain feelings of calmness, joy, love, and acceptance through hearing appropriate music at church. Babies and creepers respond by looking, smiling, and cooing when they see a teacher's face and hear him sing. Infants are soothed when they hear quiet music from a cassette tape or recording. Creepers show delight, excitement, and curiosity when they hear the musical sounds of wind chimes and musical toys such as music boxes, shake and roll rattles, and cradle gyms.

Toddlers and twos continue to enjoy listening to music. They are able to recognize simple songs which they have heard many times, and they feel secure when they hear these familiar tunes. A child learns to sing and to speak by imitation. When he hears a song repeatedly, he will begin to sing it. Quiet background music blends and softens abrupt noises, and creates a pleasing atmosphere in a room. Bright, cheerful (but not loud) music encourages happy play among the children. Discovering musical sounds in homemade instruments such as shakers or drums brings satisfaction to the child who is learning through hearing many kinds of sounds. (See chapter 15, "How to Make Additional Teaching Materials.")

Threes, fours, and fives are continuing to develop the skill of listening. They are able to sing the songs they have heard. They can distinguish differences in sounds and are challenged by a sound-matching game.

Older preschoolers may listen to music and then respond through movement or the use of instruments. An example of this experience is an activity using recorded music and inviting the children to skip, jump, walk, or tiptoe in response to the tempo, rhythm, or volume of the music.

Moving

● Mrs. Johnson holds eight-month-old Lisa on her lap and sings the song "Can You Clap Your Hands?" (p. 64).† Lisa laughs, kicks her feet, and claps her hands, imitating Mrs. Johnson's claps.

● Jason, age two, awkwardly marches around the room, beating an oatmeal-box drum and chanting a song of his own creation.

● At age four, Amy sits near the record player and claps her hands, nods her head, and taps her toes, following the directions she hears in the song "Clap Your Hands" (p. 65).†

Each of these children is responding to music through movement. Each response varies with the age and development of the child. The fact that preschoolers are seldom still is realized by all teachers. Children are naturally active. Through movement, they develop in the following areas:

● Control and development of arm and leg muscles;
● Coordination in the use of hands, arms, feet, and legs;
● Ability to think and respond;
● Skill in listening to and following directions;
● Use of abundant energy in an acceptable fashion;
● Expression of emotions—joy, excitement, tension, and frustration.

A word of caution

Many researchers agree that the preschooler can think about only one thing at a time. When a song suggests motions, the child thinks about the motions as he carries them out. When he is thinking about motions, he cannot also think about the words or the meaning of the words; thus, it is best for the child to move to songs that contain words about moving: "Clap your hands"; "Nod your head"; "Shake the tambourine." *Avoid adding motions to songs with spiritual concepts* (songs about God, Jesus, the Bible, and church). The words and the message of the song are important and have more value when the child's attention is not diverted to motions.

Making music

Preschoolers of all ages can make music. The kind of music they make depends, in part, upon their level of development, their coordination, and their individual creativity.

Tie jingle bells to a baby's shoes or ankles. He kicks and hears the sound his movement makes. He may or may not associate the sound with his action, but he is making and hearing a musical sound, nonetheless. A creeper plays the game pat-a-cake and makes a music sound with his hands. Later in his development, the nonrhythmic claps will become rhythmic.

As language develops, so does the ability to sing. Preschoolers who have heard singing will begin to sing alone or with others. Twos and threes often make their own music as they chant, hum, or sing about things they are doing at the moment.

Singing and making music with instruments may be a part of a planned group experience for threes, fours, and fives. Music-making in a group should be informal, using the child's creativity as much as possible.

The goal for the teacher should be to help the child learn concepts and experience personal satisfaction through music. Drilling for perfection in performance is not desirable, nor does it lead to the reaching of the goals of teaching.

When Can Music at Church Be Meaningful for the Preschooler?
Music may be meaningful for the preschooler when individual needs are being met or when the music relates to his activities. The key to success is the flexibility and initiative of the teacher. Music may be planned, scheduled, or spontaneous. Music may enhance every part of the session from the arrival of the first child to the departure of the last child.

• *Greeting.*—When a preschooler arrives at the door, greet him with a song such as "I Am Happy" (p. 38).† When music can be heard near the door, the child may feel calmed, welcomed, and encouraged to enter the room.

• *Teaching through activities.*—Music may be used in many ways as children participate in activities. Sing to a baby as you rock him or change his diaper. Sing with a toddler who is building with blocks. Sing a Bible-related song such as "God's Beautiful World" (p. 56)†† to a four-year-old who is interested in the nature area. Activities can be enriched by including a variety of musical activities. The book *Guiding Fours and Fives in Musical Experiences* by Baker, Butler, and Key contains helpful information regarding the use of musical activities.

• *Transitions.*—Music can help the children and teachers change smoothly from one portion of the session to the next. Sing the song "It's Fun to Work" (p. 83)† with children who are putting materials away. Provide several instruments for use by children as they arrive at the group-time area.

• *Group time.*—Music is an important part of group time for threes, fours, and fives in Sunday School and Discipleship Training. A song or game may be used to begin group time. The Bible story may be followed by a related song. For example, sing the song "Jesus Loves Children" (p. 18),† after the Bible story about Jesus and the children. A song such as "I Thank You, God" (p. 5),† may lead to a group prayer time. Singing the song "I Make Music, Too" (p. 33),† gives an opportunity to use instruments in the group setting. When the children need relaxation, the song "Stand and Stretch" (p. 91),†† gives the opportunity for movement.

• *Extended session.*—The transition from the Mission Friends, Preschool choir, Sunday School, or Discipleship Training session to the extended session can be aided by the skillful use of music. Soft background music helps to maintain a calm atmosphere in departments for babies, creepers, and toddlers. Instead of background music, a musical game or an activity using instruments may hold the interest of twos through fives. This involvement will keep their attention away from the unsettling change of teachers which is occurring.

A snack is usually served during extended session. As the snack is served to each child, the teacher may sing: "Thank you, God, for Jason's cracker. Thank you, God." The song should be repeated using each child's name when he is served.

Quiet music enhances rest time. Often the children relax in response to soft volume and slow tempo. Instrumental music is ideal for encouraging rest.

When activities are included in the extended session, spontaneous music as well as planned musical activities may be provided. Often the preschoolers wish to repeat activities used earlier in the session. This repetition is an excellent carry-over and the children's wishes should be granted.

Outdoor play may be an extended session activity. Singing about the natural world is especially meaningful to the child who is enjoying the out-of-doors. A child's social behavior may be affected when he hears the teacher near the slide sing: "Mark takes his turn. Amy takes her turn." Music played on a portable cassette player carried outside adds a new dimension to running, hopping, and jumping. A child may prefer to sit in the shade and play with sand, rocks, or small toys as he listens to music. Preschoolers may enjoy spontaneous singing when a teacher sits on the grass and strums an Autoharp, guitar, or MiniHarp.

● *Departure.*—Sing as a child leaves as well as when he arrives. Parent and child will appreciate hearing the teacher sing: "Jenny is happy. Jenny is happy. Jenny came to church today," as they leave the room. Quiet background music contributes to a calm atmosphere when parents are arriving and children are leaving the room.

Where May Music Activities Take Place?

Music is not limited by location. Music can occur anywhere an individual is present. Singing uses the voice, a God-given instrument which we have all the time. Hands are always available for clapping, and ears can hear musical sounds anywhere.

Where can babies and creepers enjoy music?

Musical sounds greet Carole at the door when she is brought into the room. This happy, quiet sound communicates to Carole: "Come in. You are welcome here." Jeff may hear many kinds of music as he lies in his crib. Mrs. Tate lifts Jenny so she can tap the wind chime, causing a jingly sound. Scott hears his teacher sing, "Jesus loves Scott" while the teacher holds him lovingly and gives him milk in a bottle. Mr. Allen carries Mary to the window so she can hear the church bells chime. Babies and creepers benefit from hearing music in every part of their room at church.

Where can toddlers, twos, and threes enjoy music?

Toddlers, twos, and threes also enjoy music in many different places. Singing, using instruments, hearing recordings, and moving to music may occur in any part of the room.

Coming in near the door,
Working puzzles on the floor,
In a corner all alone,
Singing on the telephone,
In the rest room washing hands,
On the playground in the sand—
Music here,
Music there,
I like music EVERYWHERE.

Toddlers may hear a song in the diaper-changing area, and diaper-changing becomes more pleasant for them. Twos and threes may sing or listen to music when they are in the rest room. They can participate in musical games outdoors, or they may create their own music while they play.

Where can fours and fives enjoy music?

Fours and fives benefit from many experiences with music. Often a music area is designated in the room. The record player, instruments, and other materials placed in that area make possible a wide variety of experiences with music; however, music should not be limited to the music area. Singing and listening may be meaningful in every area of the room. Music may be combined with other activities. For example, children in the art area may make a song rebus, or an activity in the nature area may include an experiment with the sounds made by striking nails of differing sizes. Note the sample rebus in chapter 15, "How to Make Additional Teaching Materials."

An excursion to the sanctuary to meet a church musician and to hear the organ or piano is a special activity appropriate for fours and fives. Take the songbook from the department and ask the musician to play songs the children know so they can sing along.

As with younger preschoolers, music may be used outdoors to enhance and enrich fours' and fives' learning and enjoyment.

Music for fun and relaxation is used in Sunday School, Church Training, Mission Friends, Preschool choir, and Weekday programs.

How May I Provide Good Experiences with Music?

A child might like to say to his teacher:
"Don't tell me about music. Let me hear music. Don't teach me music by talking about it. Let me make music. Let me use my ears and my voice and my hands to make music and respond to music. Then I will understand what you're talking about."

Provide for listening to music

● *Learn songs to sing.*—A teacher need not be a soloist to sing with preschoolers. Every teacher should sing often during each teaching session. Learn the songs in the songbooks *Songs for the Young Child,** *More Songs for 4's & 5's,** *Music for Today's Children,** *Easy Songs for Early Singers,** *Sing a Happy Song,** and in current curriculum materials. Sing these songs spontaneously whenever opportunities arise. Two cassette tapes are available from Baptist Book Stores to help teachers know how to use music with preschoolers. *Teaching Music to Preschoolers* (younger preschoolers) and *Using Music with Older Preschoolers* may be used in training sessions, weekly workers' meetings, or teachers' homes.

● *Secure the necessary equipment.*—Listening to music can be greatly enriched through the use of a record player or cassette tape player. An appropriate record player for Preschool departments is operated manually, plays at both 33⅓ and 45 RPMs, and is portable. A cassette player which may be battery- or electrically-operated is desirable. Suitable record players and cassette players are available through Baptist Book Stores.

• *Collect a variety of recordings or tapes.*—Curriculum materials frequently recommend specific recordings and tapes. As you build a collection, maintain variety and balance by including quiet instrumental music, songs from Preschool songbooks, and music for active participation. The following chart may be helpful as you categorize your recordings:

	Quiet Music	Songs to Sing	Activity Music
Baby, Creeper, and Toddler	*Music for Quiet Times* (recording) *Sounds of Praise* (recording) *Hymns for Quiet Times* (recording or cassette)	*Music for Preschool A* (cassette tape) *Easy Songs for Early Singers* (cassette tape)	*Music for 1's and 2's* (recording)
Twos and Threes	*Sea Gulls . . . Music for Rest and Relaxation* (recording) *Hymns for Quiet Times* (recording or cassette)	*Music for Preschool B* (cassette tape) *Easy Songs for Early Singers* (cassette tape)	*Songs for the Young Child* (songbook and recording)
Fours and Fives	*Music for Rest Time* (cassette tape) *Preschool Music Recording Hymns for Quiet Times* (recording or cassette)	*More Songs for 4's & 5's*, Vols. 1, 2, 3, and 4 (songbook, cassette) *Music for Today's Children*, Vols. 1, 2, 3, and 4 (songbook, cassette) *Music for Preschool C* (cassette tape) *Sing a Happy Song* (songbook, cassette)	*Walk in a Circle* (recording) *Moving Here and There* (recording) *Music Is Fun* (recording)

Additional recordings may be collected for each category.

• *Help fours and fives learn how to handle equipment and recordings.*—Preschoolers learn quickly when shown the correct way to use materials. Say: "Pick up recordings by the edges with your fingertips (demonstrate). When you finish using the record player, move the arm to its resting place."

• *Store equipment properly.*—Turn off the record player or cassette tape player at the end of each session. Place recordings in the correct jackets and store them standing vertically, not laying in a stack. Place each cassette into the proper storage box to prevent dust from collecting on the tape.

A series of SkilPaks has been developed to assist Preschool choir leaders in the use of music with boys and girls. Each of these SkilPaks

126

consists of a 60 minute cassette recording and a booklet containing activities, response sheets, fact sheets, and summary pages to go with the information on the cassette. The SkilPaks now available are: *Selecting, Teaching, and Leading Songs; Accompanying Preschool/Children's Singing;* and *Developing Tone Matching and Singing Skills.*

Provide for moving to music

• *Plan the department so that adequate space is available.*—If chairs and tables take up valuable floor space, remove these furnishings from the room. Refer to pages 105-132 of *Basic Preschool Work* for guidelines on room arrangements.

• *Make certain that the department is safe.*—As preschoolers move, they will lean, stumble, lose their balance, and fall. The room should be free of small throw rugs, floor heaters, sharp-edged furniture, and glass objects: anything that could hurt the child who bumps an item, falls on it, or walks into it.

• *Be realistic in your expectations.*—Do not expect every child to be successful in every kind of movement. For instance, some five-year-olds cannot skip, and some two-year-olds cannot tiptoe. Most children will enjoy trying if you allow them the freedom to develop at their own pace.

• *Provide accessories to make moving fun.*—Colored silk scarves and crepe paper streamers may be waved to the tempo and rhythm of the music. A folded-paper hat makes marching fun. Other accessories may be provided from time to time.

• *Encourage children to use their imaginations.*—Suggestions such as "How would you move if you pretended to be an elephant (rabbit, bird)?" will help boys and girls become involved in creative movement.

Provide for making music

• *Teach songs that the child can sing.*—Good songs for preschoolers meet these three criteria:

1. Range—from middle C up to A. Preschoolers' voices are very limited and may be strained if pushed beyond their natural range.

2. Text—words that are literal and concrete. Preschoolers cannot understand symbolism or abstractions. Songs containing symbolic phrases such as "I will make you fishers of men" are not appropriate. Select songs carefully so that the words are meaningful and do not promote distorted images for the child.

3. Rhythm—steady beat. Preschoolers are not yet coordinated enough to sing or use instruments in complicated rhythms.

• *Teach songs in a variety of ways.*—Sing, and the child will learn the song through hearing it often. Play recorded songs as background music, or invite children to sing along. Let older preschoolers make a rebus to help them learn a new song. (Note the sample rebus in chapter 15, "How to Make Additional Teaching Materials.") Give the children many opportunities to hear and sing the song informally. Repetition is a key to learning songs.

• *Use an Autoharp.*—Place an Autoharp on the floor, a low table, or your lap. Help the child learn to strum the instrument as you press the chord bars. Preschoolers who are concentrating on strumming may not be able to sing at the same time. A 12-chord Autoharp, available through Baptist Book Stores, is recommended.

• *Use a piano.*—Appropriate musical opportunities can be provided without a piano, and a piano is not needed in a room for children younger than four. A piano is beneficial in departments for fours or fives for use in Preschool choir activities. Accompaniments for songs should be played simply. See page 73 in the book *Guiding Fours and Fives in Musical Experiences** by Baker, Key, and Butler for specific guidelines. Note the placement of a piano in the four- and five-year room arrangement on page 124 of *Basic Preschool Work* by Terrell.*

• *Purchase a variety of instruments.*—Baptist Book Stores carry a wide variety of musical instruments. Those instruments appropriate for baby, creeper, and toddler departments include: MiniHarp, baby bell, bell rattle, cradle chimes, and Pull-a-Tune Bluebird Music Box. These items are available at toy and department stores. Instruments for twos through fives include resonator bells, step bells, drums, triangles, cymbals, finger cymbals, wood blocks, sand blocks, rhythm sticks, and tambourines.

• *Make a collection of homemade instruments.*—Homemade instruments are less expensive than commercial instruments. Homemade instruments can provide good experiences for the children and are often more enjoyable because of the use of familiar objects such as cardboard boxes, plastic bottles, or wooden spoons. See chapter 15, "How to Make Additional Teaching Materials" for specific instructions on making several homemade instruments.

• *Make games which use music.*—Preschoolers can enjoy making music and can learn Bible-related concepts through games. Games are sometimes described in *Bible Story Time Teacher, Preschool Bible Teacher A, Preschool Bible Teacher B,* and *Preschool Bible Teacher C.*** Refer to *The Music Leader* for games used in Preschool choirs and the magazine *Start* for musical games used in Mission Friends. See chapter 15, "How to Make Additional Teaching Materials" for additional suggestions regarding games which use music.

Guiding musical activities

The role of the teacher in music activities is two-fold:
to make music available for the child, and to teach Bible truths through music.

As you teach preschoolers, keep these guidelines in mind:
Some do's . . .

• Accept each child's individual response to music.
• Provide for musical experiences if you are in a multi-age department. Music need not be limited by the age of the children.
• Give specific instructions for the use of equipment.
• Be flexible. Take into consideration the child's interests, abilities, and other influencing factors such as weather and time of day.
• Change the words of songs in order to use the child's name.
• Be a teacher who enjoys music.

And some don'ts

● Don't drill or teach a song line by line. Find meaningful ways to repeat the song. *Use* a song with a preschooler rather than *teach* a song to the child.

● Don't use songs with symbolic language. Rather, select songs that are literal in language.
Symbolic: "I'll stand alone on the Word of God"
Literal: "I open my Bible, And what do I see? A picture of Jesus; He loves you and me."

● Don't use motions with worship songs. The motions distract from the meaning of the song. Use motions with relaxation songs such as "Stand and Stretch," (p. 91).††

● Don't put preschoolers under pressure to rehearse, give programs, or wear choir robes. They will enjoy these activities when they are older. For the preschooler, however, these activities create tension and distract from the use of music as a teaching method.

Summary

Much more music is *caught* than *taught.* As preschoolers learn through music at church, they catch much more than music education. They catch the feelings of joy and love which we as Christians experience and express. They catch Bible truths through words they sing and hear. They catch a feeling of self-worth through participation in music activities. They catch wonder and reverence—the beginning of worship.

The information contained in this chapter is only the beginning. Specific suggestions and directions for using music in the department are given in session plans found in *Bible Story Time Teacher,*✻✻ *Preschool Bible Teacher A,*✻✻ *Preschool Bible Teacher B,*✻✻ *Preschool Bible Teacher C,*✻✻ *The Music Leader,*✻✻ and *Start.*✻✻✻ In addition, ideas for using music in the home are often found in the home books *Beginning, Living,* and *Growing,*✻✻ and the leisure-reading leaflets *Look and Listen, Music Time,* and *Share.*✻✻✻

Personal Learning Activities

1. List five specific benefits which the children in your department can gain through good experiences with music.
2. Look through the current issue of your teaching periodical *(Bible Story Time Teacher; Preschool Bible Teacher A, Preschool Bible Teacher B, Preschool Bible Teacher C;* and *The Music Leader**;* or *Start***).* Find suggestions in the periodicals for (a) listening to music, (b) moving to music, and (c) making music.
After your next teaching session, put a check mark in front of each time you actually used music in that session.
4. Look through the cabinets in your department. Gather all the recordings, instruments, and other music materials. Decide what materials you lack and initiate plans to purchase or make the items. Organize a storage system for instruments and other materials. Some suggestions

for organizing these materials are found in the *Preschool/Children's Choir Plan Book.*

Materials for Further Study

Baker, Susan, Glennela Key, and Talmadge Butler. *Guiding Fours and Fives in Musical Experiences.* Nashville: Convention Press, 1972.

Bedsole, Betty. *Building an Effective Preschool Choir.* Nashville: Convention Press, 1977.

Waldrop, C. Sybil. *Understanding Today's Preschoolers.* Nashville: Convention Press, 1982.

Haystead, Wesley. *You Can't Begin Too Soon: Guiding Little Ones to God.* Glendale: Gospel Light, 1974.

Hildebrand, Verna. *Introduction to Early Childhood Education* (Chp. 13), 2nd edition. New York: Macmillan Publishing Co., 1976.

Mandell, Muriel, and Robert Wood. *Make Your Own Musical Instruments.* New York: Sterling Publishing Co., 1959.

Moore, Jane. *Movement Education for the Young Child.* Nashville: Broadman Press, 1979.

---

[11]HOLY BIBLE *New International Version,* Copyright © 1978, New York Bible Society. Used by permission. Subsequent quotations are marked NIV.

---

*Available from Baptist Book Stores.

**Available by writing Customer Service Center, 127 Ninth Avenue, North, Nashville, Tennessee 37234; or by calling toll free 1-800-458-2772.

***Available from Woman's Missionary Union, P.O. Box 830010, Birmingham, Alabama 35283-0010.

Chapter 10—How to Teach Through the Use of Nature Materials

A. Wayne Coley

Mr. David brought a shallow pan and bread crumbs to church. Before the session, he set the pan in a grassy area, put water into the pan, and spread the bread crumbs around the pan of water. Later Mr. David and Jeffrey went for a walk outside to watch the birds play in the water. Sparrows and robins were fluttering and bathing in the water. The bread crumbs had been eaten. Jeffrey squealed with delight, and the birds flew into a nearby tree. "Flying, flying, up so high, Jeffrey sees the birds," sang Mr. David. "God gave us eyes to see the birds, Jeffrey. Thank you, God, for the birds and for Jeffrey's eyes."

Why Do We Use Nature Materials with Preschoolers?

A preschooler learns through his five senses. He learns through watching, listening, tasting, smelling, and touching. Firsthand experiences are vital to a child's learning.

The world to a preschooler may be like a foreign land to an adult. The child's world is filled with strange sights, curiosities, and new adventures. Preschoolers should have firsthand experiences with nature, rather than adults trying to tell them about the world of nature. The use of nature materials allows preschoolers to have firsthand experiences with things God has made.

Providing nature activities can open up a world of excitement and wonder for a child who is learning about himself and about the world around him. Nature experiences can help the child in developing more accurate concepts about God. These concepts help the child develop a faith which can affect his Christian experience later in life.

Some values of using nature materials

Nature materials are not hard to find. No matter where you live there is something of nature which a child can enjoy. Nature materials which are common in a preschooler's everyday world are much more desirable and have more value than exotic, strange materials which are unfamiliar to the child. Don't expect Jay to tell you about sand dollars, seashells, or starfish if he has never been to a beach or seen the ocean. Introduce these things to him, but do not fill the nature area with many new and unfamiliar items.

• A preschooler can enjoy sensory experiences with nature materials and increase his knowledge about the natural world.

- The child becomes more aware of the world around him through nature activities.
- The child learns to enjoy beauty in the natural world.
- The teacher's attitude, songs, and conversation about nature help the child experience awe and wonder.

Who Can Learn Through the Use of Nature Materials?

All preschoolers, from the tiny baby to the five-year-old, can learn through experiencing nature materials. The kinds of materials and activities will be determined by the age of the preschoolers. A teacher's chief concern in using nature materials is to make the items safe for the children to handle or mouth.

Researchers tell us that after two months babies begin to finger surfaces, moving their hands back and forth. They are learning through touch as well as sight. In the first three months, the baby discovers through his eyes that objects have color and form. Later he discovers through his hands that objects have softness, hardness, wetness, dryness, smoothness, texture, and fuzziness. Nature materials provide many possibilities for babies to have new touching experiences. As babies see and touch live nature items, teachers can use simple words to describe the items (animals, grass, fruit, vegetables, or trees). Regardless of the age of the children you teach, the nature activities chosen are only limited by the imagination of the adult.

Which Nature Experiences Are Appropriate?

As we think of providing opportunities for appropriate nature experiences for preschoolers, there are some guidance suggestions to be considered:

- Provide experiences for preschoolers which involve the use of as many of their five senses as possible. For example, all preschoolers, babies through five-year-olds, enjoy water play.
- Change the nature materials each month or more often. Most nature shelves have such sameness that neither teachers nor preschoolers "see" the materials when they come into the room. The nature materials should be simple, fresh, new, clean, safe, and give enjoyment. A teacher telling a child, "Don't touch that," takes away the joy of the experience. The teacher should encourage the child to discover the nature items with the use of his senses.
- Give the preschooler a chance to discover the nature items before showing the materials to the child. A teacher would need to hold the nature item for the baby to see or hold the baby so he could see the animal, flower, or other item. In a room for creepers through five-year-olds, place the material in the nature area and allow the children to discover the nature items. Be nearby to give guidance when necessary.
- Answer a child's questions simply and in terms he can understand. Do not feel you have to give a lot of detail. Too much information may cause a child to lose excitement and interest in the item. One three-

year-old said, "He 'splained and 'splained and I got tired." The child will think twice before going into the nature area again.

• Avoid referring to nature materials as *magic*. When you plant a seed, water it, and place the seed where the sun will shine on it, the seed begins to grow. The growth of a plant is not magic; God planned for plants to grow this way.

• Express your attitudes about nature materials and give thanks to God for the items. This procedure will help preschoolers learn to have similar feelings and to express these feelings for themselves.

• Help preschoolers become aware of God's wonders where they live. Babies though toddlers enjoy being taken outside for a short walk. The teacher can talk to them about the sky, the leaves on the trees, the birds singing, and smelling a flower. Twos through fives enjoy nature walks. Teachers can make these walks rewarding for the children as they thank God for nature items he has made. Teachers need to be more conscious of God's creations outside their windows. Learning about God's world must be experienced.

• Help all preschoolers have a growing awareness that people can help care for God's world. Preschoolers can enjoy a goldfish or small animal and help feed the pet. They can also help water a plant.

The following is a listing of some appropriate nature activities for preschoolers. Descriptions of many of these experiences are given on pages 134-139.

Making a terrarium (4-5); viewing an acquarium (2-5); taking a touching walk (2-5); going on a seeing walk (T-5); participating in a hearing walk (2-5); taking a smelling walk (3-5); looking-for-a-color walk (2-5); collecting-items walk (2-5); doing float and sink experiments (2-5); touching different textures (2-5); smelling spices (2-5); tasting foods (T-5); feeling items in a bag or box (2-5); picking up items with magnets (4-5); observing items with a magnifying glass (4-5); making bird feeders (3-5); matching sound cans (3-5); blowing bubbles (3-5); experimenting with water play (2-5); making a collage of nature items (2-5); making and using wind chimes (3-5); pressing leaves between waxed paper (3-5); examining a bird's nest, a wasp nest, or a cocoon (2-5); examining shells (2-5); examining corn or wheat (2-5); examining seed (2-5); examining flowers (2-5); preserving a spider web (3-5); planting seed (2-5); planting bulbs (2-5); rooting a sweet potato (3-5); growing grass or alfalfa sprouts on a sponge (2-5); planting lima beans in a glass container between blotter paper and soil (2-5); making orange juice, ice cream, butter, peanut butter, or apple sauce (3-5); taking care of small pets such as a gerbil, a guinea pig, a hamster, or a rabbit (2-5); observing bugs in containers (2-5); visiting a zoo, a pet shop, or a farm (2-5); listening to night sounds or listening to a tape of night sounds (3-5); watching birds in a cage (2-5); observing plant roots in a clear plastic container (2-5); looking at books on nature (3-5); making nature books from seed catalogs (2-5).

How Are Nature Materials Used Effectively?
The following nature ideas can be used with most preschoolers:
Observing goldfish

For this nature activity you will need a plastic fish bowl, water, gravel, two small snails, plants from a pet shop, fish food, and goldfish. Let the water set twenty-four hours before putting the fish into a bowl. This procedure allows the chlorine to evaporate from the water. Place the gravel, a plant, two snails, and the fish in the water. Feed the fish only a couple of drops of food. Overfeeding is harmful to the fish. The water will not need changing for several weeks. Prepare another container of water so the chlorine can evaporate before the water is changed.

As a child looks at the goldfish, sing the song, "Goldfish Swimming," (p. 58). † Talk to the child about the fish. Tell him that God made goldfish. Many preschoolers want to put their hands into the water. Advise preschoolers to keep their hands outside the bowl. Say, "Thank you, God, for the goldfish."

Participating in water play
Spread a plastic cloth on the floor. Put a plastic pan on the cloth and put water in the pan. Take off a child's shoes. Hold a baby or creeper so his feet touch the water. Talk to him about his feet and about the water. Sing, "Splashing, splashing, Amy likes to splash her feet in the water."

Toddlers like to play in the water. Provide cups and other items for pouring water. Put a smock on the children to help keep them dry.

Twos through fives like to experiment with things that sink and float in water. Next to a pan of water, place a cork, a feather, a leaf, and a large bolt. Let one item sink to the bottom and say, "The bolt sank to the bottom of the pan." Then add a feather and ask, "Does the feather stay on the water (float) or sink into the water?

Blowing bubbles
Take the children outside and allow them to blow bubbles. Preschoolers enjoy seeing bubbles float toward the sky. They also enjoy trying to pop the bubbles. Teachers can use dishwashing detergent and straws or homemade bubble wands. Encourage the boys and girls to look for the different colors which appear in the bubbles when the sun shines on them.

Listening to wind chimes
Hang a wind chime in the room. Allow a small child to touch the chime and listen to the sounds the chime makes. Say, "Thank You, God, for ears to hear the wind chimes."

Caring for small animals
Bring into the room a small cage and a small animal such as a guinea pig, a hamster, a gerbil, or a rabbit. As the child looks at the animal, talk about how the animal looks, how he eats, and the kind of food he eats. Allow children to touch the animal. Ask how its fur feels. Thank God for the animal and for hands to feel its fur. Be aware of allergies children may have to animal fur. Also, check your state health department regulations regarding the use of furry animals in Preschool rooms.

Observing bugs
A homemade container can be made using a plastic quart bottle and nylon hose. Cut four sides out of the bottle and slide it into the hose. Put a wire twist, plastic tie, or rubber band around the end of the stocking. Put a bug such as a cricket, a grasshopper, or a butterfly into the container. Children can look at the bug. Return the bug to its natural habitat following the session. Sing the song "Cricket Chirping," (p. 59).† Then use the Bible thought "God made the grasshopper" (Amos 7:1).

Caring for a bird
Preschoolers enjoy looking at birds. Bring a parakeet in its cage into the room. If the bird sings, say, "Thank You, God, for ears to hear the bird singing." You can also thank God for eyes with which to see the bird.

Check to see if any of the preschoolers are allergic to feathers.

Planting seed
Place grass seed, bird seed, or alfalfa seed on a wet sponge. The seed

will begin sprouting in a couple of days. Remember that preschoolers may expect the seed to grow immediately. You may want to start the seed a few days before the session to show what the seed will look like when they sprout.

Planting nonpoisonous bulbs and seed
Use a shallow bowl, soil, and plant bulbs or seed. Allow the children to put the bulbs or seed in dirt.

Planting carrots
Cut off approximately ½-inch from the tops of several carrots. Put the cut side in a saucer of water, leaving a small portion exposed. Pretty pebbles add color as carrots sprout and grow. The pebbles also provide space for the plant to sprout. Place the saucer in a sunny windowsill. Sing, "God made the carrots for you and me."

Hanging flowers
Inside or outside, a basket of petunias hanging by a window invites many comments about God helping flowers grow.

Tasting fruit
Inform parents of plans for tasting activities and check on specific allergies to food. Peel an apple, a pear, or a banana, and cut the fruit into bite-sized pieces. Allow the children (T-5) to taste the small pieces of fruit. Thank God for giving us tongues with which to taste food. Avoid feeding younger preschoolers anything other than that which is sent by their mothers. Babies and creepers could easily get choked on pieces of fruit or vegetables.

Making a bird feeder
Let a child drop small seed such as alfalfa, seed for birds, or small beans in the little sections of a pinecone. Set the pinecone in a soft margarine tub with a small amount of water. Small rocks will help hold the pinecone upright. The cone will close overnight. Sprinkle water over the cone each day, and the seed will sprout after three or four days. Keep the cone wet, and the seed will grow for several weeks. Sprouting seed in a cone can be a group activity. In departments for older preschoolers, each child could fix a "sprouting" cone. The cone can also be used as a bird feeder.

1. Pinecones stuffed with bread
Another activity with pinecones is to let the child stuff soft bread crumbs into the sections and tie a piece of yarn to the top of the pinecone. Let each child take his cone home for a bird feeder or hang it in a tree close to a window at church.

2. Another bird feeder
Let the child fill the sections of a pinecone with suet. Provide a dish with some birdseed in it. The child can roll the cone in the seed and the seed will stick to the suet. A piece of yarn may be tied to the top of the cone so that it can be hung in a tree.

Saving containers
Save containers such as ice cream cups that have dome lids and clear plastic boxes in which after-shave is packaged. The child can plant

136

different small plants such as ground cover, beans, and seed that are fast sprouting. (Try the activity at home first.) The child can put small gravel or a little sand in the bottom of the box, then add some potting soil, and plant a rooted cutting of a plant. The child can see the types of soil as the plants grow.

Planning a nature shelf
For a nature shelf at church, obtain a shallow plastic container or line a small box with plastic or foil. Let the preschoolers, even two-year-olds, have the joy of helping plant seed that will sprout within a short period of time.

Watering plants
Provide two or three live plants for the child to water each Sunday. A shampoo bottle with a push-up spout can be cleaned and kept for a good watering bottle. Preschoolers enjoy filling the watering bottle. Encourage preschoolers to take turns watering the plants as teachers talk with the children about the things "God gives us to enjoy."

Observing tree blossoms
Place a small limb of fruit blossoms with the fruit. For example, display apricot blossoms, fresh apricots, and a picture of apricots. Use fruit blossoms that are available in your area. As a child looks at the limb and piece of fruit, say: "God planned for these apples to grow from apple tree blossoms. Thank you, God, for the apple."

Seeing corn products
Provide an ear of corn and several corn products (corn meal, corn bran cereal, corn flakes, or corn chex cereal) for the children to taste.

Observing a caterpillar
A caterpillar can be caught, placed in a jar, and observed as it forms a cocoon, and then changes into a butterfly. The time involved in this process will vary according to the area of the United States in which the learning experience takes place. Use pictures of a caterpillar, cocoon, and butterfly, or a story from *Look and Listen, Growing***, or a book about butterflies.

Examining locust
In July or August catch a live locust and display it with the dry shell from which the locust has emerged. This shell is much smaller than the locust, as the insect does not have wings until after it emerges, from the shell. The locust is fully formed in the shell. The opening on its back shows how the locust came out of the shell. When viewing the locust, say, "God planned for the locust to look like this."

Making a leaf book
Make a leaf book, using a photograph album. Press two or three small leaves or one or two large leaves in a catalog for a few days. Place only one or two kinds of leaves on a page in the album. Label the leaves. This cataloging can be done all year and leaves that are changing colors can be included.

Finding small flowers

After a rain on the desert, in springtime, very small flowers can be found. Some of these blossoms are the size of a pinhead or slightly larger.

Planting nonpoisonous flowers

If there is an area on the churchyard, such as between a sidewalk and the church building, request permission for the Preschool departments to plant flowers. One or more departments could be involved in this experience. Prepare the soil ahead of time and let five-year-olds plant the seed. Keep the pictures from the packages on display in the room. When the flowers begin to bloom, take the pictures of the empty packages outside and let the children discover which flowers are blooming.

In this same area, plant Easter lilies (or other spring bulbs) after they have stopped blooming. These plants will grow and bloom the years following. In essence, planting the bulbs is an investment which will yield benefits to preschoolers of the future.

Observing a spiderweb

A nature activity that can have value to preschoolers is capturing a spiderweb. Locate a spiderweb in the yard; spray it with enamel paint, any color you want; and press a piece of tile, cardboard, or wooden board against the wet web. Hold the web very steady for about three minutes. The paint dries quickly. Break the web off where it is attached to the bushes and it will maintain its shape on the board. Preschoolers can feel the ridges of the spiderweb. You can preserve the web by spraying it with a clear shellac, but the children cannot feel the ridges. Say, "Thank you, God, for fingers to feel the spider web."

Using a magnifying glass

An investment of a few dollars in a good magnifying glass or magnifying cube will provide opportunities for discovery and excitement for a preschooler. Flowers, buds, and leaves reveal unexpected beauty. These are often overlooked without the aid of a magnifying glass. A magnifying cube can be ordered from The Nature Company, P.O. Box 7137, Berkeley, California 94707.

Note: Using a magnifying glass is not a firsthand experience. Since the glass makes the item look larger, the child may think of this activity as magic. A child who is just beginning to observe nature materials needs to use his senses.

Observing wheat

Place wheat and wheat products on the nature shelf. Let the boys and girls taste the wheat products. Wheat bread, wheat cereal, and wheat crackers are possible choices for this tasting experience. The wheat activity is appropriate when the Bible story of Ruth is used.

Seeing an aquarium

Line the bottom of a gallon jar with aquarium gravel. Add a variety of aquarium plants. Fill the jar with water. If chlorinated water is used, remove the chlorine by allowing the water to stand in an open jar for several days. Add one or two small snails and two tropical fish or a goldfish. Tropical fish include guppies, black mollies, and swordtails.

Cover the jar with a lid. If the lid is left on the aquarium, no cleaning or feeding is necessary. Keep the aquarium out of the sun. The life expectancy of the fish, snails, and plants may vary from several months to a year or more depending on various factors related to the balanced aquarium.

Going on field trips
Get written permission from parents for children to go on field trips after the site has been selected. In most cases the field trip will be at a location close to the church. The trip may be to a farm, a zoo, a fire station, or a park. Before the trip, make a list of things which you can alert the children to observe. Assign teachers to be responsible for a specific group of children. Also, decide if you will walk or ride to the site and arrange for adequate adult supervision.

When Are Nature Materials Used?

Since nature materials help a preschooler learn about God's world, every Preschool department should offer opportunities to explore items in the natural world during each session.

Throughout the session the child should have opportunities for experiences involving nature.

Babies, creepers, and toddlers can enjoy nature experiences outside the room as teachers take them for short walks. Many preschoolers who are upset can easily be calmed by the use of nature activities. Greeting a child at the door with a pretty flower, talking about the flower, and allowing the child to touch the flower often calms the child. Outdoor walks can have the same calming effect.

Twos, threes, fours, and fives should have opportunities for experiences with nature during activities. Many nature activities do not require constant teacher guidance. Any activity which the child can experience himself has more value than those directed by a teacher. Nature experiences such as tasting foods, planting seed, and sink or float experiments may need guidance by the teacher.

Nature walks for small groups or the entire department are a favorite activity with twos through fives, but they require adequate adult supervision and safety.

Nature materials can also be used during group time with threes, fours, and fives. Talking about a smelling game used during activities could encourage the children to join group time. Talking about the seed they planted, a nature walk, and what they saw or collected could be part of the conversation of group time.

Nature materials can be used anytime with preschoolers.

Where Do Nature Activities Occur?

Every Preschool department should have an area designated for nature materials. This area can be a shelving unit, a window ledge, or the floor. Select an area near a window since plants need sunlight. Place nature materials where preschoolers can handle and examine the items. Put only a few nature items in the area, since too many nature items tend to discourage use of the area. Place objects such as shells, bird nests, and leaves on colored construction paper to enhance their appeal.

Nature experiences can occur by looking out a window, looking at a potted plant, or while observing a fish or a small animal. Nature experiences can occur outside the Preschool department as well as inside the department room.

Some plants are dangerous for use with preschoolers

When using plants with preschoolers, always use live plants. Artificial nature materials have little, if any, value to a preschooler.

There are many plants which are harmful if eaten. Here is a list of some of those plants:

Plant	Toxic Part
Azalea	all parts
Bird of Paradise	green seed pods
Burning Bush	leaves
Caladium	all parts
Caster Bean	seed
Columbine	berry
Cyclamen	tuber
Daffodil	bulb
Delphinium	all parts, especially seed
Dieffenbachia	all parts
Elephant Ear	all parts
English Ivy	leaves
Four O'clock	root, seed
Hens and Chicken	all parts
Holly	berries
Hyacinth	bulb, leaves, flower
Hydrangea	leaves, buds
Iris	root
Jerusalem Cherry	all parts
Lantana	all parts, especially berries
Larkspur	all parts, especially seed
Lily-of-the-valley	all parts
Mistletoe	berries
Mock Orange	fruit
Morning Glory	seed
Mountain Laurel	all parts
Narcissus	bulb
Oleander	leaves
Philodendron	all parts
Pinks	seed
Poinsettia	all parts
Potato	seed, sprouts
Rhododendron	all parts
Scotch Broom	seed
Spider Lily	bulb
Sweet Pea	stem

For further information on poisonous plants contact your regional poison control center or write:

Fourth General Hospital Poison Control Center
400 South 28th Street
Hattiesburg, MS 39401

There are many other plants with nonpoisonous parts which are appropriate for use with preschoolers. The important thing to remember is that preschoolers need to become more aware that plants grow.

Death and other crises

Have you ever walked into the department and found the goldfish dead? What did you do? Please do not throw the goldfish into the trash can.

A chapter on nature materials would not be complete without giving some attention to the area of death.

Children should gradually get used to the idea that death is a normal part of the life cycle. When a child's pet dies or when a pet at church dies, allow the children to mourn and bury the animal. Do not rush out to replace the pet. This action would demean the child's love for the animal and also cut short the important grieving period.

Sam found the goldfish dead one Sunday. Before the teacher could ask what should be done with it, Sam said, "Lets have a funeral and bury it." The other five-year-olds agreed. The teacher gently took the dead fish out of the aquarium, wrapped it in a paper towel, and placed it on a chair. Sam said: "God, this is a goldfish. He once was alive, but now he's dead, amen." The preschoolers and their teachers took the goldfish outside and buried it in the church yard. For several weeks the children wanted to go outside to see the place where the goldfish was buried. They soon began asking if they could get another fish.

Children should always be told the truth in crisis situations. When a child asks where his dead pet goes, do not tell him "pet heaven." Simply say, "He died." Helping a child deal with the death of a pet makes him more aware that death is a natural part of life. Also, it partially prepares him to cope with the death of a family member or friend.

Summary

Look at the nature area in the department in which you teach. Are the nature materials new and exciting each week, or do the items have dust and spider webs (a form of nature) formed around them? Are children forced to go into the nature area, or do they go because they have learned you will have something exciting there each session? Review these values of using nature materials:

- The child enjoys sensory experiences (seeing, hearing, smelling, touching, tasting).
- He becomes more aware of his surroundings.
- The child learns to enjoy beauty.
- He responds more easily to new situations.
- The preschooler learns to take care of his surroundings.
- He begins to associate God with his experiences.

Do you keep these values in mind as you plan nature activities for each session?

Turn back to the first part of the chapter and review the guidance suggestions. Decide now that you will review these suggestions often. A child's only association of the natural world with God may be what he experiences in your department.

> "A child's world is fresh and new and beautiful, full of wonder and excitement. It is our misfortune that for most of us that clear-eyed vision, that true instinct for what is beautiful and awe-inspiring, is dimmed and even lost before we reach adulthood."[12]

Personal Learning Activities

1. Exploring nature materials with children is a matter of becoming receptive to what is around you. Go on a nature walk to discover what we take so much for granted—God's beautiful world. Look at the sky—its different shades, its moving clouds, its stars by night. Listen to the wind; feel it upon your face; see it blow the leaves on the trees; hear the leaves as they swish back and forth. Watch the rain; listen to the sounds it makes as it hits the ground or the windowpane.

2. Designate an area to store nature items, pictures, and catalogs to be used in nature activities.

3. Subscribe to magazines with nature pictures such as *National Geographic* and *Ranger Rick*.

> "If a child is to keep alive his inborn sense of wonder . . . he needs the companionship of at least one adult who can share it, rediscovering with him the joy, excitement and mystery of the world we live in."[13]

Are you that kind of teacher? I hope so.

Materials for Further Study

Carson, Rachel. *The Sense of Wonder*. New York: Harper and Row, 1965.

Hildebrand Verna. *Introduction to Early Childhood Education*, (chp. 8).

Shuttlesworth, Dorothy. *Exploring Nature with Your Child*. New York: Harry N. Abrams, 1980.

Stein, Sara Bonnet. *About Dying*. New York: Walker and Co., 1974.

Watrin, Rita, and Paul Hanley Furfey. *Learning Activities for the Young Preschool Child* (Part 10). New York: D. Van Nostrand Co., 1978.

[12]Rachel Carson, *The Sense of Wonder*, (New York: Harper and Row, 1965), p. 42.
[13]Carson, *The Sense of Wonder*, p. 42.

*Available from Baptist Book Stores.
**Available by writing Customer Service Center, 127 Ninth Avenue, North, Nashville, Tennessee 37234; or by calling toll free 1-800-458-2772.

Chapter 11—How to Teach Through the Use of Puzzles

Jewell Wells Nelson

Here is a puzzle for you. What do clothespins, shoe boxes, egg cartons, and boot strings have in common? All of these items can be used in making puzzles for preschoolers.

Puzzles are materials for preschoolers which present difficulties to be solved with mental ingenuity, patience, and physical coordination. A puzzle presents a challenge to a child since the pieces must be manipulated in order to be completed.

In a broad sense, puzzles overlap into many areas of the Preschool department, or out-of-doors. Large plastic pop beads and nesting cups are puzzle toys used by babies, creepers, toddlers, and twos. Sorting pebbles or leaves into matching piles on the playground may be classified as a puzzle activity for four- and five-year-olds. When a creeper places the receiver properly on the toy telephone, he has solved a problem or worked a puzzle. When an older preschooler buttons a button or ties a shoelace, he has solved a problem or worked a puzzle.

Keep the preceding definition of puzzles in mind. Think of safe, interesting, problem-solving activities for preschoolers as you read this chapter. Underline the values of each puzzle and ideas that relate to the age group which you teach.

Why Use Puzzles with Preschoolers?

Puzzles are problem solving activities which lay a foundation for later problem solving. A baby grasps a space rings teether in the right way to benefit from the chewy edge. The creeper fits one pop bead inside the Fill-n-Dump Milk Bottle for his own satisfaction. A toddler puts the star shape into the Tupperware Shape-O ball. The two- or three-year-old fits a wooden inlay puzzle together and returns it to the puzzle rack. The four- or five-year-old fits a twenty-piece floor puzzle together. Each age child has progressed from one stage to another. The more experiences each age child has in solving manipulative problems, the easier each new challenge becomes.

Color, shape, and texture of puzzles stimulate the senses of seeing and feeling. Tasting, smelling, and hearing may also be stimulated as a child works a puzzle matching real fruit or sets of film (sound) cans. Preschoolers learn through their five senses. Puzzles involving actual products or experiences help stimulate all five senses.

Pulling things apart and putting things together intrigues preschool-

ers. Some puzzles offer opportunities for preschoolers to take items apart and put the pieces together.

Language development can be a part of puzzle activities. When a teacher claps his hands and exclaims, "Right!" as a creeper drops a pop bead into a box, the child may soon clap his hands and repeat "Right!" in response to his own performance. Fours and fives can learn not only to talk about wooden inlay puzzle pieces, but also about objects depicted in the puzzles. Increasing word knowledge can be a part of puzzle activities.

Making choices is a lifelong responsibility. Puzzles offer opportunities to make choices of the right pieces for the right places. There is a choice of which puzzle to work or whether to work a puzzle or do another activity.

Puzzles often can be completed in only one way. Finding that one way is a challenge to the preschooler. At other times there may be several ways to work a puzzle. This activity provides an opportunity for the child to use his imagination and solve a problem.

Completing a puzzle or a puzzle activity builds self-esteem.

Recognition, association, matching, and classification are big words, yet these skills are essential elements in a child's educational development. Puzzle toys, puzzles, and puzzle games offer opportunities for preschoolers to recognize, associate, match, and classify.

Social interaction is valuable as preschoolers learn to be together in puzzle activities. Preschoolers can learn to take turns and respect other children's rights to work puzzles.

In contrast, working a puzzle can also be a time for a child to be alone and enjoy his solitude.

A teacher can observe emotional, mental, and physical growth as a child works in the puzzle area. A teacher can determine ways to help the child either by interacting or by observing the child. (A more difficult puzzle may be needed to challenge a child, or an easier puzzle might prevent a child from experiencing frustration.)

Through puzzles a child can learn to follow directions. "Get a puzzle," "Work the puzzle," "Put the puzzle away" are appropriate directions for preschoolers.

A child can learn through puzzles to accept responsibility. Once he chooses a puzzle, the child should complete the puzzle (if necessary, with the teacher's guidance) and then return the item to the puzzle rack.

Puzzles can motivate a child to be involved in another area of interest, or vice versa. A puzzle about animals can spark interest in a book. Also, a book about animals can encourage a child to work the puzzle "Animals."

Puzzles can be fun. When preschoolers have a happy time in their Preschool department, they want to return to church.

Puzzles develop large and small muscles in the arms, hands, and fingers. This muscular development is essential for future handwriting experiences.

Constructive puzzle working helps prevent destructive boredom. Puzzles and puzzle activities can stimulate creativity and imagination. After working the puzzle "Going to Church," one child said, "I'm gonna build a big church with blocks."

Bible-related teaching involving songs, story conversation, and Bible thoughts can be used as children enjoy puzzles.

Who Benefits from the Use of Puzzles?

As you review the values of puzzles, you will see how beneficial puzzles can be as a child grows. Puzzles can help stimulate physical, mental, emotional, social, and spiritual growth. Each age child builds upon previous experiences as he manipulates a familiar puzzle, a new puzzle toy, or a puzzle activity.

A wise teacher will provide puzzles to suit the age of the child. Preschool Bible Teacher A,** Preschool Bible Teacher B,** Preschool Bible Teacher C,** Bible Story Time Teacher,** The Music Leader,** and Start*** give ideas for using puzzles with each age child in the Preschool-related organizations.

Which Kinds of Puzzles May Be Used with Preschoolers?

There are puzzles involving matching, sorting, identifying, progression, manipulation, sensory experiences, classifying, recognition, association, and sequence. Some puzzles may be grouped in more than one category.

There are puzzles you can buy. There are puzzles to be made. Use bought and homemade materials. The number of puzzles you have will be determined by your need, your budget, and your willingness to make puzzles.

Homemade puzzles are often not as durable as some commercial puzzles. An egg carton puzzle is not as durable as a wooden-inlay puzzle; therefore, close supervision with homemade puzzles will enable the puzzle to last longer. Wooden inlay puzzles can be left in the puzzle rack from session to session. Homemade puzzles may need to be used for a session and then stored for later use.

Once you make a puzzle, you may think of a way to use the same idea for a completely different puzzle. Look at throwaways and think about how they can be used in a puzzle activity.

  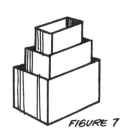

TAPE AROUND OPEN END

FIGURE 7

Stacking and nesting (See Figure 7)   (2-5)

Materials: Boxes, clean spray can caps, cans, plastic measuring cups, plastic tumblers, and plastic bowls (with or without lids)

Guidance: The stacking or nesting puzzle is completed by fitting varying sizes of boxes, caps, cups, tumblers, or bowls together. If cans are used, smooth the edges of the cans with pliers and then put tape around the open edge to make the cans safer. Felt circles cut and glued inside the bottom of each can will help reduce noise as one can is dropped into another.

Babies, creepers, and toddlers enjoy working puzzles in different ways. Two- through five-year-olds often enjoy this activity, too.

FIGURE 8

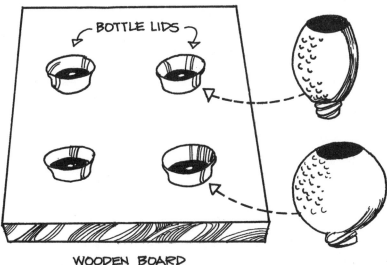

WOODEN BOARD

Upside down plastic bottle puzzle (See Figure 8)   (2-5)

Materials: Smooth board (approx. 14 by 14 ins.), four short plastic bottles with lids, nails, hammer, and a pencil.

Guidance: Lemon juice comes in a plastic lemon-shaped bottle. Vitamin C comes in an orange-shaped bottle. These bottles are suggested for an upside down bottle puzzle. Put each lid on its bottle. Turn the bottles, lid side down, on the wooden board. Leave room around the upside down container for untwisting the container from the lid. Draw a circle on the board where each lid sets. Unscrew the bottles from the lids. Nail each lid to the place where it was setting.

To work the puzzle a child may screw each bottle into the original lid. Twos and threes can work a four bottle puzzle. Fours and fives will be challenged if there are a few more plastic bottles (different kinds).

147

Clothespin and box puzzle (See Figure 9)   (T-5)

Materials: Colored clothespins, plastic tape to match each color of clothespin, and a box (shoe box or shirt box)

Guidance: Along the edge of the box, overlap 1-inch strips of tape at least an inch apart. The puzzle is worked by clipping a clothespin over the corresponding color of tape. For example, a green clothespin will be clipped over a green piece of tape on the box edge.

Toddlers can work this puzzle without colored tape. Push-on clothespins are added to the edge of a box. Twos are beginning to discern colors. Use red, blue, green, and yellow clothespins and tape for twos. Two or three pieces of each color of tape placed at random around the edge of the box presents a workable challenge for twos. Threes, fours, and fives can work this puzzle with increasing numbers of clothespins and colors.

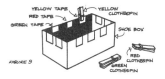

Put-things-into puzzle (See Figure 10)   (C-5)

Materials: Sturdy egg carton, six pairs of safe objects such as: two small pinecones, two cotton balls, two lids from baby food jars, two small empty plastic bottles, two sea shells, and two spools. (Twelve spools paired by color or size could be used instead of the different objects.)

Guidance: The puzzle is worked as children put matching objects across from each other into the egg carton.

FIGURE 10

The same objects may be used in another way at another time. Two small baskets, boxes, or plastic bowls are needed. The pairs of objects are placed on a table or the floor. The puzzle is worked by putting one of each matching object into each container. This puzzle is increased in

148

difficulty with fours and fives by using more objects or the same objects in different colors or sizes. For example, two spools may be used, one red and one blue, or two lids may be used, one large and one small.

Adapt this puzzle for creepers and toddlers by using one container and several safe objects. Pop beads or large spools may be used with a large oatmeal box or plastic dishpan. Younger preschoolers will enjoy simply dropping the objects into the container and dumping them out.

Puzzle board I (See Figure 11)   (C-5)
Materials: Square of smooth plywood, bolt lock, latches, hinges, light switch, slide lock, window lock, screws, and a screwdriver.
Guidance: Mount various types of locks and a light switch for preschoolers to manipulate. The complexity or simplicity of the puzzle board depends on the age of the children who use the puzzle. Creepers and toddlers may enjoy turning a light switch and sliding a bolt lock. Older preschoolers enjoy hinges, locks, and even a sneaker nailed to the board for lacing.

Teachers may choose to use real locks, light switches, and screws instead of placing them on plywood.

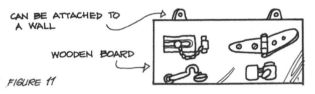

CAN BE ATTACHED TO A WALL

WOODEN BOARD

FIGURE 11

Puzzle board II (See Figure 12)   (2-5)
Materials: Fasteners such as zippers, buttons and button holes, grip fasteners, belt with buckle, and ribbon; hammer; nails; and a board.
Guidance: Secure each fastener on fabric so it will open and close easily. Attach each fastener to a smooth board with nails or a heavy-duty stapler. Attach the ends of the belt so that it can be buckled and unbuckled. Place the ribbons close enough together so that they can be tied into a bow.

Older preschoolers will be able to fasten most of these fasteners Younger preschoolers can learn to zip zippers and fasten grip fasteners.

CAN BE ATTACHED TO A WALL

WOODEN BOARD

FIGURE 12

Puzzle in a lid (See Figure 13)   (2-5)
Materials: Shallow box lid, picture (fruit, vegetable, animal, or extra teaching picture) cut to fit inside the lid, cardboard to fit inside the lid,

glue, scissors, clear contact plastic, and colored tape.
Guidance: Glue the picture to the cardboard. Bind the edges of the picture with colored plastic tape to give a guiding border to the puzzle. Cover the picture with clear contact plastic. (See chapter 4 of this book or the backs of teaching picture sets for instructions on mounting pictures.) Cut the mounted picture into large puzzle pieces. Reinforce the corners of the lid with tape. The puzzle is worked by placing the pieces of the puzzle together inside the box lid. The edges of the lid provide a frame for the puzzle and make working it easier.

FIGURE 13

REINFORCE CORNERS WITH TAPE

LID

Floor puzzle I (See Figure 14)   (2-5)
Materials: Large poster (a farm scene or a large picture of fruit or vegetables from a grocery store display), large poster board, glue, scissors, and colored plastic tape.
Guidance: Glue the large picture onto an equally large piece of cardboard. Bind the edges with colored tape. Cut the picture into large puzzle pieces. Twos and threes are able to work a six- to nine-piece floor puzzle. Fours and fives are able to work twelve- to fifteen-piece floor puzzles. A twenty-piece floor puzzle may be appropriate for some older preschoolers. Cut the puzzle pieces large enough for easy handling.

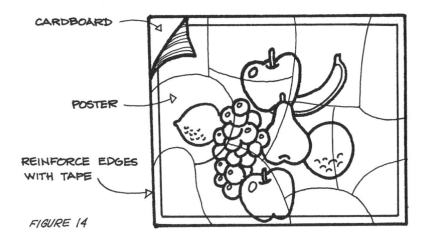

CARDBOARD

POSTER

REINFORCE EDGES WITH TAPE

FIGURE 14

Floor puzzle II (See Figure 15)   (T-5)

Materials: Large corrugated cardboard (approx. 2 by 2 ft.), scissors, spools or wooden cabinet doorknobs, and glue.

Guidance: Cut a square out of one or two sides of the cardboard. Glue a spool or knob in the center of each square for a handle. A toddler can lift the square out and place it back.

A more difficult puzzle can be made by cutting one or two squares or circles out of the center of the large cardboard. The younger pre-schooler is challenged by getting the shape out and putting it back into its proper place.

Additional shapes can be cut for older preschoolers.

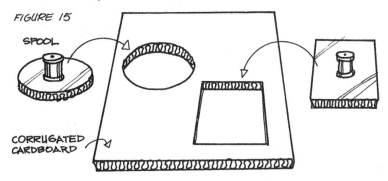

FIGURE 15

SPOOL

CORRUGATED
CARDBOARD

Gadget puzzle (See Figure 16)   (T-5)

Materials: Shallow box lid from large box; safe gadgets, such as a measuring cup and spoon, animal-shaped cookie cutter, jar lid, dough-nut cutter, felt-tipped marker, and plastic tape.

Guidance: Reinforce the corners of the box lid with tape. Place the gadgets in the lid so that there is about an equal amount of space between each one. Draw around each gadget with the marker. The puzzle is worked when a child places each gadget on its own outline.

A toddler and two-year-old can place two or four gadgets in the lid. Fours and fives can place a larger number of gadgets in a larger lid.

FIGURE 16

REINFORCE
CORNERS
WITH TAPE

SHALLOW
LID

Cube puzzle (See Figure 17) (T-5)

Materials: Two identical boxes (such as pint milk cartons); newspaper; scissors; plastic tape; two of the same issues of outdated home pieces *Beginning*, *Living*, or *Growing***; clear contact plastic; and glue.

Guidance: Stuff one empty box or carton with newspaper. Secure the box with tape. Cut six pretty pictures from one issue of the magazine. Paste a picture on each of the six sides of the box. Cover the entire box with clear contact plastic. Do exactly the same procedure with the other box or carton using the second issue of the magazine.

A toddler or two-year-old works the six-sided puzzle by placing the corresponding picture side by side; then he turns the boxes and tries to match the two additional pictures. One or two more pairs of puzzle boxes increase the challenge for twos and threes. Fours and fives enjoy several pairs of the picture cubes to sort and match. Each pair of cubes contains different matching pictures.

FIGURE 17 PICTURES FROM OUTDATED *BEGINNING,* LIVING, OR GROWING

BOX

Sequence puzzle (See Figure 18) (2-5)

Materials: Squares of bathroom tile or heavy cardboard, a book that is no longer usable but contains a sequence story, felt, clear contact plastic, glue, and scissors.

Guidance: Cut pages from a book that show a sequence (a child waking, eating breakfast, dressing, and playing outside for example). Glue each picture onto a tile (or square of cardboard). Back each tile with felt. Cover the entire tile (including the felt side) or piece of cardboard, with clear contact plastic.

A child works the puzzle by placing the tile (or cardboard) pictures in order.

The same idea may be used by covering two tiles (or squares of cardboard) with floral paper, two with striped paper, and another pair of tiles with a solid color. The puzzle is worked as a child pairs each tile with the matching tile.

Twos through fives enjoy these puzzles. Matching pairs of tiles is easier for twos. Sequence puzzles are enjoyed by fours and fives.

FIGURE 18   SEQUENCE PUZZLES FROM WORN BOOKS

TILES

OR

Muffin tin puzzle (See Figure 19)   (T-5)
Materials: Muffin tin, cardboard, scissors, decals (fruit, bird, animal, or vegetable decals which are available from card shops), clear contact plastic, and glue.
Guidance: Cut cardboard discs the size of the bottom of each muffin tin cup. You will need two discs for each muffin cup. Stick matching decals onto two of the discs. Continue until you have two look-alike discs for each muffin cup. Cover each disc with clear contact plastic. Glue one set of discs into the bottoms of the muffin tin cups.

To work the puzzle, a child will place a matching decal disc on each disc in the muffin tin.

Toddlers can work a four- to six-cup muffin tin puzzle. Twos through fives would be challenged with a six- to twelve-cup muffin tin puzzle.

FIGURE 19

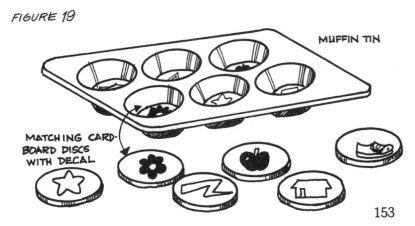

MUFFIN TIN

MATCHING CARD-
BOARD DISCS
WITH DECAL

153

Space saver puzzle (See Figure 20)   (T-5)
Materials: Felt, bristle stripping that sticks together, scissors, tape, and a felt-tipped marker.
Guidance: Cut a square of felt (2 by 2 ft.). Cut assorted colors of felt pieces into circles, squares, rectangles, and triangles. Each shape should be approximately four inches across. Lay the large piece of felt on a table. Place the shapes at equal intervals on the large piece of felt. Draw around each shape with the marker. Onto each outline sew a piece of bristle stripping. Also, sew a piece of the bristle stripping onto each separate shape to match its outline on the large felt piece.

Hang the large felt piece at a child's eye level on the wall with wide book binding tape. Do not use tacks. The puzzle is worked as a child sticks each separate shape to its outline on the felt fabric. The puzzle can be worked on a table if space permits. The bristle stripping is not needed for a flat surface.

Older preschoolers enjoy the hanging puzzle with six to ten pieces. Younger preschoolers will need a simple adaptation of the puzzle (two to four pieces) without the matching bristle stripping. Also, the younger preschoolers need to work the puzzle on a flat surface.

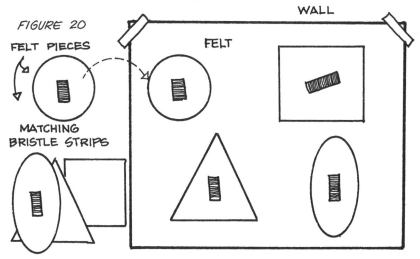

FIGURE 20
FELT PIECES
MATCHING BRISTLE STRIPS
WALL
FELT

Shoe box lace-up puzzle (See Figure 21)   (2-5)
Materials: Sturdy shoe box, hole punch, notebook hold reinforcements, and a boot string (or two different color shoe strings).
Guidance: Discard the shoe box lid. Cut a fourth out of each side of the box so the sides are alike. Cut a half off of one end of the box. You will have a basic high-top shoe shape (without the top part where the tongue is usually located). Punch holes for lacing along the cut sides only. Reinforce the holes with notebook hole reinforcements. The boot string will be used for lacing the shoe. If two colors of shoe strings are used, tie the two strings together to make one long string.

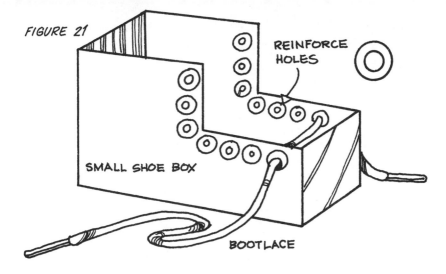

FIGURE 21

REINFORCE HOLES

SMALL SHOE BOX

BOOTLACE

This puzzle is appropriate for twos and older. Younger twos and toddler may get a similar threading experience by stringing large spools on a boot string. The lacing and threading technique is a good prerequisite for handwriting.

You can buy puzzles
Puzzles can be purchased from the Baptist Book Store, toy departments, school supply stores, hobby shops, and through catalogs.

What are the guidelines for purchasing puzzles for preschoolers?
● Pictures depicted in puzzles to be used at church need to be realistic. Animals do not wear clothes, so animals in puzzles are more realistic if they do not wear clothes. Nursery rhymes and fairy tale picture puzzles are not suggested for Preschool departments for this same reason. Use realistic pictures when teaching through the use of Bible conversation, songs, Bible thoughts, and stories.
● Purchase a few good, durable, wooden inlay puzzles rather than several inexpensive cardboard puzzles.
● Two to six pieces in a puzzle are suggested for creepers and toddlers. Two to ten pieces in a puzzle are enough for twos and threes. From ten to twenty pieces are suggested for fours and fives. Refer to your teacher's guide for a list of specific puzzles which are recommended for the age group which you teach.
● Paint used on puzzles must be nontoxic.
● Puzzle toys and puzzles need to be free of sharp edges and free of pieces small enough to swallow.

When Are Puzzles Used at Church?
Puzzles and how to use them need to be a part of the planning for Sunday School, Discipleship Training, Mission Friends, Preschool choir, Mother's Day Out, kindergarten, and any other weekday activities with

155

preschoolers. Puzzle activities suggested in *Preschool Bible Teacher A, Preschool Bible Teacher B, Preschool Bible Teacher C;*** and *Bible Story Time Teacher* can be used anytime preschoolers are at church. If you teach in extended session you will also find puzzle ideas in the packets *Extended Session for Babies and Ones, Extended Session for 2's and 3's,* and *Extended Session for 4's and 5's.* If you teach during special events at church, an undated unit will give ideas for teaching through the use of puzzles. Also, Vacation Bible School materials suggest ways to use puzzles. *The Music Leader* and *Start* also suggest puzzle usage.

In most of these organizations puzzles are suggested during activity time.

Where Can Puzzles Be Used?

Locate puzzles in a well-lighted, out-of-the-way place in the department room. A low table with three child-sized chairs can be used. A puzzle rack, or container, is also a good place for puzzles; however, puzzles are not limited to one corner of the room. Babies, creepers, and toddlers enjoy puzzle toys and puzzles in a crib, on the floor, and even out-of-doors. A clean floor is a suitable place for two- through five-year-olds to work puzzles, especially if space is limited. Have you used a wall puzzle in limited space? (See suggestions of homemade puzzles, p. 147.)

Fours and fives can make puzzles in an *art* activity. The cube puzzles or puzzle boards may be in the *block* area. The book *Who Lives Here?* and other puzzle books can be in several parts of the room. Stacking measuring containers or sorting things can take place in the *homeliving* area. There are *musical* puzzle games (which bell matches the sound on the piano) which four- and-five-year-olds enjoy. Leaves glued to cardboard squares and covered with clear contact plastic can be matched in the *nature* area. Putting a Bible story picture puzzle (with few pieces) together in *group time* can help recall a Bible story. Threes, fours, and fives can see how many different kinds of leaves they can find out-of-doors. They may look for red nature items, green objects, soft objects, or hard nature items. Do not limit puzzles to a corner of the room. Puzzles can be used in every area.

How Are Puzzles Used with Preschoolers?

Carefully read chapter 2, "How to Teach Through Activities."

Puzzles can be used effectively during teachable moments with preschoolers. Teachers may use Bible conversation, Bible thoughts, Bible stories, and songs in the puzzle area. Teachers can teach responsibility as children enjoy puzzles.

The Bible can be on the floor near a puzzle or puzzle toy. As a creeper crawls toward the Bible, the teacher can touch the Bible and say: "Bible. This is the Bible." Fours and fives can talk about the Bible as they are working puzzles. They can talk about a puzzle depicting a Bible-related subject. Conversation and puzzles go well together.

156

While a three-year-old works a puzzle, use a Bible thought. Say: "In the Bible we read, 'God gave us eyes to see.' You can see the puzzle pieces with your eyes."

Perhaps the puzzle "Grandmother Reads a Bible Story" used with fives will give an opportunity for you to say: "That puzzle makes me think of a story in the Bible. The story is about a boy named Timothy." Continue by telling about young Timothy and Grandmother Lois.

As a toddler works the puzzle "Birds I See," sing the song "God Makes Little Birds," (p. 9)† or sing the song "I Like to Go to Church" (p. 27)† as a four-year-old works the puzzle "Going to Church."

Say a thank-you prayer as the baby tugs and pulls at a puzzle toy. "Thank you, God, for Scott's hands. Thank you, God, for happy times at church."

Puzzles can lead into other areas for more teachable moments. After a five-year-old finishes the floor puzzle "The Farm," say: "There is a book about the farm on the bookrack. Get the book and we will read it." Corn in its husk in the nature areas can provide an opportunity to talk about farming.

Puzzles and pictures are compatible. The puzzle "Jesus and the Children" corresponds with *Read-to-Me Bible Story Pictures, Set 1,* Picture 10, "Jesus and the Children."** Place the puzzle and the picture in the puzzle area of four- and five-year departments. As a child works the puzzle, he may refer to the picture to determine where a piece of the puzzle goes.

Bible story pictures may be cut from outdated literature. Each picture is pasted onto construction paper. The construction paper is then cut into a puzzle. Each puzzle is placed in an envelope. Older preschoolers may choose to work one of the puzzles and recall the Bible story that goes with the picture.

Older preschoolers learn responsibility when a teacher gives positive guidance in the puzzle area. To a child who needs help in finishing a puzzle, say, "See if this piece fits here." When a child has finished a puzzle, say, "Now, you may put the puzzle back in the rack (or container)."

Help preschoolers learn to take turns by saying: "Mark, let's water the plants. After that, perhaps someone will be finished with a puzzle, and you can have a turn," or "When Joe finishes with the puzzle, it will be your turn."

*Preschool Bible Teacher A, Preschool Bible Teacher B, Preschool Bible Teacher C,*** *Bible Story Time Teacher; Start,* and *The Music Leader* are good sources for other teaching ideas to use as children enjoy puzzles, puzzle toys, and puzzle games.

Care and storage of puzzles

How teachers care for and guide the use of puzzles will help determine how valuable puzzles will be to preschoolers.

Use only a few puzzles during a session. Babies, creepers, and toddlers will enjoy two to four puzzle toys and one or two wooden inlay puzzles during a session.

Twos and threes may have access to two to three wooden inlay puzzles, during activities. One other special puzzle activity, such as a homemade puzzle, may be available for middle preschoolers.

Fours and fives will enjoy three to four wooden inlay puzzles during activities. One or two special puzzles or puzzle games may be used as session plans suggest.

Cleanliness is important.

Babies, creepers, and toddlers taste-test even puzzles. Liquid soap, water, and a soft cloth can be used to wipe washable puzzle toys and puzzles. The soft cloth is recommended because germs grow in damp sponges.

Make handling wooden inlay puzzles easier by cutting lightweight cardboard the size of each puzzle piece. Glue each piece of cardboard into its indention in the puzzle frame. The piece placed into the puzzle frame will then be raised a bit above the frame so a child's fingers can remove each puzzle piece.

For easy identification, mark each puzzle piece to go with its frame or container. For example, on the back of the wooden inlay puzzle "Animals," mark the number "1." On the back of each of the eight pieces that go into that puzzle, mark a number "1." If puzzles should get mixed up, it is easier to sort the pieces if each puzzle is marked to match its frame or container.

One way to replace a lost wooden puzzle piece is by using wood putty. Press foil into the indention of the missing puzzle piece. Press wood putty into the indention. Let the putty dry for at least twenty-four hours. Lift the foil and the piece out of the puzzle. Sand rough edges. Paint the new puzzle piece with nontoxic paint.

Puzzles can be valuable to more children if a puzzle resource center is established in the Preschool area or media center. All Preschool puzzles could be kept in the resource center and checked out as they are needed. Teachers can plan for a session and then go to the resource center to get puzzles to enhance the session's theme or activities. If suggested puzzles are not available, teachers can substitute others from the resource center.

Puzzles in the Preschool Bible Teacher A Resource Kit, Preschool Bible Teacher B Resource Kit, Preschool Bible Teacher C Resource Kit, * * and *Bible Story Time Teacher Resource Kits need to be mounted on cardboard (or as instructions suggest) and filed for easy accessibility and future use.* These puzzles can also be in the resource center.

Summary

Puzzles are materials or activities which present a challenge to a child's ability to solve problems. Puzzles are used at church to aid preschoolers' growth—physically, mentally, emotionally, socially, and spiritually. While preschoolers enjoy puzzle activities, teachers can capture teachable moments to relate Bible conversation, songs, stories, and positive guidance.

Puzzles can be bought or made. Puzzle games can be used with older preschoolers. Puzzles, puzzle toys, and puzzle games need to be a part of the learning experiences planned for preschoolers at church.

Proper care and usage of puzzles and puzzle toys extend their usefulness.

Personal Learning Activities

1. Make one or more of the suggested homemade puzzles. Use that puzzle(s) with preschoolers. Evaluate the experience.
2. Collect catalogs containing puzzles. See if puzzle toys or puzzles pictured in the catalogs can be made by you or someone you know.
3. Use the guidelines for purchasing puzzles as you plan to buy puzzles for preschoolers.
4. Make an inventory of puzzles for preschoolers in your church. Replace any necessary pieces. Discard puzzles or puzzle toys which do not meet safety standards. Categorize puzzles and puzzle toys according to the age of a child for which they are best suited.
5. Set up a resource center for puzzles in your church.

Materials for Further Study

Following are names of companies which produce some acceptable puzzles, puzzle toys, puzzle games, and puzzle holders. Any time you purchase a puzzle-related item, use the guidelines for selecting good puzzles.

When you shop, look for such names as: Broadman; Childcraft; Creative Playthings; Fisher-Price; Gabriel; Judy; Kohner, Inc.; Knickerbocker Toy Co.; Lauri; Mattel; Milton Bradley; Playskool; Romper Room Toys; and Tupperware.

Some sources for catalogs include:

—Baptist Book Store, The Sunday School Board, 127 Ninth Avenue, North, Nashville, Tennessee 37234.

—Childcraft Education Corp., 20 Kilmer Road, Edison, New Jersey, 08817.

—Creative Playthings, 33 Loring Drive, Framingham, MA 01701.

—Fisher-Price Consumer Products, 636 Girard Ave., East Aurora, New York, 14052.

—Matttel Toys, Attn.: Consumer Affairs, 5150 Rosecrans Avenue, Hawthorne, California 90250.

—Tupperware (Check in your local phone book.).

*Available from Baptist Book Stores.
**Available by writing Customer Service Center, 127 Ninth Avenue, North, Nashville, Tennessee 37234; or by calling toll free 1-800-458-2772.
***Available from Woman's Missionary Union, P.O. Box 830010, Birmingham, Alabama 35283-0010.

Chapter 12—How to Use the Bible with Preschoolers

Dixie Ruth Crase

A wide variety of developmentally appropriate books is of inestimable value in young children's lives. Picture books shared with a baby sitting in the lap of a teacher or parent help lay the foundation for warm, positive feelings associated with reading. Throughout the Preschool years, books help children understand themselves, others, and their world. Books may open doors to new vocabulary, reinforce concepts, and provide an avenue for expression of feelings. The word *Bible* comes from *biblia,* meaning "books." The Bible is a special book which may become a meaningful part of preschoolers' experiences.

This chapter will suggest the significance of the Bible in teachers' and children's lives. Because much of the Bible is primarily written for adults, appropriate Bible thoughts for use with babies, creepers, toddlers, twos, threes, fours, and fives will be identified. A Bible thought is *the main truth in a Bible verse stated in terms which a child can understand.* When to use Bible thoughts, stories, pictures, and songs will be discussed in this chapter. Proper placement of the Bible will encourage babies, creepers, and toddlers to touch the pages and look at the pictures. Older preschoolers begin to associate Bible thoughts with planned activities in the department.

Why Are Bible Thoughts, Pictures, Stories, Songs, and Conversation Used with Preschoolers?

The Bible is used with preschoolers so they can become more aware that:

1. God made the natural world;
2. God made us;
3. God loves us;
4. Jesus loves us;
5. We can love and help one another;
6. We can thank God.

God made the natural world.—The natural world envelops a newborn from birth. As his vision develops he can see flowers in the garden and trees swaying in the wind. The teacher says: "God made the trees. Thank you, God, for the trees." A creeper or toddler watches the goldfish swimming in a clear plastic container placed on the floor. His

teacher may sing the song, "Goldfish Swimming," (p. 58)† A young preschooler understands a tone of voice expressing marvel and enjoyment of God's natural world.

Twos' and threes' mobility expands their encounters with the natural world. Alert teachers help children become increasingly aware that God planned for fruit, birds, and animals. When twos and threes drink orange juice, look at a picture of birds, or feel a kitten, the teacher can say: "God made the _____. Thank you, God, for the _____."

Older preschoolers' enjoyment of the natural world may be expressed when a teacher opens the Bible to Psalm 147:16. The teacher may say, "God gives snow," as the children watch snowflakes fall on the windowsill.

God made us.—To begin life as a cherished creation of God is surely each child's birthright. When Stephanie is held to hear the wind chimes in the baby department, the teacher may say: "Thank you, God, for ears to hear the chimes. Thank you, God, for Stephanie's ears."

As a three-year-old mixes yellow and blue tempera paint, he delights in discovering another color. His teacher may say: "God gave us eyes to see. I'm glad God planned pretty colors for us to see."

An older preschooler can begin to recognize the marvel of his body. Place a snapshot of a five-year-old on a piece of construction paper. Below the picture print, "I am wonderfully made" (Ps. 139:14). Positive feelings about self make a good beginning in an increased awareness that God made us.

God loves us.—An innate need to experience love seems to be a universal condition of newborns. Young preschoolers can experience God's love through warm, sensitive, caring adults. When children develop a sense of trust in themselves and others they are helping to lay the foundation to trust God. As a creeper pats the Bible, his teacher says: "The Bible tells about God. God is good." A teacher's smile helps to convey true gratitude for a loving God.

As a group of threes looks at a picture of a family, they are invited to tell what mothers do for them. Their teacher may say, "I'm thankful God planned for special people to care for us." He may open the Bible to 1 Peter 5:7 and say, "God takes care of you."

When a teacher reads the book *Where Are You, God?* by Watson, an older preschooler begins to recognize that God is near and that he is with us.

Jesus loves us.—When Jeremy is being rocked, his teacher sings, "Rocking my little one, rocking my little one, Jesus loves Jeremy . . ." A two-year-old may be greeted with a picture of Jesus and the children. A teacher smiles and says, "Jesus said, 'You are my friends.'"

Older preschoolers are interested in their new abilities. They can cut with scissors, hop on one foot, and button large buttons. As a teacher delights in a preschooler's new accomplishments, he may say: "Your body is growing. Jesus grew and became strong, too."

We can love and help one another.—As two creepers discover each

162

other, their teacher may gently sing, "Love one another . . ." The teacher helps set the stage for an easy touch and a positive encounter. When diapering a toddler, invite him to hand you the clean diaper. Say, "Thank you for helping, Timmy."

Watch for expressions of kindness by threes in the homeliving area. Say: "Allison, thank you for letting Dawn sweep the floor. The Bible teaches us to be kind. You were kind to let Dawn sweep the floor."

An unstructured art activity may require fours and fives to take turns with bottles of paste. As children select collage items, say, "You are taking turns with the paste. The Bible says, 'Be kind.' You are being kind when you take turns with the paste." Positive expectations often bring about positive results. In response to Bible stories, older preschoolers share experiences they have had with their families. Teachers can reinforce Christian parents' teaching. You may say: "I'm glad you helped rake the leaves. The Bible says, 'Children, obey your parents.' You obeyed your father when you raked the leaves."

We can express our thanks to God.—When welcoming a toddler, stoop to the child's eye level and sing softly, "Todd likes to come to church . . ." Happy times at church include thanking God. Toddlers catch your spirit of gratitude.

When twos and threes look at a picture of Jesus in the temple, a teacher may tell a Bible story about Jesus' experience. He may say: "Jesus went to church. Wade and Sandy come to church, too."

Older preschoolers begin to understand that the Bible teaches us to love God. Our expressions of love for God include thanksgiving. Fours and fives enjoy matching a piece of colored construction paper to a Bible marker of the same color. A teacher helps each child "read" his Bible thought. The markers may include the Bible thought "Be glad and sing happy songs" (Ps. 9:2).

Who Can Understand Bible Thoughts, Pictures, Stories, Songs, and Conversation?

Each age group in the Preschool Division can become increasingly aware of appropriate Bible thoughts. The characteristics of babies, creepers, toddlers, twos, threes, fours, and fives help us know what the children can comprehend.

Babies

From the moment of birth, babies are learning. Initial learning experiences occur when babies use their senses. As a baby is held and fed, his physical needs are being met. A teacher may sing: "Jesus, Jesus, I love Jesus . . ." What is the baby learning? He is learning to associate the pleasures of food, warmth, and a pleasant voice with words he hears about Jesus. This happy time at church helps to lay a foundation for understanding the Bible thought, "Jesus loves us" (Rev. 1:5).

A teacher places an orange in Jonathan's crib. As Jonathan touches the rough texture of the orange, his teachers say: "God made the orange. Thank you, God, for the orange."

Creepers

A Bible is placed on the floor. This book is opened to a picture of Jesus in the temple. As a creeper approaches the Bible, Dawn's teacher sits beside her. The teacher says: "Dawn, see the picture of Jesus. Jesus went to church. Dawn comes to church, too."

Toddlers

As preschoolers learn to pull themselves up, stand alone, and walk, they are excited about their new abilities. A teacher who shares their excitement may say: "God made us. God planned for Anthony to have strong legs. Thank you, God, for Anthony's strong legs." To Allan, the teacher may sing, "You're growing, growing . . ."

Toddlers may begin to use single words. As Cleo looks at a picture book of birds, a teacher may say, "Cleo, show me the bird." When children enjoy word games, they are increasing their vocabulary and their awareness for God's creative abilities. Cleo's teacher says: "Thank you, God, for birds. The birds have nests."

Twos

While Leslie tries to stack cardboard blocks, Michael may push them over. A teacher may sing, "Stack, stack, stack the blocks . . ." To Michael the teacher may say: "Leslie likes to stack those blocks. You may stack these blocks." When children are playing happily, say: "The Bible says we are to love one another. You showed that you love Leslie when you let him stack some of the blocks. Thank you, God, for friends." Invite Michael and Leslie to look at *Read-to-Me Bible Story Pictures, Set 1,* Picture 12, "Jesus and the Children."** Say: "Jesus had friends. Some of Jesus' friends were children."

Threes

Three-year-olds begin to imitate tasks of adults. Pretending to cook, clean, shop, and drive to work is fun. Threes also enjoy helping adults with real tasks. Given a sponge to wipe a table, Eldon may clean with enthusiasm. Express your appreciation for his assistance. You may sing: "Thank you, God, for helpers. Thank you, God."

While walking through colorful fall leaves, a teacher may talk with threes about the trees and their beautiful leaves. An open Bible may have a leaf marking the Bible thought, "God made the trees" (Gen. 1:11).

Fours

A set of slides portraying different farm animals or zoo animals may be placed on a table or on the floor. A battery-operated hand viewer is available for fours to individually see the slide collection. As Jim views each animal, he may name the animal, describe the sound it makes, or tell what the animal eats. Bookmarks may have animal pictures on them. They may be placed in the Bible at Genesis 1:25 and Psalm 104:14. Jim's teacher says: "God made the cattle. God makes the grass to grow for the cattle to eat."

Fives

A quiet rest/listening time on the grass or mats may follow snack time on

164

a summer day. Invite fives to close their eyes and listen for outdoor sounds. They may hear the sounds of traffic on a nearby street. They may hear the sound of the lawn sprinkler or birds singing. A teacher says, "The time of the singing of birds is come" (Song of Sol. 2:12).

Which Bible Thoughts, Pictures, Stories, Songs, and Conversation Are Used with Preschoolers?

Preschoolers' introduction to the Bible should be positive, meaningful, and doctrinally sound. Developmentally appropriate experiences related to the Bible help lay the foundation for a true appreciation of the Bible's significance.

Positive introduction to the Bible

As you study the Bible thoughts suggested for each Preschool age group, catch the positive, happy approach which each thought conveys. The preschooler's delight in his body and his abilities are celebrated. Child and teacher can proclaim, "God made us." The sun shining on the clouds prompts a positive response to be shared with a preschooler. Open the Bible to Psalm 104:3 and say, "God made the clouds." God's goodness is recognized in his many gifts to us. Fours' and fives' increasing awareness of God's ultimate gift is expressed when they note the marker at 1 John 4:10. Say with a child, "God loved us and sent his Son."

Meaningful introduction to the Bible

Bible thoughts, pictures, stories, songs, and conversation need to have meaning to the child. Memorization and ritual have no place in building a clear understanding of Bible truths. Bible thoughts which use concrete, tangible words or phrases are better understood by preschoolers. Todd likes to splash the small amount of water in the plastic dishpan. His teacher says: "God made the water. Thank you, God, for water."

Natural World Pictures, Set 2, Picture 2, "Fruit"** is placed on the floor in the toddler department. Allison looks at the picture and holds a banana. Her teacher might sing: "Thank you, God, for bananas. Thank you, God." He may peel the banana and invite Allison to taste a slice of the banana. The Bible is opened to Psalm 136:25 as the teacher says: "God gives food to us. Thank you, God, for the banana."

Playing outside on a sunny day, two- and three-year-olds delight in chasing soap bubbles. A teacher may place the open Bible on the grass. As Eloise sits and watches a bubble, her teacher may say, "God makes the wind blow the bubbles."

Fours and fives enjoy the Bible story about Miriam. These older preschoolers can describe how Miriam helped her mother. A marker at Exodus 20:12 helps older preschoolers understand that the Bible teaches us to obey our fathers and mothers. Older preschoolers can suggest ways they help in their families.

Doctrinally sound introduction to the Bible

First experiences are vital because they help lay the groundwork for subsequent learnings. Preschoolers should be taught ideas and concepts which can be built upon as they mature in their understanding of the Bible. In the following list, note the Bible thoughts to use with babies, creepers, and toddlers, twos and threes, and fours and fives.

Bible Thought	Reference	Age Designation*
Church		
"I like to go to church."	Psalm 122:1	A B C
"I was glad when they said, 'Let us go to church.'"		C
"Sing thanks to God."	Psalm 147:7	C
"Bring an offering to church."	Malachi 3:10	C
"Jesus went to church."	Mark 11:15	A B C
"Bring an offering."	1 Chronicles 16:29	C
"Be glad and sing happy songs."	Psalm 9:2	B C
"It is a good thing to give thanks."	Psalm 92:1	C
"We work together."	1 Corinthians 3:9	A B C
"We are helpers."	2 Corinthians 1:24	A B C
"Help one another."	Galatians 5:13	A B C
"Be kind to each other"	Ephesians 4:32	B C
"Love one another."	1 John 4:7	B
"Let us love one another."		C
Family		
"Love your father and mother."	Exodus 20:12	C
"We work together."	1 Corinthians 3:9	A B C
"We are helpers."	2 Corinthians 1:24	A B C
"Help one another."	Galatians 5:13	A B C
"Be kind to each other."	Ephesians 4:32	B C
"Children, obey your parents."	Colossians 3:20	C
"Love one another."	1 John 4:7	B
"Let us love one another."		C
"Jesus loves us."	Revelation 1:5	A B C
God		
"God made the flowers."	Genesis 1:11	A B C
"God made the fruit."		
"God made the grass."		
"God made the trees."		
"God made the moon."	Genesis 1:16	A B C
"God made the sun."		
"God made the stars."		
"God made the birds."	Genesis 1:21	A B C
"God made the fish."		
"God made the cows."	Genesis 1:25	A B C
"God made the cattle."		C
"God looked at everything he had made and he was very pleased."	Genesis 1:31	C
"God made the trees."	Genesis 2:9	A B C
"Say thank you to God."	Psalm 136:1	B
"Give thanks to God."		C
"God gives food to us."	Psalm 136:25	A B C
"God made me."	Psalm 139:14	B C
"I am wonderfully made."		C
"Sing thanks to God."	Psalm 147:7	C
"God makes the wind blow."	Psalm 147:18	C
"God sends the autumn (season) rain."	Jeremiah 5:24	C
"God sends the rain."		A B
"God sends the spring rain."		C
"God made the grasshopper."	Amos 7:1	A B C
"Look at the wonderful things God made."	Job 37:14	C
"God is good to us."	Psalm 73:1	A B C
"God made the summer."	Psalm 74:17	B
"God made the winter."		B
"God has made the summer."		C

"God has made the winter."		C
"It is a good thing to give thanks."	Psalm 92:1	C
"God made the ocean and the dry land."	Psalm 95:5	C
"God made the water."	Psalm 104:10	A B C
"Love God."	Mark 12:30	C
"God gives us things to enjoy."	1 Timothy 6:17	C
"God loves us."	1 John 4:10	A B C
"God loved us and sent his Son."		C

Natural World

"God made the flowers."	Genesis 1:11	A B C
"God made the fruit."		
"God made the grass."		
"God made the trees."		
"God made the moon."	Genesis 1:16	A B C
"God made the sun."		
"God made the stars."		
"God made the birds."	Genesis 1:21	A B C
"God made the fish."		
"God made the cows."	Genesis 1:25	A B C
"God made the cattle."		C
"God looked at everything he had made and he was very pleased."	Genesis 1:31	C
"God made the trees."	Genesis 2:9	A B C
"God makes the grass grow."	Psalm 104:14	A B C
"God makes the grass grow for the cattle."		C
"The moon shines in the night."	Psalm 136:9	A B C
"The stars shine in the night."		A B C
"God gives food to us."	Psalm 136:25	A B C
"God makes rain."	Psalm 147:8	A B C
"God makes the grass grow."		A B C
"God gives food to animals."	Psalm 147:9	B C
"God gives food to birds."		B C
"God sends the snow."	Psalm 147:16	B C
"God makes the wind blow."	Psalm 147:18	C
"The flowers grow."	Song of Solomon 2:12	A B
"The flowers grow and bloom."		C
"The time of the singing of birds is come."		C
"God sends the autumn (season) rain."	Jeremiah 5:24	C
"God sends the rain."		A B
"God sends the spring rain."		C
"God makes the lightning flash with the rain."	Jeremiah 10:13	C
"God makes the lightning flash."		B
"God gives the moon and stars for a light by night."	Jeremiah 31:35	C
"God gives the sun for a light by day."		C
"The sun shines in the day."		A B C
"God made the grasshopper."	Amos 7:1	A B C
"The birds have nests."	Matthew 8:20	C
"God made the clouds."	Job 36:27	B C
"Look at the wonderful things God made."	Job 37:14	C
"God made the summer."	Psalm 74:17	B
"God made the winter."		B
"God has made the summer."		C
"God has made the winter."		C
"God made the ocean and the dry land."	Psalm 95:5	C
"God made the water."	Psalm 104:10	A B C
"God gives us things to enjoy."	1 Timothy 6:17	C

Self

"I like to go to church."	Psalm 122:1	A B C

		A	B	C
"I was glad when they said, 'Let us go to church.' "				C
"God made me."	Psalm 139:14		B	C
"I am wonderfully made."				C
"God gave us ears to hear."	Proverbs 20:12	A	B	C
"God gave us eyes to see."		A	B	C
"God gave us ears to hear and eyes to see."				C
"Be glad and sing happy songs."	Psalm 9:2		B	C
"God is good to us."	Psalm 73:1	A	B	C
"God made us."	Psalm 100:3	A	B	C
"Jesus said, 'I love you.' "	John 15:9	A	B	C
"Jesus said, 'You are my friends.' "	John 15:14-15	A	B	C
"Work with your hands."	1 Thessalonians 4:11			C
"God loves us."	1 John 4:10	A	B	C
"God loved us and sent his Son."				C
"Jesus loves us."	Revelation 1:5	A	B	C

Jesus

		A	B	C
"Jesus was born in Bethlehem."	Matthew 2:1			C
"Jesus lived in Nazareth."	Matthew 2:23			C
"Jesus said, 'Let the children come to me.' "	Matthew 19:14		B	C
"Jesus went to church."	Mark 11:15	A	B	C
"Jesus grew and became strong."	Luke 2:40			C
"Jesus grew."	Luke 2:52	A	B	C
"Jesus grew tall."		A	B	C
"Jesus had friends."		A	B	C
"Jesus said, 'I love you.' "	John 15:9	A	B	C
"Jesus said, 'You are my friends.' "	John 15:14-15	A	B	C
"Jesus said, 'Love one another.' "	John 15:17	A	B	C
"Jesus went about doing good."	Acts 10:38			C
"Jesus loves us."	Revelation 1:5	A	B	C

Others

		A	B	C
"A friend loves at all times."	Proverbs 17:17			C
"Jesus had friends."	Luke 2:52	A	B	C
"Jesus said, 'You are my friends.' "	John 15:14-15	A	B	C
"Jesus said, 'Love one another.' "	John 15:17	A	B	C
"We work together."	1 Corinthians 3:9	A	B	C
"We are helpers."	2 Corinthians 1:24	A	B	C
"Help one another."	Galatians 5:13	A	B	C
"Be kind to each other."	Ephesians 4:32		B	C
"Love one another."	1 John 4:7		B	
"Let us love one another."				C

---

*A = baby, creeper, toddler
B = twos and threes
C = fours and fives

When Are Bible Thoughts, Pictures, Stories, Songs, and Conversation Used with Preschoolers?

In Deuteronomy 6:1-9, Israel is instructed to teach children ". . . when thou sittest in thine house, and when thou walkest by the way, and when thou liest down, and when thou risest up." From arrival to departure, recognize and capture teachable moments to use Bible-related material with preschoolers.

Arrival

Preparation for children's arrival begins in a weekly workers' meeting. As teachers and directors study *Preschool Bible Teacher A,***

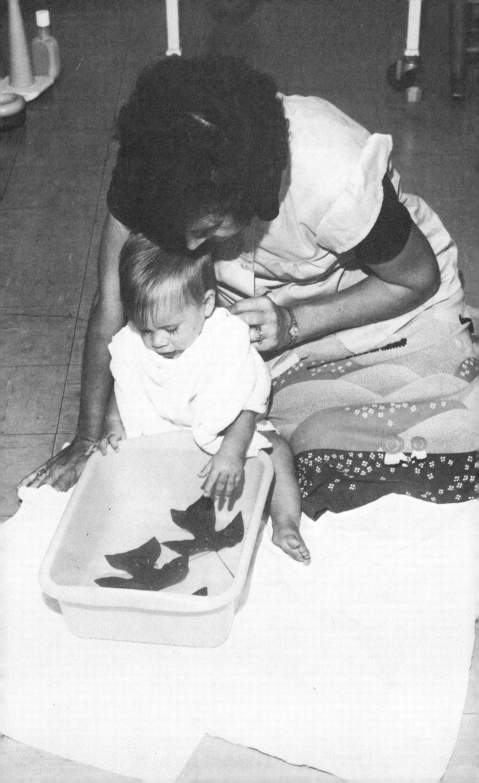

Preschool Bible Teacher B,** *Preschool Bible Teacher C,*** *Bible Story Time Teacher,*** *Start,**** or *The Music Leader,*** they note recommended Bible thoughts and stories for each session. Note the suggestions regarding the use of Bible thoughts and Bible stories in chapters 2, 3, and 13 of this book.

Listed below are a few situations which may occur when using Bible-related materials as preschoolers arrive.

As baby Susan arrives at the door to the department, the director greets Susan's parents and welcomes Susan with *Present-Day Pictures, Set 1,* Picture 10, "Pop Beads." He may say: "God gave us eyes to see. Thank you, God, for Susan's eyes to see the pop beads." When Mrs. Anthony receives Lyndal, she places him on the floor near the Mini-Harp. She may sing and play the song "My Best Friend Is Jesus." (p. 99). ***

In the toddler department, the director sits near the door to welcome Amy and thank her parents for bringing her. He holds a flower for Amy to see, smell, and touch. He says: "God made the flowers. Thank you, God, for flowers."

Twos and threes who have regularly attended well-planned sessions will usually be happy to arrive at their department. As Todd arrives, invite him to pet the puppy in the cardboard box. You may sing the song "Doggy, Doggy," (p. 60).†

Greet fours and fives on their eye level. Smile and acknowledge parents' presence. Avoid lengthy conversations which will detract from the significance of a child's arrival. As the director sits near the door, he will hold a Bible open to Mark 11:15. When Ted arrives, the director says: "I'm glad you came to church, Ted. The Bible teaches that 'Jesus went to church.' "

During the session the teachers can plan to do some of the following activities.

Activities

As Todd watches the bird mobile above his crib, his teacher may sing: "Blue, blue bird, Oh, Todd can see the bird. God gave Todd eyes, so he can see the bird" (tune, "God Gave Me Eyes," p. 7). Place wrist or ankle bells on a child who is moving about on the floor. As the bells ring, sing: "Jingle, jingle, jingle, jingle, Sandy rings the bells" (tune "Pitter, Patter," p. 50).† Say: "Sandy likes to come to church. She likes to ring the bells." Respect individual choices of activities. Allan may enjoy watching and listening to Sandy's bells; however, he may not like for the bells to be placed on him.

Twos and threes are ready for a variety of fresh, attractive activities in the department. Place the Bible in the homeliving area. A flower serves as a marker for Genesis 1:11. As Kathy notices the flower, say: "The Bible tells us, 'God made the flowers.' "

Place the book *God's Summer Gifts* by Linam on the bookrack. As fours and fives listen to a teacher reading the book, they may talk about their own experiences in summer. Encourage children to express their feelings and ideas. In the conversation, share the Bible thought, "God made the summer" (Ps. 74:17).

Transition (movement from one part of the session to another part of the session when several activities take place—for example, the movement from activity time to group time in three-, four-, and five-year departments)

When preschoolers have been involved in a variety of activities, they may need refreshments or a rest. Babies and creepers may need their diapers changed. The younger the child, the more individualized his schedule will be. As you feed Jack pureed carrots, share the Bible thought, "God gives food" (Ps. 136:25).

Toddlers may enjoy eating snacks together as they sit on the floor. When each toddler eats his cracker, say, "Thank you, God, for crackers." As Madeline drinks her orange juice, open the Bible to Genesis 1:11 and say, "God made the fruit."

Twos and threes can help teachers return Blockbusters to a low shelf and straighten the homeliving area. As Julie wipes the art table with a damp sponge, say: "Thank you for helping, Julie. The Bible says, 'We are helpers' (2 Cor. 1:24)."

As fours and fives mature, they are more aware of the schedule for each session. They begin to understand the importance of good housekeeping in preparation for group time. As Jennifer carefully replaces the books on the bookrack, sing the song "It's Fun to Be Together," (p. 17).††† You may say: "Jennifer, you are such a good helper! The Bible teaches us to do what is good."

Group time

Threes, fours, and fives enjoy coming together for a special time with their friends. The director may sing a song or talk quietly with children as the teachers and children are preparing for group time. After directing a relaxation game, the director opens the Bible and tells the Bible story. If the Bible story is about a family, children may be invited to relate their own family experiences. After listening to the Bible story of David helping his father take care of the sheep, Lisa may tell about feeding her dog. The director may say: "God made the animals. I am glad God planned for us to help care for animals." Older preschoolers may want to thank God for their pets.

(See chapter 13, "How to Lead Group Time Experiences" for further details regarding group time.)

Extended session

Every adult who is in contact with children is teaching. Extended session provides an opportunity for teachers to continue the Sunday School or Church Training learning experiences through the worship service. During extended session, teachers have more time to extend a child's awareness of the Bible. Preschoolers learn by repetition. Hearing Bible thoughts, stories, and songs introduced in the first part of the session reinforces learning. A Bible thought used in a variety of situations helps children recognize the significance of Bible truths. A teacher may share

the Bible thought "God gives water" (Psalm 104:10) as children wash hands, drink water, watch a goldfish swimming, or listen to the rain on the window. Five-year-olds may reenact a Bible story they have heard during group time. Children have an opportunity to play a different role during extended session.

Departure

As parents arrive, one teacher stands or sits near the door. Children's personal belongings are placed outside the department or near the door. When parents knock softly, a teacher brings their child to them. Other teachers and children continue appropriate activities. A toddler and his teacher may play and sing the song "Roll the Ball," (p. 80).†
Twos and threes may be looking at the book *I'm Glad God Thought of Mothers* by Cachiaras. Their teacher may share the Bible thought, "I like to go to church" (Ps. 122:1). He may describe an activity which each two- or three-year-old enjoyed during the session. Most children enjoy this short story about their experience.

Parents appreciate a positive, encouraging word or note about their child's activities. Brief handwritten notes to the parents of younger pre-schoolers may reinforce biblical teaching in the home. Sarah's note may read: "My teacher said, 'God made the winter.' I felt the snow in a plastic dishpan. The snow was cold."

Where Are Bible Thoughts, Pictures, Stories, Songs, and Conversation Shared with Preschoolers?

In Matthew 18:20 Jesus taught that "where two or three are gathered together in my name, there am I in the midst of them." Surely this reminds us that wherever preschoolers are, they can be learning Bible truths. In each session, teachers need to be sensitive to teachable moments which occur in the department. Babies and creepers can respond to Bible pictures, songs, and conversation as they rest or play in their cribs or swings. While they are being held or rocked, they may have warm, loving experiences associated with appropriate Bible thoughts.

Toddlers may begin to understand the significance of the Bible when it is placed on the floor near the cardboard blocks. A teacher sitting on the floor may open the Bible to a picture of Jesus. When Steven stacks the blocks, his teacher says: "You are growing, Steven. See the picture of Jesus. Jesus grew, too."

Twos and threes will join a teacher singing about their activities. As Greg paints at the easel, his teacher sings: "Blue, blue paint, Oh, Greg can paint with a brush. Thank you, God, for pretty paint and brush" (tune "God Gave Me Eyes," p. 7).†

Older preschoolers enjoy walks outside their department. During Discipleship Training, Mission Friends, Preschool choir, or extended session, take a short walk when the moon and stars are shining. In a brief Bible story include the Bible thought "God gives the moon and stars for a light by night" (Jer. 31:35).

How Are Bible Thoughts, Pictures, Stories, Songs, and Conversation Used with Preschoolers?

Bible truths are transmitted to preschoolers by teachers who—
- Are growing in their personal study of the Bible;
- Understand how preschoolers learn;
- Recognize the significance of weekly workers' meetings to prepare for using the Bible in each session.

In order to give, teachers need opportunities to receive. Receiving a new insight into Bible passages renews our enthusiasm for sharing with others.

A private time for individual Bible study and meditation is an invaluable contribution to one's Christian life. You may want to follow the recommended daily Bible readings included in the teacher's periodicals *Preschool Bible Teacher A, B, or C.*** The program help *Guidelines for Bible Study for Workers with Preschoolers and Children*** offers encouragement and practical suggestions to increase your commitment to serious Bible study.

Opportunities for adult fellowship and concentrated periods of Bible study may be offered by your church during January Bible Study. Attend associational and statewide conferences or Baptist Doctrine Studies with special emphasis on Bible exposition. Glorieta and Ridgecrest Baptist Conference Centers provide inspirational sessions focusing on application of biblical truths to teaching preschoolers.

Preschoolers may learn Bible truths as they—
- Taste, touch, look, listen, and smell;
- Develop eye-hand coordination;
- Practice large motor skills;
- Interact with appropriate learning materials;
- Are challenged but not frustrated;
- Experience feelings of success and accomplishment;
- Repeat happy experiences;
- Relate to other children;
- Imitate and identify with significant adults;
- Find their physical, social, emotional, mental, and spiritual needs are being met;
- Associate positive, meaningful Bible thoughts with their experiences.

Preparing to use the Bible during each session
The significance of weekly workers' meetings in advance of each session is difficult to exaggerate. Weekly workers' meetings provide opportunities for the following:
- *Evaluation of previous sessions.*—How was the Bible used with each baby, creeper, toddler, two-, three-, four-, or five-year-old? Did Georgia pat the Bible gently as her teacher sat on the floor with the Bible in his lap? Did Eric repeat the word *Bible* when he heard his teacher singing the song "The Bible Is a Special Book" (p. 102)†††? Did three-year-old Patty name her family members when she heard the Bible story of Baby

Obed? Were four- and five-year-olds successful in matching Bible thoughts and present-day pictures?

● *Visitation assignments and sharing.*—As teachers share results of visiting in children's homes, each preschooler is better understood. Individual needs of children are more likely to be met in subsequent sessions. During home visits, five-year-olds may enjoy the book *I Go to School* by Mason. A teacher who has visited in a child's home is more likely to know the name of his school (kindergarten or day-care center). He may say, "You're growing, and the Bible says, 'Jesus grew.' "

When each teacher assumes responsibility for visitation and outreach to specific members and prospects, ministry to families is less haphazard. Needs and concerns of parents become a matter of prayerful attention by teachers. Parents can be encouraged to continue using Bible thoughts, story conversation, and prayer thoughts in the home. The quarterly home pieces *Beginning, Living, Growing,*** or *Bible Story Time Younger Pupil* and *Bible Story Time Older Pupil* may reinforce Bible truths used in a Preschool department if they are delivered to the home of each child.

● *Promotion of church-wide emphases.*—Preschool teachers will help plan teaching-learning experiences for preschoolers when adults are involved in special meetings, study courses, or revivals. Materials from the teachers' periodicals are applicable whenever preschoolers come to church. Bible truths should be included in each session.

● *Inspiration and renewal of efforts.*—Teaching is hard work. Understanding young children and their parents requires persistent dedication to the task. The plus of Bible teaching in a quality program is most likely to occur when teachers are uplifted by fellow laborers who love each other. Children are sensitive to a spirit of caring and cooperation among adults. Negative or indifferent feelings among teachers do little to promote a positive, warm introduction to Bible truths.

● *Preparation for each session.*—Follow the weekly workers' meeting suggestions and guidelines appearing in your teacher's guide (*Preschool Bible Teacher A, Preschool Bible Teacher B, Preschool Bible Teacher C, Bible Story Time Teacher, The Music Leader,*** or *Start****). Note the Bible teaching aim for each session. As you study, complete a department plan sheet for workers with babies, creepers, and toddlers; twos and threes; or fours and fives.

Become familiar with biblically-related resources suggested in *Preschool Bible Teacher A.* Use these at appropriate times with individual babies, creepers, and toddlers during each session. Practice singing recommended songs. Think of a specific child and situation in which you plan to use each Bible thought.

Pray as you study the Bible background material provided in *Preschool Bible Teacher B* and *Preschool Bible Teacher C.*** Review the suggested Bible thoughts and Bible story. As you prepare materials for activities, note how Bible truths can be taught through art, blocks, homeliving, music, nature, and puzzles. Adapt the suggestions to fit the children in your department.

When you prepare for a group time experience for threes, fours, and fives, practice telling the Bible story. Appropriate songs, games, and relaxation before and after the Bible story will encourage children to listen attentively.

Planning for each session includes preparation for extended session. Remember that some children will only experience the extended session while their parents attend the worship service. Careful preparation is required if all children are to have a positive, meaningful experience while learning Bible truths.

Summary

The significance of the Bible in a Christian's life is readily acknowledged. Growing spiritually requires regular study and daily application of biblical principles. To fail to read and heed the Bible's message is to limit our effectiveness as teachers. What we say to children is important. What we do with children is more important. What we are as Christian teachers is infinitely more important. This chapter has looked at why the Bible is used with preschoolers. Which Bible thoughts can be understood by each specific age group has been considered. When and where to use Bible thoughts, pictures, stories, songs, and conversation has been discussed. Appropriate methods to use in communicating Bible truths to preschoolers have been explored.

Personal Learning Activities

1. Read the program help *Guidelines for Bible Study for Workers with Preschoolers and Children.*** Decide on a time, place, and method to proceed with your personal Bible study.

2. If your department does not have an appropriate Bible, purchase a copy of the Holman *Read-to-Me Bible.** This Bible contains 44 Bible stories, 36 full-color illustrations, and special helps for parents and teachers of preschoolers.

Materials for Further Study
Filmstrip
How to Use the Bible with Preschoolers

Free Help
Davis, Cos. *How a Preschooler Learns About God.*

Books
Caldwell, Max. *Witness to Win* (chapter 5). Nashville Convention Press, 1977.

Haystead, Wesley. *You Can't Begin Too Soon: Guiding Little Ones to God.* Glendale, California: Regal, 1974.

Uland, Zadabeth. *Bible Teaching for Preschoolers.* Nashville: Convention Press, 1984.

Waldrop, Sybil. *Moral and Spiritual Development.* Nashville: Broadman Press, 1982.

Ligon, E. M., L. W. Barber, and H. J. Williams. *Looking at Me.* Nashville: Broadman Press, 1979.

---

*Available from Baptist Book Stores.

**Available by writing Customer Service Center, 127 Ninth Avenue, North, Nashville, Tennessee 37234; or by calling toll free 1-800-458-2772.

***Available from Woman's Missionary Union, P.O. Box 830010, Birmingham, Alabama 35283-0010.

Chapter 13—How to Lead Group-Time Experiences

S. Alfred Foy

Is group time needed? Is group time important? How can group time be effective and not chaotic? Some directors feel that group time is a waste of time since children are sometimes hard to "manage." Other directors are heard to say, "Let us get through our play, so that we can get to the learning activities."

What Is Group Time?

Group time is a time when teachers and children gather for teaching-learning experiences. These experiences may include singing songs, playing games, looking at pictures, using the Bible, praying, and hearing a Bible story. A short group time is recommended for a three-year department. A longer group time is planned for a four- or five-year department. The activities of group time give children opportunities for self-expression. At the same time, children are learning to work and cooperate in a group effort. Every activity planned should contribute to the child's physical, mental, social, emotional, and spiritual development.

Who Is Involved in Group Time?

People are social beings. They usually enjoy doing things with others. Threes, fours, and fives are beginning to become more aware of other people. They are beginning to relate positively to other children and adults.

Group time contributes to the children's social development, providing opportunities for them to do things together. The child is encouraged to follow directions and take turns. Thus, he is beginning to be more aware of the rights and interests of others.

Group time provides opportunities for cognitive (capable of being reduced to factual knowledge) learning experiences. The activities are more structured and the child is not given as much freedom of choice. However, group time needs to be flexible to allow for the children's interests and needs.

The following factors must be considered as group-time plans are made:

- Three-, four-, and five-year-olds like to do things. They want to be a part of "where the action is."
- The older preschooler is active and finds it hard to sit still very long.

- The preschooler is able to think for himself; however, he does not think like an adult.
- Children ages three, four, and five like to talk, but they also like to listen.
- Even though the child enjoys time alone, he also likes to work with others.
- Group time provides opportunities for developing listening skills.
- Group time provides moments of quiet meditation and awe and wonder on the child's level. Group time gives preschoolers some opportunities for corporate "worship" experiences; however, group time should not be designed to be a miniature worship service. Worship is a conscious communion with God, and most preschoolers are not mature enough to make this choice. Group time is also not to be thought of as preparation for worship service attendance. Even though some of the same elements of a church worship service are used, the child is not "preparing to worship."
- Group time should give the child opportunities to sit, stand, touch pictures, hold the Bible, listen to recordings, "read" Bible thoughts, listen to a Bible story, play games, sing, talk to God, and talk about things of interest to him.

Even though group time contributes to the child's total growth, this segment of the session is *not* necessarily the most important part of the session. Group time does serve as a time to enhance learning that has taken place during activities.

When Is Group Time Conducted?

Group time is best planned for the last part of the session. The amount of time designated is dependent upon the children's maturity and attention span. A maximum five- to ten-minute group time is recommended for threes; fours can participate in a fifteen-minute group time; and twenty to twenty-five minutes is recommended for five-year-olds. The time segment for group time may be gradually extended throughout the year up to the maximum indicated for each age.

Chronological age may not always be the determining factor for the length of group time. Since growth and maturity rates of children vary, the interest and experience of the group must also be considered in determining the length of group time.

Where Is Group Time Conducted?

Group time should take place in the same room in which the children were involved in activities. A smaller room may need some rearrangement of furniture to provide adequate space for group time. Tables and other furniture can be pushed against the wall. The best place for group time is facing the longest wall in the room. The children should not face the door. Arrange chairs for children and teachers in a semicircle. The director sits in the center of the semicircle. Group time begins as soon as one or two children arrive at the semicircle. The children and other teachers sit in the semicircle so that no child is sitting behind another child. Children and teachers can bring chairs from the activity areas and help form a semicircle. The semicircle arrangement gives each child eye contact with the director. This arrangement also allows some space for moving about. A semicircle gives children a feeling of not being crowded.

Group time can also be effective with children sitting on the floor. Children can sit on a carpet, an area rug, or individual mats.

All teachers need to be involved in the group. Teachers sit with the children rather than behind them. They participate in group-time activities without monopolizing conversation. Teachers sing with the children. They listen to the Bible and play games. Teachers take part in prayer time as requested by the director.

How Does the Director Handle the Transition Between Activities and Group Time?

The transition period between activities and group time is very important. Children need time to complete activities they have begun. They need time to put away materials and clean up spills. An unhurried transition contributes much to the success of group time. The director informs the children and teachers in each area that it is time to stop activities and come to the group. The children are not required to bring Bibles, home books, or other materials to group time.

As she moves from activity to activity, Mrs. Green may quietly say: "When you have finished your painting, it will be time for group time." "Sam, we need helpers to put away the blocks so we can have group time. Let's stack all the long blocks like this. James can stack all of the short blocks on the next shelf." Similar instructions and encouragement can be given in each activity area. Be patient as children work to put away materials. If chairs are used in group time, the child can bring a chair to the group-time area.

Singing songs such as the following helps the child feel good about what he is doing to help.

"Susan is a helper, Susan is a helper.

She is putting up the blocks.

Susan is a helper" (Tune "I Will Be a Helper," p. 10).††

Learning continues during the transition. Children should not feel there is a break between activities and group time.

A clear understanding of where to put materials helps children do a better job. Using instructions such as: "Hurry and put up the dishes" or "You've only got a few minutes to finish the puzzle" may confuse the child and produce careless work. The statement, "In five minutes it will be time for group time" does not mean a great deal to a preschooler with his limited concept of time.

As teachers and children complete activities and put away materials, the department director gathers materials to use in group time. Mrs. Green, the director, takes her place in the center of the semicircle with

all the materials she will need for group time. As children come to the group-time area, the director begins an activity with them. Suggested transitional activities may include some of the following:

- Conversing about activities;
- Talking about the children—what they are wearing, how they are growing, ways they helped during activities;
- Playing name recognition games;
- Listening and participating with an activity recording such as *Walk in a Circle**;
- Playing games recognizing colors, shapes, and friends;
- Playing guessing games—guess what is missing;
- Singing songs such as "There's No One Exactly Like Me," (p. 12),†† using a child's name instead of the word *me*;
- Making up additional words to a familiar song such as "I'm Growing," p. 30†. Sing: "We can put on all our clothes," or "We can reach up very high";
- Playing instruments;
- Moving to music;

Elements of a good group time
- Singing (Music).—Singing is a vital part of group time. Singing a familiar song is one way to unify the group. Children enjoy singing songs which they know. Sometimes the director can sing a new song for the children and then ask them to sing the song; however, new songs are best introduced during activities, giving the children several opportunities to hear the song.

Singing songs can be done at any time during the group time. It is usually best, however, to sing a song near the beginning of group time. Songs can be used to introduce the Bible story. A song can be sung after showing a picture or after conversation. Sometimes the children may suggest songs to sing. At other times a song may be used as a prayer.

A piano is not necessary to accompany the singing. If a piano is in the room, it should be a studio-sized piano and in tune. The pianist should be one of the teachers in the department. An Autoharp or ChromAharP provides an effective accompaniment for singing in group time; however, children can often learn and use a song more quickly as they listen to the director sing unaccompanied. Encourage the children to listen as the song is sung. Then say, "Sing all of the words you can remember." Avoid drilling on the words of the song. Sing the entire song so that the children can learn all of it.

Be familiar with the song so you can sing it without the songbook.

Introduce the song informally. "That Bible verse reminds me of a song." Start singing the song without telling the children the title of the song.

Use only two songs in succession.

Sing the song without expecting the children to sing; then ask the children to sing with you.

Use the song rather than *teach* the song.

Grouping all the music activities into a "music period" is not the best procedure. Asking a musician to come to the room and "have the music" is not desirable. Songs chosen for group time should relate to the focus for the session. Avoid motions with songs that deal with spiritual concepts; otherwise the children will concentrate more on the motions than the biblical truths. Motion songs can be used for relaxation; however, the motions should be natural and not symbolic.

A child may have difficulty singing with a recording until he knows the song well; however, a recording of a song can be an effective means of introducing the song. Recordings provide opportunities for listening experiences. Recordings are also a good source of relaxation songs and activities.

Using only one song at a time on a recording is recommended. A good manually-operated record player is recommended for use in the room.

Simple percussion instruments can be used with songs. Use only a few instruments at a time. Two or three children can play instruments while the other children sing.

Show a child how to play an instrument before he is given the instrument to play. Be selective about the instruments that are used with a song. Use instruments that enhance a song and make it sound musical. Children can take turns playing the instruments. Suggested instruments to use in group time include: Autoharp, ChromAharP, resonator bells (use only selected bells), step bells, drums, triangle, cymbals, finger cymbals, rhythm sticks, wood block, tone block, sand blocks, tambourine, and bells (wrist, loop, stick, and jingle clogs).

● *Conversation.*—Talking and listening are important parts of group time. "I want to tell you something" is the desire of most young children. Teachers need to be willing to listen. Children become more aware of others as they listen to other children talk about their experiences. Listening to the child, the director may learn—

● What the child is like,
● How the child feels,
● What the child thinks,
● What the child has done,
● What the child may do,
● Questions the child wants to ask,
● How to meet the child's needs.

The children should feel that they are expected to talk and that the director is interested in what they have to say. The director sets an example for the children to follow when he listens without interrupting. The child has a natural desire for self-expression. Opportunities to express his thoughts and feelings to a willing listener may help the child feel that he is important.

Conversation can be about an activity related to the child, related to a song or picture, or about natural happenings.

- *Prayer.*—Opportunities for children and teachers to talk to God need to be scheduled during group time; however, the best prayer experiences are spontaneous. A "prayer time" is difficult to plan with preschoolers.

The director may suggest: "I feel like saying thank you to God for my friends. Would you like to pray?" Encourage children to pray using their own thoughts and words. Never correct a child's prayer.

The use of quiet music may help create a mood for prayer. Or after telling the Bible story, the children may be in a prayerful mood. After reading thoughts from the Bible, children may want to talk to God.

Most of the prayers of preschoolers are thank-you prayers. The child needs to be encouraged to feel that prayer is important. The children learn to pray from adult examples. The words "Thank you, God" mean more to a child than the words "We thank thee." Hearing a teacher pray in the child's language helps a child know how to pray. Teachers need to be careful to direct prayers to God. Children may be confused with an interchange of *God* and *Jesus* in a prayer. Use only a few sentences to help the child feel more confident in expressing what he feels.

Ask children to volunteer to pray; then call on the volunteers, giving them an order to follow. "Ben may talk to God first; then it will be Marie's turn. I will pray last." Do not call on a child to pray unless he volunteers. Every child who wants to pray should be given the opportunity.

Children should not be expected to assume a position when praying or repeat the words of the teacher's prayer. The director may say: "Most people like to close their eyes when they pray. I am going to close my eyes; you may want to close your eyes, too."

The director who has experienced the naturalness of a child's prayer will find this a rewarding and refreshing experience.

- *Telling the Bible story.*—Effective telling of the Bible story may help impress upon the child's mind the importance of the story. These elements contribute to an effectively told story:
  1. Sit in a child-sized chair or on the floor.
  2. Establish eye contact with the children.
  3. Avoid use of props while telling the story (puppets, flannel-graphs, and pictures) because preschoolers will be mainly concerned about the props and miss the biblical truth.
  4. Avoid use of gestures.
  5. Introduce the story carefully. Use conversation, a picture, or a song to stimulate interest before telling the story.
  6. Open the Bible to the correct reference for the story before you begin the story.
  7. Begin the story without using the title.
  8. Know the story well enough so that you do not need notes.
  9. Practice telling the story prior to the session.
  10. Talk softly, slowly, and distinctly in a low-pitched voice.

184

11. Include a child's name to hold his interest in the story. For example, "John, the shepherds were excited over the angel's news." This is also a good way to involve a child who is not listening or who interrupts.
12. Pause for a few seconds after telling the story to give children an opportunity to respond and ask questions.
13. After telling the story, show a picture related to the story. Ask children to tell what is happening in the picture, or ask children to name the characters in the picture. Never hold a picture for the children to look at while telling the Bible story because the children will concentrate on the picture and miss the biblical truths in the story.
14. Tell the story using these four points:
    a. *A good beginning to catch the interest of the listeners.*—Introduce the leading characters. Establish the answers to the questions who, why, and where.
    b. *A natural series of events, with each event in the story presenting a clear and complete picture.*—Use words to inspire imagery. Cause the listener to want to know what happens next. The events should be in correct sequence, and one event should lead into the next event.
    c. *A strong climax.*—The events should lead to the climatic event or the high point of the story.
    d. *A conclusion.*—After the climax, the story should quickly conclude. Avoid moralizing. Let the story speak for itself. Pause after telling the story to give the children an opportunity to think about the story.

Preparing to tell the Bible story
Study chapter 3, "How to Teach Through Story Conversation and Stories." When preparing for a session, read the story as printed in the teacher's guide at least two times; then close the teacher's guide. Try to think of the central Bible truths emphasized in the story. Recall the main characters, places, and events. Open the teacher's guide and read the story again, making mental note of the sequence of events and conversation; then tell the story aloud. Read the printed version again to see if you included important facts, characters, and events. Tell the story aloud again. You may want to tape the story using a cassette recorder. Listen to the tape and make notes of areas that need improvement. Do not try to memorize the printed version of the story. Think of ways you can make the story exciting and natural sounding.

Using the Bible.—The director needs to leave the Bible opened to the correct reference for the Bible story while telling the story. The child can sense and see that the basis for the story comes from the Bible.

The Bible needs to be accessible to every child to hold and look at during activities and group time. The child should be allowed to handle the Bible. As the director uses Bible thoughts with the children, they should be encouraged to look at the shaded verse in the Bible. A good practice is to mark all Bible thoughts in the Bible used during group time with a colored lead pencil or a fluorescent marker. Where wording differs from the King James version, write in the margin the words to be used with the children.

Simple and colorful Bible markers can be made using two-inch gros-grain (a strong close-woven corded fabric usually of silk, rayon, or cotton) ribbon or colored construction paper strips. The child can be asked to choose a marker or find a marker of a particular color. Open the Bible to the marked verse, point to the words, and read them to the child and the group. The child or the group may repeat the Bible thought. However, mere repetition of the words does not assure the child's understanding of the verse.

Bible-related conversation about the Bible story and Bible thoughts helps the child become more aware of the importance of the Bible. Looking at the printed words may impress upon the child that the words he hears are found in the Bible. Avoid giving rewards for learning Bible thoughts. Children learn Bible thoughts as they discover that the thought helps them know what to do. *Preschool Bible Teacher A, Preschool Bible Teacher B, Preschool Bible Teacher C, Bible Story Time Teacher, The Music Leader,*** and *Start**** do not designate memory verses. Selected Bible thoughts are used session after session, providing repetition for the child.

Using pictures.—All pictures used in the room should be on the child's eye level. For example, during group time, place the pictures used in departments for older preschoolers on the picture rail. If pictures are placed on a tackboard, place rolled masking tape on the back of each picture. Pictures may also be propped against the wall on the floor. Children enjoy touching and holding pictures.

Pictures can be used in group time to stimulate interest in the Bible story; relate to a Bible thought; illustrate a song; provide information for the children, more clearly impressing upon them the desired thought; prompt conversation about positive actions; and give the child a greater awareness of the natural world.

Possible picture activities may include:

- Designate a child to hold a picture and take the picture from child to child for them to see.
- Ask a preschooler to come and place his finger on a named object or person in the picture. Say, "Which person in the picture do you think is David?"
- Ask a child to match a Bible thought and picture. Ask, "Can you see a picture that reminds you of the Bible thought _____?"
- Use pictures for story recall. Ask: "What is happening in the picture?" "Who are the people in this picture?" "What do you think happened before what you see in this picture?" "What do you think will happen next?"
- Ask children to look at the picture and tell something about it.
- Use a picture to think of a song to sing.

186

- Give a clue and ask the children to find the picture matching that clue.
- Stimulate a child's thinking about the picture. Say: "I see a picture of a family enjoying the outdoors. Can you find that picture?"
- Participate in a picture walk. Walk in small groups to find pictures placed around the room. Stop at a picture. Look at it. Then sing a song, recall a Bible story, use a Bible thought, or just talk about the picture.
- Ask several children to hold pictures. Read or quote a Bible thought. The children try to decide who has the picture that matches the Bible thought.
- Plan an activity with "picture posing."—Ask the children to assume the positions of the characters in the picture.

Games and relaxation.—A relaxation game gives children opportunities to release muscular tension. A well-planned game can be a learning experience as well as a relaxation. For example, a picture walk encourages conversation about the displayed pictures while the children move about the room. Use games for a specific purpose. Sometimes relaxation is needed, but let the game be a means to an end and not the actual end.

A game used early in group time may help the children feel at ease. A game may encourage a shy child to participate in the group. Games may help develop a group feeling. Games provide opportunities to recognize visitors and new members. A game may help children learn the names of the other children.

A game can serve as a unifying activity to maintain the children's interest. For example, play a game at the end of the session as children begin to leave with their parents.

Games give children opportunities to practice taking turns, being thoughtful, and calling names. Select games carefully to avoid overstimulation. Avoid using the same game too often over a period of time. Select games to use inside that make the least possible noise, remembering that some noise is to be expected. Select games which have few rules and do not have a winner.

Types of games to consider include:

- Name games,
- Pretend games,
- Guessing games,
- Relaxation games,
- Story recall games,
- Riddles,
- Leader games,
- Song games,
- Recordings.

Group time for three-year-olds

Since the attention span of a three-year-old is very short, start with a short two- or three-minute group time at the beginning of the year. Then increase the time spent in group time gradually, to a maximum of ten minutes by the end of the year. A five-minute, fast-paced group time is recommended.

Although the same elements are used in group time for threes, do not attempt to use all of the elements each session.

Sit on the floor for group time with threes to create a more informal setting. The children should not be expected to stay in a perfectly formed semicircle. Allow for squirming and interruptions from the children.

The Bible story is used with the children during activities. During group time, the director can retell the story. Capitalize on the children's interest and wanting to add story details. Keep their interest in the story recall by weaving the child's name into the discussions before the story.

When children become tired and restless, conclude group-time activities and move to other activities in the room. If group time is held at the end of the first session, teachers can help children begin to take turns using the rest room in preparation for snacks during the extended session.

Handling problems during group time

Some problems may surface during group time. For example, Mark and Walter always become rowdy when sitting beside each other. Separate the two boys at the beginning of group time by asking a teacher to sit between them, or play a "change places" game to place children where they will not be tempted to be disruptive.

The director should not have to stop group-time activities to correct a behavior problem. Other teachers can move to the children when the

problem occurs and take steps to correct the disruption.

Sometimes a child may refuse to take part in group time. A hesitant child should not be forced to come to group time. Allow the child to sit quietly away from the group. He should not be allowed to play with activity materials. The child is given the choice of being a part of the group or sitting quietly and observing. A teacher may want to quietly encourage the child to become a part of the group.

Interruptions from children are to be expected during group time. These interruptions may communicate that the child is bored, interested, curious, does not understand, or needs clarification on a certain point. The child should feel free to interrupt; however, the director may say to the child: "Thank you. We need to talk about that. Will you remind me to talk about _____ when we are through with our Bible story?" The director needs to decide whether the interruption is a sincere attempt to gain more information or if the child is deliberately being mischievous. Weave the child's name and his interruption back into the group-time plans.

Sometimes group time is chaotic because children are not interested in what is going on. Ask yourself these questions:

• Have the children been sitting for a long time? If the answer is yes, then involve them in a relaxation game or activity.

• Am I trying to "cover material" rather than help children learn? Evaluate your approach. Did you begin with the children's needs and interests in mind?

• Is group time fast paced? If children do not seem interested in a planned activity, move immediately to the next activity. Be flexible and shift plans to accommodate the interest and mood of the children. You may try the activity later in the group time.

Summary

Remember that:

- Group time is a time when children are just beginning to develop social skills. Be patient. Do not expect them to do everything you want them to do during the first few sessions.
- The best plans may not always work. Plan alternate activities that can be used.
- Children should not be expected to sit still during group time. Expect wiggling, squirming, and talking.
- Be calm. Speak softly and clearly. Give simple and complete instructions about what the children are to do.
- Children learn more from a director's attitude than from what the director might say. Do you exemplify a Christian attitude?
- The last activity is a transitional activity. Teachers from the first session will be leaving as extended session teachers arrive, or parents arrive to get their child. Ask parents not to enter the room, but to knock on the door. A teacher should gently tap the child on the shoulder and take him to the door. Gather his personal belongings and artwork for him to take home. Avoid loud talking at the door. The other children can continue playing a game. Continue the game until only one or two children remain. Then ask these children to help straighten the room and put away materials until their parents arrive. Do not allow a child to leave the room without his parents or another adult who has been previously designated to come for the child.

Listening to activity recordings, reading a book, looking at a filmstrip, and playing a guessing game are examples of good closing activities.

After all the children have gone, the director and teachers should check the room to see that all materials have been put away. The room needs to be ready for the next group to use.

Personal Learning Activities

1. List two values of group-time experiences.
2. Name the elements that may be effectively used in group time.
3. Think about group time in your department. What are some ways you can improve its effectiveness?

Materials for Further Study

Waldrop, C. Sybil. *Understanding Today's Preschoolers.* Nashville: Convention Press, 1982.

Uland, Zadabeth. *Bible Teaching for Preschoolers.* Nashville: Convention Press, 1984.

Terrell, Jerry. *Basic Preschool Work.* Nashville: Convention Press, 1981.

---

*Available from Baptist Book Stores.

**Available by writing Customer Service Center, 127 Ninth Avenue, North, Nashville, Tennessee 37234; or by calling toll free 1-800-458-2772.

***Available from Woman's Missionary Union, P.O. Box 830010, Birmingham, Alabama 35283-0010.

Chapter 14—How to Teach Through the Use of Audiovisuals

Helen Young

The word *audiovisuals* includes an extensive number of items that involve the sense of hearing and the sense of sight in teaching and learning. The general use of the word in this chapter applies to tape recorders, tape players (many machines both record and play), and tapes; filmstrip projectors, filmstrips, and filmslips (short filmstrips); slide projectors and slides; motion picture projectors and films. Teaching pictures, record players, and recordings are mentioned only incidentally, since their use is dealt with in chapters 4 and 9. Some smaller audiovisual-type materials are also mentioned.

Many churches have media centers stocked with audiovisual equipment and materials. Persons who serve there can train teachers to use audiovisuals. Media center personnel usually are glad to have suggestions about items to purchase. Churches who do not have audiovisual equipment can borrow these items from neighboring churches or state or associational offices. Using audiovisuals that have recently been produced for preschoolers will increase teaching opportunities.

Why Use Audiovisuals with Preschoolers?

If available educational media are helpful to preschoolers, it is the responsibility of their teachers at church to use these media to make Bible truths more meaningful.

Preschoolers learn much through their senses of sight and hearing. New types of equipment and material create new interest in learning.

Pictures rapidly increase knowledge and appeal to young children. There often is added interest when all or part of a visual moves.

Learning to listen is a skill with which young children need help. Some audio materials for preschoolers encourage them to listen and to respond verbally, physically, or visually.

Who Uses Audiovisuals That Correspond with the Abilities of the Child?

A baby, creeper, toddler, or two-year-old usually responds positively to soft music arranged to create happy moods. The baby in a bed may respond only with an attitude of contentment. The facial expression of a creeper may show surprise when there is an abrupt change in the intensity of recorded sound. The toddler may respond with happy, springing motions to some types of music. Appropriate tapes used on a

tape player are useful as background music in all Preschool rooms.

During the last three or four months that a child is in a room for twos, he may be able to give attention while one, two, or three frames of a filmslip are shown. A filmstrip projector and a filmslip with frames that have meaning without being used as a part of a story may be shown in a department for older twos.

A three-year-old may be encouraged to say a few words into a tape recorder. If this happens, hearing his voice played back delights him. He may also listen to animal sounds one at a time and learn to match each animal sound with a corresponding picture of that animal. Such sounds may be on a vinyl recording for a record player or a cassette tape.

A three-year-old may enjoy five or six frames of a filmslip.

The four- or five-year-old can learn from filmstrips that are arranged in story form. He also can profit from an occasional ten-minute film, if he is familiar with situations similar to those pictured.

Slides shown with a projector or slide viewer are interesting and helpful to an older preschooler. The child can operate some projectors and viewers.

Which Audiovisuals Are Available for Preschoolers?

The Church Audiovisual Equipment Plan (CAVE Plan) of The Sunday School Board makes audiovisuals available to churches at very reasonable prices. For details, write Broadman Sales, MSN 120, 127 Ninth Avenue, North, Nashville, Tennessee 37234. A good supply of tapes, filmstrips, and films suitable for use with preschoolers are available through this plan.

Filmstrips are available through Baptist Book Stores; films are available through Baptist Film Centers. A few filmstrips that Baptist Book Stores carry can also be ordered by using the Undated Form. This form accompanies the church literature Dated Form, used to order Sunday School, Church Training, and Church Music periodicals. A limited supply of audiovisual materials that are coordinated with curriculum units are also in *Preschool Bible Teacher A Resource Kit,*** *Preschool Bible Teacher B Resource Kit (2's & 3's),*** *Preschool Bible Teacher C Resource Kit (4's & 5's),*** and *Bible Story Time Teacher Resource Kits,*** which are listed on the church literature Dated Form along with Preschool periodicals.

Audiovisual materials desirable for preschoolers include:
Collections of songs that may be used as background music
- *Music for Preschool A* (cassette for tape player)*—for use with babies, creepers, and toddlers
- *Music for Preschool B* (cassette)*—for use with twos and threes
- *Music for Preschool C* (cassette)*—for use with fours and fives
- *Preschool Music Recording*—for use with fours and fives
Collections of musical numbers that help create a restful mood—
- *Music for Rest Time* (cassette)*—for use with all preschoolers

- *Hymns for Quiet Times* (recording or cassette)*—for use with all pre-schoolers
- *Songs for the Young Child,* Vol. 1-4 (recordings)*
- *Songs for the Young Child,* Nos. 1-2 (cassettes)*
- *More Songs for 4's and 5's,* Vol. 1-4 (recordings)*
- *Sea Gulls: Music for Rest and Relaxation* (recording)*
Filmstrips—for use with fours and fives
- *God's Plan for People* (with cassette)*; (with vinyl recording)*
- *Myself and Others* (with cassette)*; (with recording)*
- *Living in God's World* (with vinyl recording)*
- "God Cares for You" Series (four filmstrips with recordings)*
- "Community Helpers" Series 1 (four filmstrips with cassettes)*
- "Community Helpers" Series 2 (four filmstrips with cassettes)*
- Stories About the Seasons" Series
- "Stories About Families" Series
Films—for use with fours and fives
- *Seeing God in Signs of Love****
- *Seeing God in Mountain Forests****
- "God's Wonders" Series (thirteen films)***
Collection of sounds for listening activities—for use with threes, fours, and fives
- *Discovering Sounds in My World* (cassette—home, church, work, transportation, animal sounds)*
Collections of Slides—for use with fours and fives
- Personal or purchased slides: animals, flowers, church buildings, houses, animal homes, seasonal pictures of a tree, children of various nationalities, and objects seen on nature walks
Miscellaneous items
- Shake 'n Roll Rattles, soft-sounding bells, wind chimes, and colorful mobiles—for use with babies
- Musical toys that play soft, happy music—for use with babies and creepers
- Push and pull toys that make interesting sounds when they roll—for use by toddlers
- Slide viewer—for use with fours and fives
- Battery-operated hand viewers with discs on which miniature slides are mounted around the edges—for use with fours and fives
- Singer/Broadman Study Mate II**** (shows on the machine magnified frames of a filmstrip)—for use with fours and fives

When Are Audiovisuals Used with Preschoolers?

There is seldom a time during a session when some kind of audiovisual could not be used with any Preschool group. Some teachers show a filmstrip on the ceiling during rest/listening time and some use musical activity recordings during outdoor time. Since the battery-operated hand viewer is small, its use is limited to individuals or small groups of children. Hand viewers are best used during activities. It is difficult to conduct other activities while a film is being shown; therefore, motion pictures are usually shown during group time.

Where Are Audiovisuals Used in Preschool Departments?

Audiovisual equipment and materials usually are not kept in Preschool rooms when not in use. If they are stored in the church media center or the central storage area for Preschool materials, the items will be safer and will be available to other teachers.

Babies, creepers, or toddlers cannot be expected to take care of a tape player. It should be placed out of reach of a child, but where teachers can operate it easily. When a teacher uses a tape player with one child or a small group, he takes it close to those involved, but protects the tape player from damage.

A flower rattle is placed in the bed with a baby, close enough for him to reach the rattle. Soft-sounding bells are placed where teachers can get the bells easily, but out of reach of the baby, if the bells have surfaces on which a baby could hurt himself. Wind chimes are hung securely at adult height in a place where clappers can swing freely. A toy that plays when a string is pulled is tied firmly to the side of the baby's bed so that he can reach the string. A mobile is fastened tightly to the bed where the baby can see it when he lies on his back.

Push and pull toys that make interesting sounds are placed on the floor in rooms for toddlers.

The filmstrip projector is placed out of reach of a two- or three-year-old when the equipment is not in use. When a filmstrip is shown, the projector is put on the floor three to five feet from a smooth, clean wall which serves as a screen while a teacher operates the projector. If a narration on a vinyl recording is used, the record player is placed on the floor close enough for the teacher to operate it.

How Do Teachers Guide Preschoolers Toward Constructive Experiences with Audiovisuals?

Most of the audiovisual learning activities for preschoolers are primarily teacher-directed, since most of the equipment is mechanical. With adequate supervision some preschoolers can, however, start and stop a tape player, turn the knob of a filmstrip projector, or put slides in a slide projector. When such help is possible, the child's feelings of self-worth may be improved because he is showing what he can do.

The baby can look at and shake a bell rattle. A teacher can enrich the experience by saying: "God gave you hands so you can shake things like the bell rattle. God gave you ears so you can hear noises." Touch the baby's hand that holds the bell rattle as the word *hand* is said and one of the baby's ears when the word *ear* is said. With such actions a teacher may help a baby to associate the name "God" with happy experiences.

A younger preschooler who is encouraged to pull the cord that makes a musical toy play may become more self-confident because of his

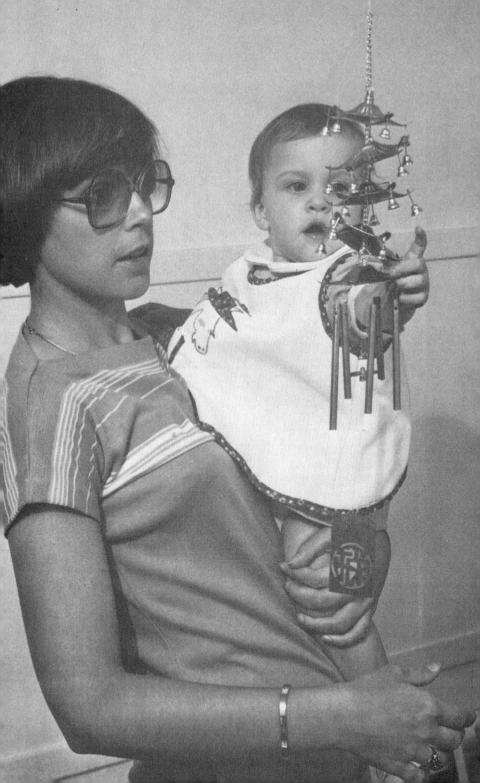

achievement. A teacher saying with a prayerful attitude, "Thank you, God, for Burt's hands," may create an atmosphere of awe and wonder in the area. If Burt shows delight by a smile, an expression of awe, squeals, or quick hand or leg movements, a teacher has a good opportunity to approve what the child has done by saying, "Burt made the Bluebird Music Box play!"

If Burt cannot pull the string on the musical toy, the teacher may do so. The child will then have music to enjoy for a while because of the thoughtfulness of a person who loves him. If the child shows signs of happiness because of the music, the teacher may say, "The music makes Burt happy!"

Babies and toddlers may be shown a picture as a corresponding animal sound is played on a tape recorder. The teacher may say: "God made the dog. The dog says 'bowwow.' " The tape recorder may then be stopped and the teacher may sing: "Doggy, doggy, Bow-wow-wow; Doggy, doggy, Bow-wow-wow; thank you, God; thank you for my doggy."

As a two- or three-year-old listens to a tape of animal sounds, he may be able to identify each of four to six pictures of animals that make corresponding sounds. If he cannot do this, a teacher may point to each picture as the sound that the animal makes is heard on the tape. Then the child may be given the opportunity to match each picture to a sound. A teacher may comment: "God made the animals. He made each kind of animal so that it can make its own kind of sound. God gave us ears to hear the animals."

A four- or five-year-old may be able to identify sounds without pictures. The cassette tape *Discovering Sounds in My World*** may be used for this activity, or a tape on which a teacher has previously recorded sounds may be used. Small rocks being shaken in a box, tin pans rattling against each other, whistles and horns being blown, persons walking in heavy boots, light switches clicking, bells ringing, and sand being shaken in a box are sounds that older preschoolers like and with which they are familiar.

Older preschoolers can help make tapes to use for activities. Each of the musical instruments children use may be played one at a time while a tape recorder is turned on; then all of the children can have a turn telling about the sounds. Fours and fives may have a deeper understanding of God after such an experience if the teacher says, "I'm glad God gives us minds so we can remember."

"I need some music," four-year-old Chris said as he got up from the floor where he had been building with blocks. A tape recorder was not in the room, so the teacher helped Chris put a recording on the record player. Listening to the recording seemed to meet a need in Chris' life. Most preschoolers feel such needs, but few can recognize and express this feeling as Chris did. The three tapes *Music for Preschool A, Music for Preschool B,* and *Music for Preschool C*** contain songs that can be used in Preschool rooms.

*Music for Rest Time** is a cassette tape which carries a collection of songs that are conducive to rest. A slightly darkened room, rest mats on the floor, and music such as that on the rest time tape help preschoolers and teachers relax during rest time.

If filmslips and filmstrips are used during group time, reading the narration or saying the narration from memory may be better than using a recording or tape. Children are familiar with the voices of their teachers; they may not understand all that was said by a person who read the narration for the recording. Best results usually come when one teacher operates the projector and another narrates. The children can hear better if the teacher who is narrating sits at the front of the room facing the boys and girls. Usually there is sufficient light from the projected picture for the reader to see well enough to read. The teacher can form the habit of looking at the picture after the narration that goes with a frame is read. This is a signal to the operator to turn to the next frame. The teacher who reads can check to see that the narration he is about to read matches the frame. The same filmslip or filmstrip may be used two or three times during a year. The value of a filmslip or filmstrip often increases as children become more familiar with its content.

As a filmslip or a filmstrip is being introduced, older preschoolers may be asked to watch for situations or items shown in the filmstrip. If the filmstrip to be shown is *God's Plan for People,* part 1*, older preschoolers may be asked to watch for things that children did at Andy's church. After seeing the filmstrip, the children may be asked to tell what they saw children doing at Andy's church. If the filmstrip *Living in God's World,** Part 1 is to be shown, older preschoolers may be asked to name parts of their bodies that help them learn. Frequently, a teacher does not have a follow-up activity after a filmslip or a filmstrip is shown. Like a good story that is well told, some audiovisual materials carry the message the teacher wants emphasized and a related activity is not necessary. If a filmstrip is being viewed by only a few and if the narration is read, there can be discussion from frame to frame.

Slides may be used in teaching older preschoolers. Conversation about each slide naturally takes place as they are shown. Slides are most helpful when arranged by groups and when only one of these groups of slides is shown during one session. For instance, one group may deal with the church which the child attends. This group may include slides of the church building, church staff members, the Preschool rooms at church, activities in an older Preschool department, church friends of different ages, and people involved in some special church projects.

The picture on a slide is placed upside down in the projector; therefore, a teacher prepares them to plainly show which side of the slide goes in the projector.

A slide viewer is used by the child himself or with the help of a teacher who looks at each slide, tells the child something about the slide, and then lets the child view the slide. If there are two or three children using the slide viewer, each child has a turn to look before the slide is changed. A portable projector can be used by a small group without turn taking, since three or four can see a frame at once.

Audiovisuals suggested in this chapter can enrich teaching. They all relate to the present-day lives of the children. No Bible story audiovisual materials are suggested, for it is important that a *teacher* tell the Bible story. (In departments for older preschoolers, this teacher is usually the department director and the story is one element of group time procedure.) There is no better way to communicate the message of a Bible story than to live by it. The teacher should sit with the Bible open to the

background passage, look directly into each child's eyes, and in a natural voice tell a well-prepared Bible story. The Bible story should undergird the session focus and the month's Bible teaching aim. As helpful as audiovisuals are, the teacher is the best visual aid.

Summary
From the time a child is first brought to church, he learns through the senses of hearing and seeing; therefore, some types of audiovisuals, from mobiles and rattles for babies to motion pictures for older preschoolers, can be used with each age group.

Audiovisuals can enrich Preschool learning experiences when appropriate materials are available for each group. Many churches have audiovisual equipment that can be used in Preschool rooms. Media center personnel perhaps will order suggested materials to use with the equipment; listings in this book may guide in selections. If you are not using audiovisual materials to the degree that you could, start doing so and add another dimension to the learning experiences of the preschoolers you teach.

Personal Learning Activities
1. Why are audiovisual materials used with each age group?
2. Name two new audiovisual items that would be practical for use in your department.
3. Where would be a good place for a tape player to be placed in your room for the next session during which you will teach?
4. Where can audiovisual equipment and materials that are shared by Preschool departments in all Preschool-related organizations be stored?
5. What is the best audiovisual aid?

Material for Further Study
Terrell, Jerry. *Basic Preschool Work.* Nashville: Convention Press, 1981.
*Media: Library Services Journal***

---

*Available from Baptist Book Stores.
**Available by writing Customer Service Center, 127 Ninth Avenue, North, Nashville, Tennessee 37234; or by calling toll free 1-800-458-2772.
***Available from Baptist Film Centers, 2930 Flowers Road South, Atlanta, Georgia 30341; 317 Guthrie Street, Louisville, Kentucky 40202; P. O. Box 161121, Memphis, Tennessee 38116; P. O. Box 19005, Greensboro, North Carolina 27410; 2622 Avenue E. East, Arlington, Texas 76011.
****Available through the CAVE Plan, Broadman Sales, MSN 120, 127 Ninth Avenue, North, Nashville, Tennessee 37234.

Chapter 15—How to Make Additional Teaching Materials

Jewell Wells Nelson

Are you (choose one or more): ____trying to save money? ____ creative? ____not creative? ____looking for new ideas? ____looking for old ideas that are good?

If you checked any of the above, this chapter is for you. Chapter 15 is a compilation of ideas from teachers of preschoolers who have seen good results from following the ideas included in the chapter.

This chapter is divided into alphabetical headings for your convenience: Art, Blocks, Books, Homeliving, Indoor Equipment, Music, Nature, Outdoor Equipment, and Outreach.

The value of each suggested item is either described in a previous chapter dealing with the same area, or the value is given with the suggested idea.

The items suggested can be made by teachers and other adults in local, associational, state, or convention-wide conferences. Learning by doing, sharing, and seeing will create greater interest and be a more valuable experience. Getting parents and other adults in the church involved in creating useful items for Preschool departments will enhance relationships and reveal talents.

Preschoolers can be included in some of the activities and in making some of the items, such as play dough and no bake cookies.

As you use each item or activity with preschoolers, reinforce the value by singing songs, using Bible thoughts, Bible conversation, and stories. (See chapters 1, 2, 3, and 12.)

Symbols by each item will help you know the approximate age for which the item is intended: *B* (baby), *C* (creeper), *T* (toddler), *2* (two-year-old), *3* (three-year-old), *4* (four-year-old), and *5* (five-year-old).

Art
(See also chapter 5, "How to Teach Through Art Activities.")
Chunky crayons 2-5
Teachers at church and public kindergartens are usually happy to discard broken crayons. You may have a collection of old crayons in your home. Place foil liners in a muffin tin. Shave or cut the crayons into each muffin tin cup. Put one color per muffin tin cup. Place the crayon-filled muffin tin in a warm oven, 200°—225° F. When the crayon bits have melted completely, remove the muffin tin from the oven. Let the muffin tin cool completely and the crayons harden. Remove the foil muffin tin

liners from the crayons. You now have large, chunky crayons. These crayons fit small hands comfortably. Preschoolers use large muscles in coloring. Give preschoolers large paper (such as the ad section from the newspaper) and let them color with chunk crayons in large strokes, circles, and scribbles.

Paint (2-5)

5 cups hot water
2 cups flour
Combine water and flour and cook about 15 minutes. Stir constantly to prevent lumping. Take the mixture off the heat and add:
½ cup soap flakes (not detergent)
   (available at discount department stores and grocery stores)
½ cup salt
Mix well.
Pour the mixture into four pint containers. Add 4 tablespoons of dry tempera to each pint of the hot mixture.

(1) Finger paint (2-5)

3 parts water
1 part powdered wallpaper paste
Dry tempera paint
Stir wallpaper paste into water and add tempera.

(2) Finger paint (2-5)

Lump laundry starch
Dry tempera
Follow the directions on the starch box for heavy starch. Add enough tempera to get the color you desire.
Finger paint can be used on a cafeteria tray or cookie sheet (with sides), or place ¼ cup of the finger paint inside a zip lock plastic bag. Place the bag on a cookie sheet or tray. Manipulating a bag containing finger paint gives the enjoyment of finger paint and play dough.

Paste (2-5)

1 cup boiling water
1 tablespoon powdered alum
1 pint cold water
1 pint flour
1 teaspoon oil of cloves
Boil 1 cup water. Add the powdered alum. Gradually add cold water to the flour. Mix until smooth. Pour flour mixture gradually into boiling alum water. Cook until it has a bluish cast, stirring constantly. Remove from the heat. Add oil of cloves. Stir. Keep in airtight containers. If the paste needs thinning, add water.

Sawdust clay (2-5)

Mix 1 cup paste with 2 cups sawdust. A thick wallpaper paste may be substituted for the homemade paste. Sand may be substituted for saw-dust. Experiment for the right consistency. Preschoolers do not need to make something from the clay. The experience of feeling, molding, pounding, and manipulating the clay is reason enough to use clay.

Blocks
(See also chapter 6, "How to Teach Through Block Activities.")
Milk carton blocks
For each block you will need two milk cartons the same size. Cut the top away from each carton. Stuff each carton very tightly with crushed newspaper. With open ends together, push one carton inside the other. Put the cartons together with masking tape. Cover the block with contact plastic. (A wood design is appropriate.)

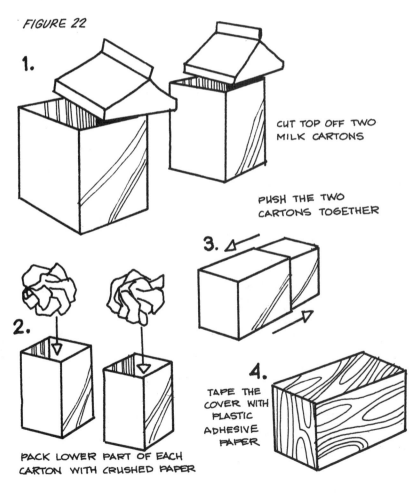

FIGURE 22

1.

CUT TOP OFF TWO MILK CARTONS

PUSH THE TWO CARTONS TOGETHER

3.

2.

PACK LOWER PART OF EACH CARTON WITH CRUSHED PAPER

4.

TAPE THE COVER WITH PLASTIC ADHESIVE PAPER

Pull toys (T)

Shoe boxes and plastic dishpans make good pull toys. Tie a cord to the end of a shoe box for a pull toy. Tie two or more shoe boxes together for a train effect. Tie a cord through the hole in the rim of a dishpan for a pull cord on the dishpan.

FIGURE 23

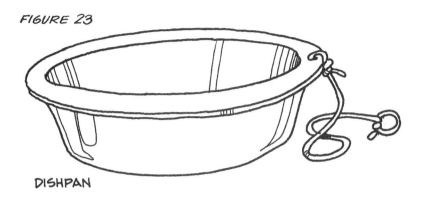

DISHPAN

SHOE BOXES

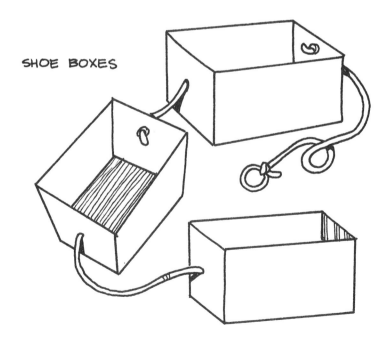

Wood vehicles (3-5)

Use the following design to make a car or truck. White glue will be
needed for assembling the car or truck. The wheels are nailed on with
#4 nails. Allow at least twenty-four hours before using the car or truck.

FIGURE 24

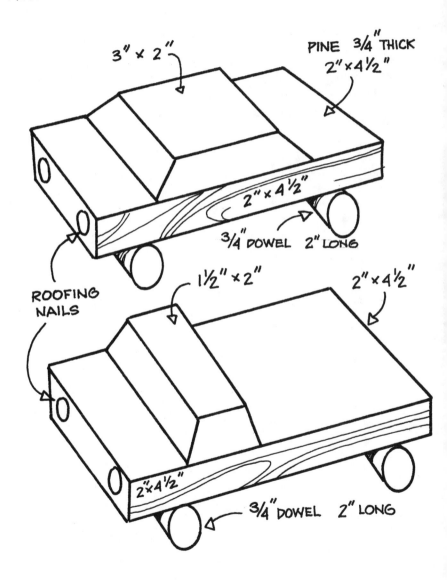

Books
(See also chapter 7, "How to Teach through the Use of Books.")

Space-saver-book-holder
You will need one regular size pillowcase (31 ins.). Measure ten inches down from the open end of the pillowcase and sew straight across (A). Measure five inches down from the stitched line and mark with a pin (B). Make a fold so that A is at the bottom of the fold and pin. Fold back down so that B is the top of the fold. Do not sew. Measure down ten inches from B. Mark with a pin (C). Make an upward fold at C and pin.

Sew along both outside edges catching A, B, and C in a straight line (D). Sew down the middle of the pillowcase (E) to form six pockets for books. Attach plastic rings (F) or cloth loops at each corner and center for attaching the book holder to a wall.

FIGURE 25

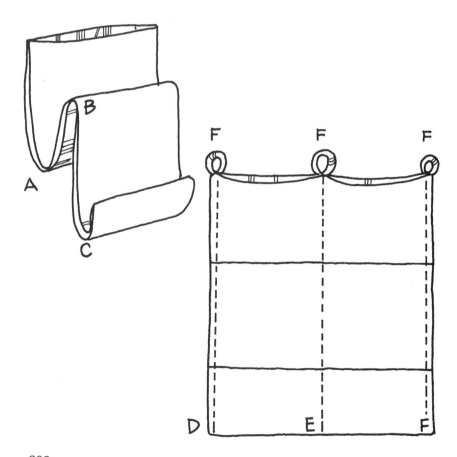

Feel book (B-5)
Select several different textures of fabric such as denim, burlap, felt, ticking, corduroy, velvet, satin, dotted swiss, and seersucker. Cut all pieces the same size (approx. 8 by 10 ins.). Cutting the fabric with pinking shears will help prevent fraying of the fabric. Place the fabrics on top of each other. Stitch with a machine along the left side of the book. The younger the child the fewer fabrics you will need. Four fabrics for younger preschoolers will be adequate.

Lightweight fabrics will be more easily handled if they are glued onto lightweight cardboard. The cardboard-fabric book can be bound at the left-hand side with string or plastic rings.

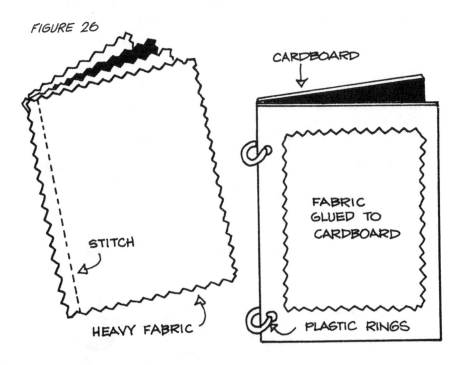

FIGURE 26

CARDBOARD

FABRIC GLUED TO CARDBOARD

STITCH

HEAVY FABRIC

PLASTIC RINGS

Homeliving
(See also chapter 8, "How to Teach Through Homeliving Activities.")
Cooked play dough (2-5)
1 cup flour
½ cup salt
1 cup water
1 tablespoon cooking oil
2 teaspoons cream of tartar
Food coloring, if desired
Mix all dry ingredients. Add oil, water, and food coloring. Cook in a stick-resistant pan or electric skillet. Stir constantly, since the mixture

thickens quickly. Cook until the dough becomes one large ball. This process takes not more than three minutes. Empty onto waxed paper. Knead until smooth and cool. Store in an air-tight container immediately.

Uncooked play dough (2-5)

1 cup flour
½ cup salt
1 tablespoon cooking oil
⅓ cup water, or enough to make the mixture as stiff as pie dough. Warm water may be used for a smoother texture.

Mix the dry ingredients. Gradually add water and oil, getting oil into the mixture as soon as it can become smoothly absorbed. Knead the dough until the mixture clings together. Add flour if the dough becomes too sticky while being used.

Mobile (B-T)

One coat hanger; three lengths of string (12 to 14 ins.); and three colored, plastic dish scrubbers make an eye-catching mobile. Attach each string onto the hanger. Tie an eye-catching colored scrubber or picture onto the other end of each string. Anything safe and colorful could be used instead of the scrubbers. Colored sponges, crushed foil, crushed colorful wrapping paper, and shiny jar lids or rings may be used. Pictures of people, fruit or animals may be used instead of scrubbers.

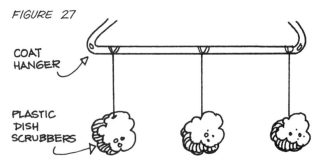

FIGURE 27

COAT HANGER

PLASTIC DISH SCRUBBERS

Indoor Equipment

Door pole

Get a hardwood dowel, about 1½ inches in diameter. (A strong broom handle will work.) The stick will need to be as long as the door is wide. Two hardwood blocks (1 by 3 by 4 ins.) are needed to hold the door pole. Four wood screws, at least two inches long, will secure the holders.

The pole needs to be placed above the children's heads. Children need to reach up to grasp the pole. They can then pull on the pole or swing on it. A mat placed under the pole will help protect children who fall.

The pole can be moved when it is not in use. Large muscle activity reduces emotional stress at any age, so use the door pole to encourage large muscle activity.

Note: The broom stick or dowel may not be strong enough for some fives to swing on.

FIGURE 28

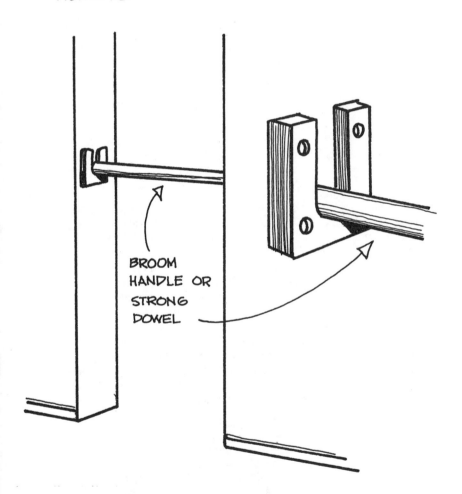

BROOM
HANDLE OR
STRONG
DOWEL

Fold-up table (2-5)
If you want to save space and money, but need a table, make a fold-up table. You will need a piece of plywood measuring about 24 by 36 inches. Attach the tabletop to the wall with hinges so it will fold up. When the table is down, it will need to be the correct height for a work

table for the age you teach. Attach legs on the outer edge of the table with hinges so the hinges will allow the legs to fold against the underside of the table. Place a hook on the wall above the table to correspond with an eye on the outer edge of the table.

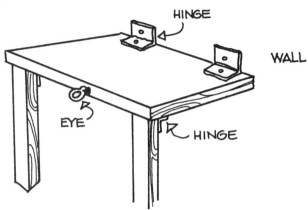

Space saver storage (B-5)

Make two sets of free-standing shelves the same size (or use commercially made book shelves). Diagrams and instructions for making open shelves may be found in the program help entitled *Make Your Own Preschool Furniture*. This packet is available through the Customer Service Center, 127 Ninth Avenue, North, Nashville, Tennessee 37234 and Baptist Book Stores. Place casters under each set of shelves for rolling. Push the shelves together with the shelving inside. Attach them at one end (top and bottom) with hinges. At the other end, connect the shelves with one or more latch hooks.

If you have limited space, the roll-away storage shelves will enable you to move the shelves into a room for activities. The storage shelves can be rolled into another room or hallway when not in use. If you share a room with another group or have all preschoolers in one room, the roll-away storage shelves are especially useful.

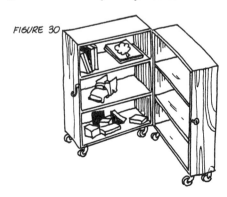

Upsize-down table

Turn a table upside down. Be sure there are no splinters, rough edges, or nail ends inside the under side of the table. Heavy cardboard or plywood nailed to three sides of the table legs makes a cozy place for quiet work. The table can be a house for homeliving, or a book nook for the book area. Children will not care that the house or book nook does not have a roof.

A small table can become a pet container for the nature area. Instead of cardboard or plywood, stretch chicken wire around all four sides of the table legs. Secure with heavy-duty staples.

For outdoors, put sand in the upside-down table for another use. Do not use walls or screen wire on the table for a sand area. Make the ends of the table legs safe. Cover each leg end with a padding such as sponge and bind with cord, or cover each end with an oven mit and tie the mit securely.

FIGURE 31

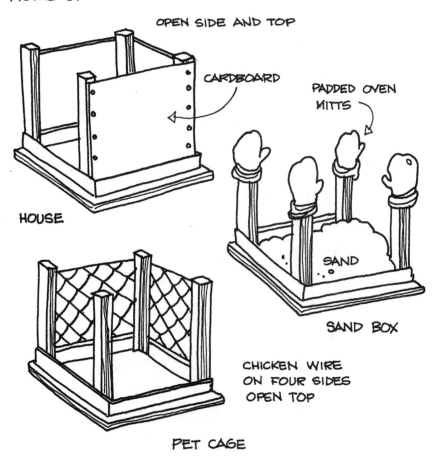

OPEN SIDE AND TOP

CARDBOARD

HOUSE

PADDED OVEN MITTS

SAND

SAND BOX

CHICKEN WIRE ON FOUR SIDES OPEN TOP

PET CAGE

Music

(See also chapter 11, "How to Teach Through Music Activities.")

Bells (B-5)

Make a wrist or ankle band with wide elastic. Sew small sleigh bells onto the band with elastic cord. Check the bells regularly to be sure they do not cut the elastic and come off.

Rebus (4-5)

Let older preschoolers make a rebus to help them learn a new song such as "We Know Spring Is Here" from the songbook *Music for Today's Children* (p. 122).

We know spring is here. We know spring is here.

(1) Budding trees, bright green leaves, all show us spring is here.

FIGURE 32

(2) Big white clouds, warm sunshine, all show us spring is here.

FIGURE 33

(3) Singing birds, growing flowers, all show us spring is here.

Select-a-song (3-5)

Cut songs from outdated copies of the teacher's guides, leaflets, or home books.** Tape each song to a 5 by 7-inch card. Place the cards in a suitable container.

During group time, songs may be selected as children take turns pulling a songcard from the container. Preschoolers can enjoy making music and can learn Bible-related concepts through games. Games are sometimes described in curriculum materials. See chapter 13, "How to Lead Group Time" for other suggestions.

Cut a 24" circle of cardboard. Section the board into six equal parts. In one section put pictures of nature items. In another section put a copy of the song "God Loves Me."

Toss a bean bag or large button. Sing about whatever is pictured in the section on which the bean bag lands.

FIGURE 34

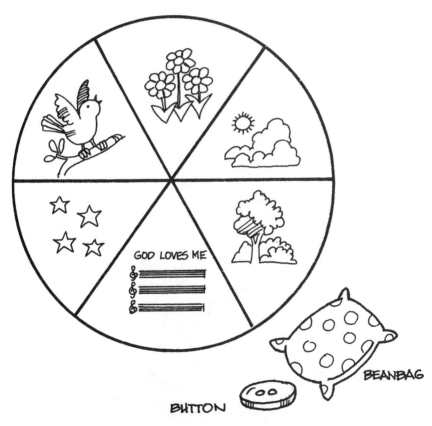

Nature

(See also chapter 10, "How to Teach Through The Use of Nature Materials.")

Plastic bags   (B-5)

A freshly-cut flower will stay fresh for days if it is sealed in a clear plastic bag. The flower can be taped near a baby's bed so the child can see the brightly colored flower. The bag can be handled by a toddler or two-year-old. Threes through fives will appreciate the pretty flower-in-a-bag in the nature area.

A large zip lock plastic bag can be used as a fish container for a baby. One small fish and water (leaving air space) sealed in the bag can be taped near the baby's bed so he can observe the moving fish. Do not leave the fish in the bag indefinitely.

Seed can be sprouted in a plastic bag. Put moist cotton in the bottom of a plastic bag. Sprinkle the cotton with grass or other seed. Tape the bag to a window. Moisture forms in the bag if the bag is closed. Moisture evaporates if the bag is open. Regulate moistness by opening or closing the bag.

Bird house

A cardboard milk carton can be made into a bird house. Cut a round hole in one side of the carton. Tie a cord through the top of the carton. Tie the other end of the cord to a tree branch outside your department window.

FIGURE 35

Outdoor Equipment

Knotted sheet swing (T-5)

For a temporary swing, securely tie a knotted sheet to a strong, low tree limb, or use any secure structure that would allow the swing to move. Toddlers and twos enjoy holding onto the knotted sheet and moving back and forth with it. Older preschoolers will enjoy swinging. They may climb the sheet, using the knots as foot holders.

Climbing on the swing as well as moving with it helps to strengthen children's large muscles. Large muscles need to be developed before finer muscles can develop properly.

Do not leave the knotted-sheet-swing exposed to the elements. Rain and sun will cause the sheet to deteriorate.

FIGURE 36

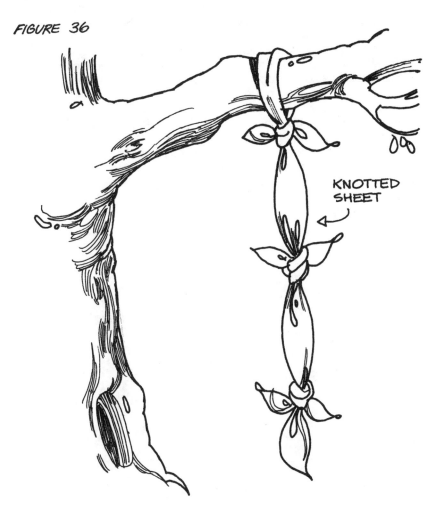

KNOTTED SHEET

217

A trucking company will probably be happy to give you one or more old tires and tubes.

● An old tire is fun to walk on. The tire can be filled with sand for a sand area. Before you fill a tire with sand, make four holes in the side of the tire that will be against the ground. The holes will allow water to drain.

● One or more tires can be placed in the ground to make a crawl-through area. Make three or four drainage holes in a third of the tire to be placed underground. Place a third of an upright tire in a trench. Fill the curve of the tire that is underground with rocks. Cover the tire securely with earth or cement so that two thirds of the tire stands above ground. Children will enjoy crawling through, around, and over the tire. More than one tire can be placed in a row to form a tunnel. Leave enough space between each tire so a child can crawl between the tires as well as through them.

● A tire swing is a favorite kind of swing. Securely tie a rope onto a car tire. Tie the other end of the rope securely to a strong limb or bar. The tire should be close enough to the ground so that the children you teach can easily get into and out of the tire swing.

● Old inner tubes are fun to walk on, sit on, crawl through, sleep on, and use in water play. Several inner tubes tied together make an interesting walking and jumping area.

The use of legs, arms, and the whole body in tire inner tube play helps develop large muscle control; eye-hand, and eye-foot coordination.

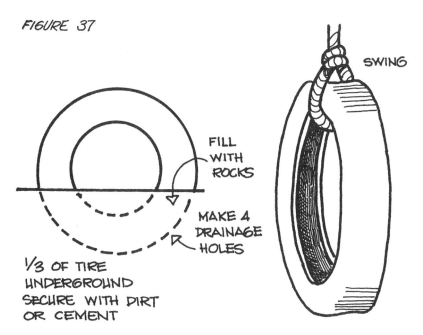

FIGURE 37

FILL WITH ROCKS

MAKE 4 DRAINAGE HOLES

⅓ OF TIRE UNDERGROUND SECURE WITH DIRT OR CEMENT

SWING

Tree bench (2-5)

If you have access to trees, consider building a tree bench. Children will enjoy climbing on the bench, sitting on it, putting things on the tree bench, putting things under it, and having a walking board around a favorite tree.

Benches around trees should be checked often for wasps and poisonous spiders.

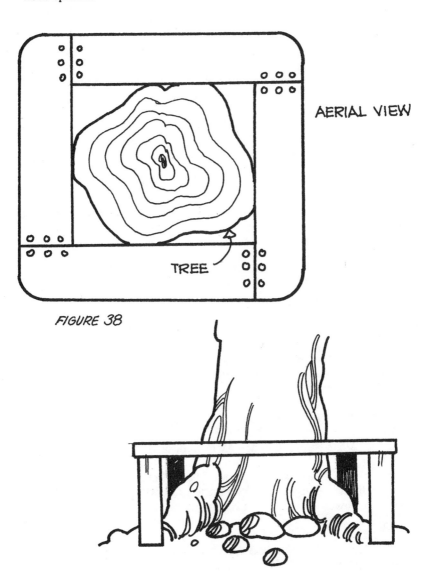

AERIAL VIEW

TREE

FIGURE 38

Outreach

Greeting cards (B-5)

Save copies of outdated issues of the home books *Beginning, Living,* and *Growing,* and the leisure-reading leaflet *Look and Listen.*** Cut appropriate songs, pictures, Bible thoughts, and Bible stories out of the magazines. Use construction paper for the card. Fold the construction paper in card fashion. The paper can be folded to fit in an envelope, or may be folded with the child's address and a return address on the outside. If this procedure is used, seal the card with tape and mail it without an envelope.

On the front of a card with an envelope, paste an appropriate picture. On the inside of the card, paste a song, Bible thought, story, or picture. Print your message with crayons, felt-tipped markers, or a pen. Possible messages are: "I love you," "We missed you," "Happy birthday," and "Get well."

Make large cards and take them to children in your department. Hand-delivered messages to the home are the very best kind of outreach. Remember the child who is regular in attendance. He likes to get pretty cards and visits, too.

Summary

This chapter has been written to whet your imagination, to help you save money, and to help you make wise use of your space. Have a purpose as you create, using these and other ideas. Each item and activity needs to have value to preschoolers.

Personal Learning Activities

1. Read chapter 15 again. Underline the suggestions that you think are practical for your situation.
2. Plan a workshop for teachers and parents; make some of the items suggested in this chapter.
3. List ideas that you have thought of as a result of reading this chapter.
4. Jot down the value and purpose of each of the ideas you listed in question number 3.

Materials for Further Study

Books

Garlow, Willa Ruth. *Outreach for Preschoolers.* Nashville: Convention Press, 1971.

Hogan, Paul. *Playgrounds for Free: The Utilization of Used and Surplus Materials in Playground Construction.* Cambridge: MIT Press, 1974.

Nelson, Jewell Wells. *Cradle Roll = Visitation.* Nashville: Convention Press, 1978.

Write to the following for pamphlets:

—Association for Childhood Education International, 11141 Georgia Avenue, Suite 200, Wheaton, MD 20902.

—National Association for the Education of Young Children, 1834 Connecticut Avenue, N.W., Washington, D.C. 20009
—Community Playthings, Route 213, Rifton, New York 12471 for the pamphlet *Criteria for Selecting Play Equipment*
—Place your name on a mailing list for the newsletter "The Growing Child," P. O. Box 1100, Lafayette, Indiana 47902 ($14.95 per year).

---

*Available from Baptist Book Stores.
**Available by writing Customer Service Center, 127 Ninth Avenue, North, Nashville, Tennessee 37234; or by calling toll free 1-800-458-2772.

The Church Study Course

The Church Study Course is a Southern Baptist education system designed to support the training efforts of local churches. It provides courses, recognition, record keeping and regular reports for some 20,000 participating churches.

The Church Study Course is characterized by short courses ranging from 2½ to 10 hours in length. They may be studied individually or in groups. With more than 600 courses in 24 subject areas, it offers 130 diploma plans in all areas of church leadership and Christian growth. Diplomas represent hours of study, knowledge and skills acquired, and approval of the sponsoring agency.

While the heart of the Church Study Course is leadership training, many courses are available for all members. Each year, approximately 900,000 awards and 170,000 diplomas are earned by adults and youth. While youth may receive credit on any of the courses, some courses are designed especially for youth. Also available in the system are non-credit short courses for children and preschoolers.

Originating in 1902 with two Sunday School courses, the Church Study Course now serves all church programs and is jointly sponsored by many agencies within the Southern Baptist Convention. Sponsors include: Baptist Sunday School Board, Woman's Missionary Union, Brotherhood Commission, Home Mission Board, Foreign Mission Board, Stewardship Commission, Education Commission, and the respective departments of the state conventions and associations affiliated with the Southern Baptist Convention.

Records are kept by the Sunday School Board for the other agencies. A state-of-the-art computer system maintains records for more than one million individual students and provides regular reports to the participating churches. After enrollment in a diploma plan(s), diplomas are issued automatically as requirements are met. Credit earned in one church is recognized in all other Southern Baptist churches.

Complete details about the Church Study Course system, courses available, and diplomas offered may be found in a current copy of the *Church Study Course Catalog.*

How to Request Credit for this Course

This book is the text for course number 12009 in the subject area: "Age Division and Special Group Characteristics of the Church Study Course." This course is designed for five hours of group study.

Credit for this course may be obtained in two ways:

1. Read the book and attend class sessions. (If you are absent from one or more sessions, complete the "Personal Learning Activities" for the material missed.)
2. Read the book and complete the "Personal Learning Activities." (Written work should be submitted to an appropriate church leader.)

A request for credit may be made on Form 725 "Church Study Course Enrollment/Credit Request" and sent to the Awards Office, Sunday School Board, 127 Ninth Avenue, North, Nashville, Tennessee 37234. The form on the following page may be used to request credit. Enrollment in a diploma plan may also be made on Form 725.

Within three months of your completion of a course, confirmation of your credit will be sent to your church. A copy of your complete transcript will be sent to your church annually during the July–September quarter if you have completed a course during the previous 12 months.

CHURCH STUDY COURSE
ENROLLMENT/CREDIT REQUEST
FORM - 725 (Rev. 1-89)

MAIL THIS REQUEST TO ➡

CHURCH STUDY COURSE AWARDS OFFICE
BAPTIST SUNDAY SCHOOL BOARD
127 NINTH AVENUE, NORTH
NASHVILLE, TENNESSEE 37234

Is this the first course taken since 1983? ☐ YES If yes, or not sure complete all of Section 1. ☐ NO If no, complete only bold boxes in Section 1.

SECTION 1 - STUDENT I.D.

STUDENT

Social Security Number

☐ Mr. ☐ Miss
☐ Mrs.

Personal CSC Number*

DATE OF BIRTH

Month	Day	Year

Name (First, MI, Last)

Street, Route, or P.O. Box

City, State — Zip Code

CHURCH

Church Name

Mailing Address

City, State — Zip Code

SECTION 2 - CHANGE REQUEST ONLY (Current inf. in Section1)

☐ Former Name

☐ Former Address — Zip Code

☐ Former Church — Zip Code

SECTION 3 - COURSE CREDIT REQUEST

Course No.	Title (use exact title)
1. **12009**	**HOW TO GUIDE PRESCHOOLERS**
2.	
3.	
4.	
5.	
6.	

SECTION 4 - DIPLOMA ENROLLMENT

Enter exact diploma title from current Church Study Course catalog. Indicate diploma age group if appropriate. Do not enroll again with each course. When all requirements have been met, the diploma will be mailed to your church. Enrollment in Christian Development Diplomas is automatic. No charge will be made for enrollment or diplomas.

Title of Diploma	Age group or area
Title of Diploma	Age group or area
Signature of Pastor, Teacher, or Other Church Leader	Date

*CSC # not required for new students. Others please give CSC # when using SS # for the first time. Then, only one ID # is required.